LIVING IN GOD'S CREATION

Foundations series

Testifying to the faith and creativity of the Orthodox Christian Church, the Foundations series draws upon the riches of its tradition to address the modern world. These survey texts are suitable both for preliminary inquiry and deeper investigation, in the classroom and for personal study.

Peter C. Bouteneff
Series Editor

BOOK 1
Stages on Life's Way: Orthodox Thinking on Bioethics
by John and Lyn Breck

BOOK 2
Seeds of the Word: Orthodox Thinking on Other Religions
by John Garvey

BOOK 3
Sweeter Than Honey: Orthodox Thinking on Dogma and Truth
by Peter C. Bouteneff

BOOK 4
Living in God's Creation: Orthodox Perspectives on Ecology
by Elizabeth Theokritoff

BOOK 5
Fellow Workers with God: Orthodox Thinking on Theosis
by Norman Russell

BOOK 4 OF THE FOUNDATIONS SERIES

Living in God's Creation

ORTHODOX PERSPECTIVES ON ECOLOGY

Elizabeth Theokritoff

ST VLADIMIR'S SEMINARY PRESS
CRESTWOOD, NEW YORK
2009

Library of Congress Cataloging-in-Publication Data

Theokritoff, Elizabeth
Living in God's creation : Orthodox perspectives on Ecology /
Elizabeth Theokritoff
p. cm. — (Foundations series ; bk. 4)
ISBN 978-0-88141-338-0
1. Human ecology—Religious aspects—Orthodox Eastern Church.
2. Orthodox Eastern Church—Doctrines. I. Title.

BX337.5.T44 2009
261.8'8—dc22

2009014898

ST VLADIMIR'S SEMINARY PRESS
575 Scarsdale Rd, Yonkers, NY 10707
1-800-204-2665
www.svspress.com

ISSN 1556-9837
ISBN 978-0-88141-338-0

PRINTED IN THE UNITED STATES OF AMERICA

For George

CONTENTS

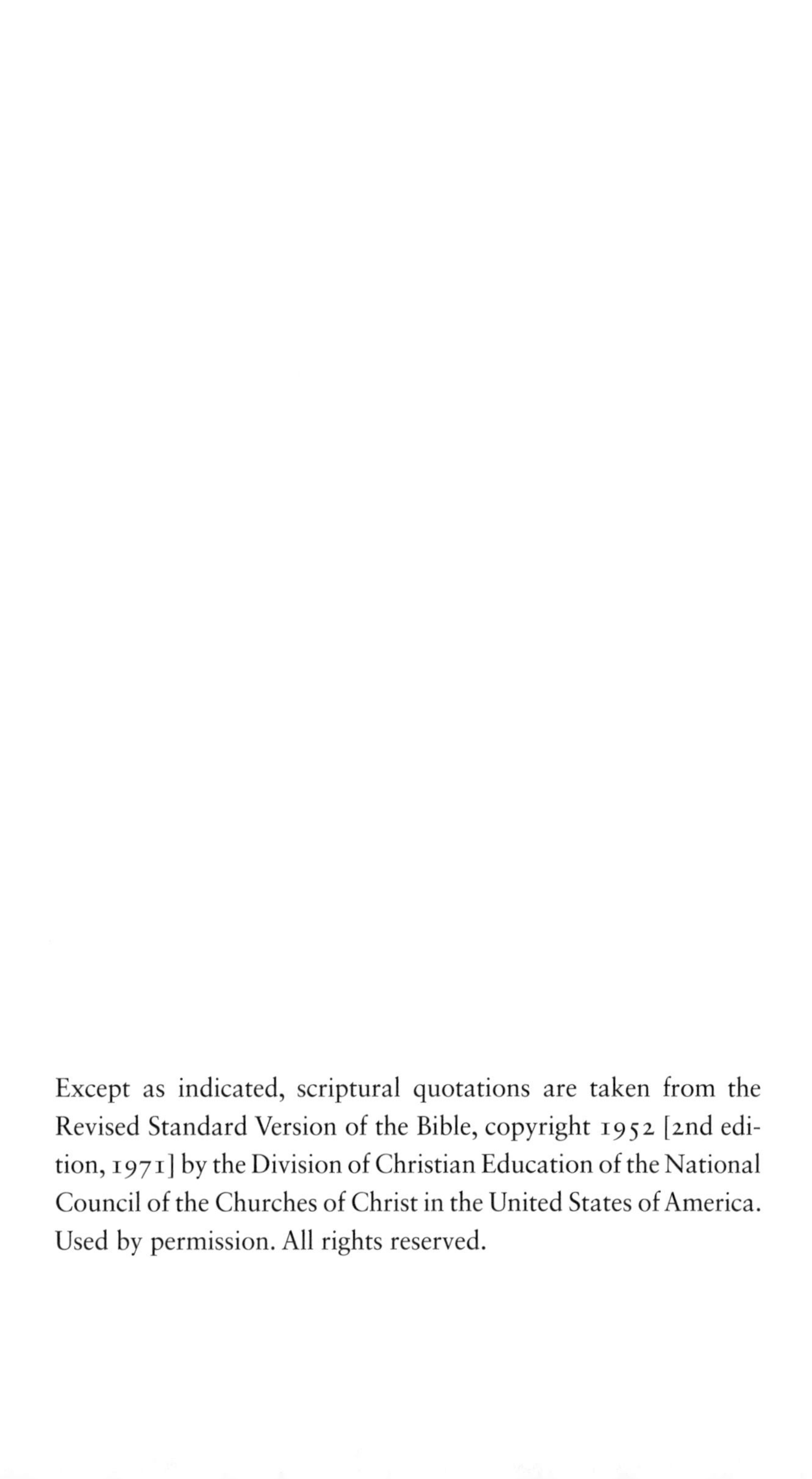

Foreword

Environmental and ecological issues have been sharply politicized in recent decades, at least in the U.S. Concern for the environment is supposed to belong to liberals—whom conservatives accuse of alarmism and fiscal irresponsibility. Conservatives, say liberals, fund studies that are predetermined to discredit environmentalist warnings, which aren't good for big business.

People in the Church are hardly immune to falling into politicized camps. They often assume that to be Orthodox Christian means to be aligned with a political ideology. Yet when it comes to the environment, the created world, and the place of humans within it, the tradition of the Church knows neither left nor right. If you turn to the Church's theological and liturgical ethos which breathes today as it ever has, it no longer matters whether you've been listening to Greenpeace or talk radio: if you want to live a truly Christian life, you must inhabit the earth in a way that is mindful of the whole of creation—humanity in particular, but also the entirety of non-human creation, spiritual and material, apart from which humanity is inconceivable.

That is the utterly convincing argument of this book. Drawing deeply from the Church's patristic, liturgical, hagiographic, and iconographic tradition, Elizabeth Theokritoff assembles a clear and compelling mosaic of the Church's collective understanding of the created world and our place in it.

Along the way to her unmistakable conclusions for how we live our lives in the world today, the author presents countless fresh and important insights on many of the fundamentals of Orthodox thought and life. Her treatment of asceticism, for example, is at once familiar in some of its contours, and yet also entirely fresh, drawing on sources we may not have encountered before, and synthesizing them in a new and personal, yet entirely genuine and orthodox way. The author also presents us with episodes from saints' lives that are completely delightful—but also deeply sobering, if we pause to take in their true message and its implications.

Indeed, chances are you may want to change some of your habits after reading this book. But if that happens, it won't be because you've felt manipulated in any way: these pages are devoid of sentimentality, hysteria, or noisy activism. No, if you change it will be because you've just been calmly convinced that this is simply the right thing to do. Theokritoff delivers common sense, Church-sense: every authoritative area of the Church's tradition tells us that the life in Christ entails a consciously holistic, deeply responsible approach to everything and everyone God has made. In the author's own words,

> The sacramental life of the Church, and the Eucharist especially, points to sharing with others. This is not presented to us as a moral imperative, something that we do because it is "the right thing." We do it because we are members of one another; we cannot truly live in any other way. (page 209)

Foreword

For many years a translator of some of the most important works of 20th century Greek-language Orthodox theology, Elizabeth Theokritoff here shows herself as what many of us have long known her to be: a scholar and a profound theologian in her own right. I know Elizabeth also as someone who lives simply, with a thoroughly natural and deep respect for the created world and for every person and animal in it. Here is someone who indeed "walks lightly on the earth." I am glad that the ideas set out in this book, which are at once integral to the Orthodox tradition and to the author's own life and thought, are here made available to a wider public. In this way we may all learn much about our Church, and even more about the awesome, glorious cosmos that God has created and that He so loves.

—Peter Bouteneff

Preface and Acknowledgements

The origins of this book go back to the summer of 2000, when the diocese of Demetrias (Volos) in central Greece launched an ambitious and far-sighted project for an Academy of Theological Studies that would organize public lecture series and conferences. The emphasis of the Academy was to be not simply on teaching basics of theology, but rather on exploring how the Orthodox Christian tradition speaks to the challenges of our times and our culture. I was privileged to be invited to take part in the first summer school, and chose as my topic "Creator and creation." It is out of those five lectures that these chapters have grown.

Those who want to explore this timely subject will not find in this book a final destination, but a series of signposts. Its aim is to point readers to the various sources within the Orthodox tradition for a theology of creation and an understanding of humans' place in it. But it does not stand alone; it is also intended to make better known the wealth of valuable writing that already exists relating Orthodox theology to environmental concerns. Much of this is tucked away in journals hard to find outside academic libraries, or in church periodicals with limited circulation. Suggestions for further reading at the end of each chapter indicate some of this material, with especial emphasis on works that the reader may have some hope of finding. Some of the less accessible sources may be cited in footnotes. But it is also worth highlighting some works of relevance to the overall theme, which cannot readily be pigeonholed in one or another chapter. Of particular note are Paul Evdokimov's seminal article "Nature," published in the *Scottish Journal of Theology* 18 (March 1965): 1–22; Metropolitan Kallistos Ware's *Through the Creation to the Creator* (London: Friends of the Centre, 1996); and John Chryssavgis's *Beyond the Shattered Image* (Minneapolis: Light and Life Publishing, 1999). Those able to get hold of any or all of these would gain from reading them in parallel with this book.

I owe a debt of gratitude to all who over the years have given encouragement to pursue this subject and helped me to develop my thinking on it, as well as to those who have contributed more directly to the shaping of this book. To Metropolitan Ignatios of Demetrias and Dr Dimitri Conomos, for the original invitation to lecture in Volos; to Evi Voulgaraki-Pisina, for her enthusiasm for the texts of those lectures and willingness to publish them; to Fr John Jillions and the Institute for Orthodox Christian Studies in Cambridge for the opportunity to give a study day on the same topic, and to all who joined in the discussion at those and other lectures; to Dr Peter Gilbert, for many discussions of theological points; to Fr John Chryssavgis, Mariamna Fortounatto, and Amelia Perkins for looking over and commenting on various chapters; to Christine Bulko and Betty Howarth for reading the manuscript at various stages; to those who reviewed the manuscript for St Vladimir's Seminary Press; to the endlessly patient and encouraging series editor Peter Bouteneff; to the librarians at Mount Tabor Public Library, whose diligence in procuring inter-library loans greatly simplified my research; and as always, to my long-suffering husband George. Whatever value the book may have is due in no small part to all those mentioned; its many remaining imperfections are my own.

Material from Chapters 1–3 has appeared in Greek in *Oikosystema kai Anthropini Kyriarchia* (Athens: Maistros, 2003). Portions of Chapter 4 have appeared in "Creation and Salvation in Orthodox Worship," *Ecotheology* 10 (January 2001): 97–108, copyright © Equinox Publishing Ltd 2001. Portions of Chapters 3, 5 and 6 have appeared, respectively, in " 'Let them have dominion': The witness of the Saints," *St Tikhon's Theological Journal* 2 (2004); "From Sacramental Life to Sacramental Living," *Greek Orthodox Theological Review* 44:1–4 (1999); and "Embodied Word and New Creation: Some Modern Orthodox Insights Concerning the Material World" in John Behr, Andrew Louth, and Dimitri Conomos (eds.), *Abba: The Tradition of Orthodoxy in the West* (Crestwood, NY: St Vladimir's Seminary Press, 2003).

A note on scriptural quotations

Unless otherwise stated, scriptural quotations follow the Revised Standard Version. Modern pronouns and verbal forms have however been substituted, in line with the usage in quotations from liturgical texts. Where a quotation is designated "Septuagint," the text has been translated directly from the Greek of the Old Testament. Psalm *numberings* always follow the Septuagint text used by the Orthodox Church, so that the psalm number is in most cases one less than that found in English versions based on the Hebrew. Verse numberings may also differ, since the Septuagint often counts the inscription of the psalm as the first verse.

Introduction

There is a story of a hermit being asked by an earnest visitor, "What do you actually do?" And the hermit replies, "I live here." *Living here*: it is a calling, a life's work—but also the most basic thing imaginable. Before anything else, we live on earth; we live in our environment. But today, we increasingly feel that this basic ground is being taken from under our feet. When we talk about our environment, it is almost always in the context of crisis, degradation, damage or loss. The very business of living as humans on the earth suddenly seems enormously problematic and complicated.

It seems strange that something so basic as our relationship with our natural environment should be a matter of lively debate and soul-searching. For most of human history, after all, this relationship must have seemed fairly straightforward. There were certain things that human ingenuity could control; humans could domesticate animals, cultivate crops, mine and smelt metals. They felled trees and built houses and ships; they developed sophisticated systems of water storage and distribution. In retrospect, we can see that they shaped entire landscapes; sometimes they would hunt a population of a certain animal to extinction, and occasionally they provoked local ecological collapse by over-using resources. But such environmental changes happened gradually, and it is unlikely that people had much awareness of the extent to which they were contributing to them. There seemed to be quite a clear dividing line between things that were subject to humans, and the workings of the natural world which were in the hands of God. Humans were on the receiving end of both nature's bounty and natural disasters, and could do little more than react to whatever nature dealt them.

Then came an age of rapid advances in science and technology. For the first time, entire civilizations felt that they were largely in control of natural forces instead of being at their mercy. People no longer felt compelled to work around or simply accept aspects of nature that were inconvenient to them: they could alter them. At the same time, radical changes were being made in the social environment: entire (or almost entire) societies could now enjoy previously unheard-of levels of prosperity and comfort. But then suddenly—as it seemed to most people—the natural world itself was in crisis. First it was the pollution of water and air and soil. Familiar animals and plants began to disappear from their former range. Now the very systems that regulate the earth show signs of strain. Holes have appeared in the ozone layer. Extreme weather—heat waves, storms and floods—threaten the lives and livelihoods of thousands at a time. Receding glaciers, vanishing sea ice and thawing permafrost threaten ways of life that have survived for centuries or millennia. Rising temperatures combined with extensive world travel bring tropical diseases to prosperous countries in temperate zones. Like a child pulling thoughtlessly at a loose thread, we watch with growing horror as the fabric of our world starts to unravel. Or perhaps we deploy a familiar human defense mechanism, and persuade ourselves that nothing unusual or disturbing is really happening.

Unfortunately, our capacity to *affect* the world as a whole is not matched by our capacity to *think in terms of* the world as a whole.

So there is a temptation to try to pigeonhole the threats we face, to cut them down to size. None of this is really our problem, the thinking seems to go. It affects something out there called "the environment": a realm of rainforests and distant wildernesses, polar bears and white rhinos, or perhaps wild flowers and birds that some of us might choose to enjoy in our spare time. Concern for all this is an optional extra, something of interest only to "environmentalists." In the view of some, such "environmentalism" is at best an irrelevance, a luxury for the rich, or a distraction from our proper concern for human welfare. At worst, it is regarded as a sinister and politically motivated plot to subvert our way of life.

It is this sort of thinking that leads people to ask why "the environment" should be of concern to Christians. On a basic and practical level, this should be easy to answer. The natural world is, after all, where we all live. So being indifferent to environmental pressures on other creatures is rather like pulling a dead canary out of a mine shaft and saying airily: "Not to worry: humans are more important than canaries." But the dead canary means potentially dead miners. Many of the issues we label as "environmental" can better be thought of as the ultimate "life issues": they concern the very life support system that our physical survival depends on. More specifically, they concern the ways in which human activity (or inaction) threatens the life of other humans, as well as other species, by making the earth a more dangerous and unhealthy place to live. So environmental concern turns out to be a matter of practical love for our neighbor, especially those most in need of our care. Most environmental problems take their toll on the poor and weak long before they affect those who can afford to live far from the landfills, upwind of the factories or power plants, and well above sea level. From the Christian point of view, there is no such thing as a discrete ideology of "environmentalism" separate from love of God and love of neighbor. Christian environmental concern is not a distraction from feeding the hungry, clothing the naked and caring for the poor, but rather a recognition of the bigger picture. It is a recognition of all that needs to happen if we are to obey the imperatives of Christian charity at the present juncture of human history.

This may explain why we need to concern ourselves with *practical* measures to address environmental problems. But why should such problems require profound *theological* thinking? In particular, why should they require a new look at our relationship to the rest of God's creation? Is this not a concession to the secular view of humans as just another animal, rather than a unique creature in the image of God?

To understand the need for the theological perspective, we need to consider what is actually involved in taking practical measures to address environmental problems. First of all, we need the honesty and courage to recognize what the problems are, how human activity is contributing to them, and how we personally are implicated. These questions can be very complex, involving an elaborate nexus of causes and effects; but they are ultimately questions of fact to which theology (or ideology) should not be relevant. In practice, however, as we all know, agreeing on facts is rarely simple. If a particular finding would oblige people to make sacrifices or change their behavior in other unpalatable ways, they will find all sorts of reasons to disbelieve it. Or it may happen that people object, on principle, to some of the solutions proposed to deal with a set of problems (such as artificial birth control, to reduce the pressure from a growing population); and instead of suggesting alternatives, as they have every right to do, they sometimes find it simpler to deny the problem. Or again, if people are convinced that the way they use the earth is perfectly legitimate—that it is fulfilling to the letter a divine mandate, for instance—then they may be less likely to accept that it could result in a litany of woes drawn straight from an Old Testament prophet's depiction of divine displeasure.

Let us suppose, however, that we can agree on the nature of at least some of the environmental threats facing us: we then come to the question of remedies. Of course, everyone is happy to embrace remedies so long as they are painless. "Technology will find a solution," people often say hopefully. There is no need to inconvenience ourselves, so the thinking goes; we can carry on living in just the same way. Now, there is no doubt that technology in various forms has played an important part in solving human problems since the dawn of civilization. But when we look at the potentials of various technologies (whether we are talking about improving crop yields, producing cleaner energy, energy efficiency or other areas) it quickly becomes apparent that few are without their drawbacks; almost none will produce a net benefit if they are not combined with difficult decisions to give up some of the things we have grown accustomed to doing. We need to entertain the possibility that "technical fixes" will not be sufficient.

It is hard to escape the conclusion that with an ever-growing human population, it is not enough for humanity as a whole to do more with less; individually, we must also learn to do less with less. This seems to point to an ethical dimension, whether we are talking about individual decisions (using products and produce that cause less pollution, driving and flying less . . .) or about policy changes at the national and international level. Of course, the latter are out of the hands of any one individual; but governments and companies have an incentive to make hard decisions only when their citizens or customers are whole-heartedly in support of the necessary changes. But is an appeal to ethics sufficient to deal with the underlying causes of environmental problems—to address these problems in such a way that they do not keep recurring? Moral failings such as selfishness and greed are often blamed for environmental destruction, and they play an obvious role in perpetuating it; yet they are hardly novel features of human nature. If selfishness and greed are the principle cause of environmental problems, why did such problems not manifest themselves millennia ago? Surely, something more must be involved.

The fact that we so readily invoke technology as a panacea reveals a feature of the modern outlook that may have much to do with today's environmental ills: a culture of control. Technology has always enabled humans to push the boundaries of what nature allows (starting with clothes and houses to protect us against the weather) or to make the most of what it offers. But in modern times, technology has increasingly been used in an attempt to defy nature's constraints altogether. There has been a very significant change in the way we view human technical skill. Instead of being seen as a further aspect of God's providence, this aspect of human ingenuity becomes a way for us to arrange the world for our own convenience, with no reference to some higher will for the world or for us. And this clearly takes us very deep into what we believe about humans' place in the world, the Creator's will for his creation and the way God uses nature to guide and teach us. As we look more closely at this whole idea of control, enormously influential as it is, we start to see why it is profoundly problematic from both a practical and a theological point of view.

What is meant by a "culture of control"? Looking around us, we repeatedly see a desire to control nature, often manifested in seemingly trivial ways. Many people regard it as quite normal, for instance, to have strawberries to eat in mid-winter, relax in a cool house in mid-summer in a subtropical climate, or sit on a well-watered lawn beside a swimming pool in a semi-desert. Or even, for that matter, to fly across oceans or continents for a weekend break. Some would see such things as harmless indulgences, which only a killjoy would object to. But such indulgences do raise expectations to levels that become increasingly unrealistic as an ever larger portion of the world's growing population starts to demand similar luxuries. And more profoundly, they reflect an expectation that nature should not be allowed to restrict us. That if I happen to feel like doing something, then neither season, nor climate, nor distance should be allowed to stand in my way.

This is not to say that efforts to control nature are always motivated by self-indulgence; one could equally point to advances in medicine which have alleviated so much human suffering over the past century, and the many inventions that have freed people from backbreaking and dangerous labor. But whatever our motives, the fact remains that the more humans pursue control over nature, the more it seems to elude us. It is not just the still-untamed power of tsunamis or volcanoes, which can turn our lives upside down—or end them—in a few minutes. More sobering still is the discovery that our very attempts to control and improve nature spawn a host of unintended consequences. Levees and channeled waterways prevent the deposition of silt, depleting the wetlands that would otherwise buffer storm surges, thus necessitating higher and stronger levees . . . Ubiquitous and convenient plastics turn out to be filling our bodies with persistent toxins. Short-lived consumer items, and layers of packaging "for your safety," create serious hazards to someone else's safety when they have to be disposed of. Those benign advances in medicine contribute to a population of unprecedented size, much of it subject to the ills of overcrowding and poverty. And in the affluent world, the cars that give us "freedom" and the electrical appliances serving our every need add relentlessly to a buildup of greenhouse gases, which deliver rising sea levels, more damaging hurricanes, the spread of tropical diseases, the thawing of permafrost to release still more greenhouse gases . . . Like the sorcerer's apprentice wrestling with his enchanted broomstick, we discover that the more we control nature, the more we need to control in order to maintain some sort of equilibrium. In short, the idea that we are in control of nature starts to look like a dangerous illusion.

Given how many of our current environmental problems have been created by previous "solutions," it seems less than realistic to expect to control our way out of them. But controlling nature is not simply an idea that fails to live up to expectations: it also has a more sinister side. The demand to bend nature to our own desires extends to other living creatures, to a degree undreamed of in millennia of domestication. The animals that provide much of our food are typically treated as disposable units for industrialized production. Crippled by over-breeding and drugs to enhance their productivity, they often spend their short lives unable to indulge in the most basic natural behavior. And at the other end of the scale, there is the no less unnatural life of the pet that is treated like a human member of the family. It may enjoy better food and medical care than the majority of the world's human population, but its scope for natural behaviors is hardly greater than the battery chicken's.

Some may counter that it is quite proper to make use of animals as we see fit. But in practice, there is usually a close parallel between how people treat animals and how they treat other humans; and we see the same pattern here. The idea of nature as something to be organized for human convenience spreads insidiously into the idea that human life is something to be organized for *my* individual convenience. In many developed societies, it is increasingly acceptable for lives to be artificially shortened by euthanasia, or artificially prolonged by costly medical procedures even when they are manifestly drawing to their natural close. New lives are artificially cut off *in utero*, or artificially initiated through elaborate fertility treatments. The common denominator is the feeling that *I should be in control*: I should not have to accept and adapt to a course of events that is not of my own choosing. In more theological terms, this can be seen as a loss of the sense that we are *creatures*—that we owe our very being to the will and love of Someone other than ourselves.

In both the more innocent and the more sinister examples of trying to control our environment, there is a failure to appreciate the bigger picture. There is little sense of existing in relationship with all others. Environmental issues are by definition concerned with the bigger picture, with our relatedness. Perhaps as never before, they confront us with the stark reality of our essential interdependence. It turns out that almost nothing we do—where we live, how far we travel and by what means, the foods and other products we buy—is a purely private matter. Once we start exploring the effects of our seemingly most trivial choices, we realize how everything ends up affecting everyone and everything else.

To the Christian, this picture of reality should have a certain ring of familiarity. We are members of one body; we pray to "*our*

Father," not "*my* Father." We are given responsibilities within our Father's creation; first and foremost, we have a responsibility towards each other, to "bear one another's burdens." If we fail to fulfill these responsibilities, everything suffers; "the land mourns" (cf. Hos 4.3).

According to this picture, we cannot with impunity reshape the world for our own convenience. We are not ultimately in control of nature: with all our creativity, we are nevertheless creatures, living in a world that is likewise God's creation. And it should be made clear at the outset that "God's creation" is not simply a pious synonym for "the environment"—though it often seems to be used that way in contemporary Christian environmental writing. "Environment" means something *around us*: it is defined in relation and in contradistinction to humans. Whether our relationship to "the environment" is couched in terms of man *versus* nature, or of man working in harmony with nature, we are still talking about two distinct entities. "Creation," however, is defined in contradistinction to the Creator alone. It is the reality to which we ourselves belong, along with everything else from archangels and galaxies to caterpillars and quarks. We can speak of living "in" creation in the sense that we speak of growing up "in" a family—referring not to a sort of container or stage set distinct from ourselves, but to a larger whole of which we form a part. Before we can establish a right attitude to the environment which surrounds us, we need a right understanding of the totality to which we and it belong—the created order.

Many people would agree that the "environmental" crisis has deep spiritual roots, having to do with how we humans see ourselves and our place in nature. But a number of the same people are inclined to look anywhere but to the Christian tradition for answers. Given that the passion for controlling and exploiting nature arose, in its modern guise, in the historically Christian West, it is sometimes assumed that the Christian tradition itself is somehow part of the problem. While this idea does not stand up to serious historical scrutiny, it has created sufficient confusion that something should be said about it.

The modern notion of the natural world as a collection of resources and commodities could arise only in a particular kind of society. On the one hand, it requires a society sufficiently *Christianized,* or at least monotheist, that it no longer sees the world as full of gods. On the other hand, it requires a society sufficiently *de*-Christianized that the natural world is distanced from the God who created it and was born into it in the person of Jesus Christ. It has been pointed out that this modern view of nature is closely bound up with the rise of the money economy and, later, industrialization. We should note, however, that these developments did not take place in the heyday of the Christian empire, but in societies where the authority of Christianity was already weakened by various factors, including the fragmentation resulting from the Reformation. Furthermore, Reformed Christianity itself had modified the traditional view of creation in some significant ways. As many Protestant writers today recognize, a preoccupation with human salvation to the exclusion of the rest of creation went hand in hand with a desire to "purge the landscape of the sacred and locate the site of God's activity entirely in the individual self."[1] Additionally, the growing concern of western Christendom with life in this world led to some impressive social improvements; but it also fostered an

[1]Michael Northcott, *The Environment and Christian Ethics* (Cambridge: Cambridge University Press, 1996), 53; cf. H. Paul Santmire, *The Travail of Nature* (Minneapolis, MN: Fortress Press, 1985), 122.

expectation of prosperity as the proper reward for godliness. None of this *caused* the exploitation of nature, but it cleared away many of the restraints that had existed in earlier times. If the large-scale destruction of God's creation came only with a narrowing of the Christian vision and the growing fragmentation of the Christian world, this suggests that the fullness of the Christian vision might well be able to point us to a better path.

For many Orthodox Christians, the environmental challenge to some of the attitudes and ways of life associated with the modern secular West is a welcome wake-up call. It is a call to recover the world view implicit in the Christian tradition, and indeed reflected in certain aspects of traditional Christian cultures. This is not to evoke the myth of a golden age of Orthodox culture. It is, however, to suggest that environmental responsibility begins with living our faith in the most mundane details of everyday life. It begins with the realization that nothing is un-spiritual and unworthy of God just because it is physical. The housewife making the sign of the Cross over a loaf before cutting it, or the grandmother censing the livestock at her evening prayers, show an awareness of God's presence in his creation that we would do well to regain.

The purpose of this book is to explore how the Orthodox Christian tradition understands nature as God's creation, and humans' place within it. This can be described as "Christian ecology," rather as we speak of "Christian anthropology" or "Christian cosmology," meaning the Church's understanding of the human being and the world, respectively. Ecology in the scientific sense is concerned with living creatures in the environment that they call home (*oikos* in Greek). That environment consists of other members of the same species, and other creatures—animal, vegetable, and mineral. A "Christian ecology," therefore, is the theological understanding of humans-in-the-world—of the "spiritual ecosystem" which makes up God's creation. This means that the Church's *ecological vision* has two equally crucial components: it involves our relationship with both the *ecu-mene* (the inhabited earth, the human community) and the *eco-system* within which we live. It also concerns the relationship of the whole to its Creator.

To explore a Christian ecology, therefore, we need to ask several questions:

- What does it mean to see the material world as God's creation?
- What is the spiritual significance of the material world, its relation to God?
- In what sense is God apart from the universe, and in what sense is he present in it?
- Is the rest of nature "fallen" as a result of human sin?

Then we can explore how the human creature fits into the picture:

- What does it mean to be a material creature, yet fashioned in God's image and likeness?
- What is the role played by other people and other creatures in our relationship with God, and His with us?

Last but by no means least, outlining an ecological vision will lead us into questions arising directly out of the present state of both *ecumene* and *ecoystem*. It is vital to come to a deeper theological understanding of God's creation and our own place in it; but this on its own will not show us how to address specific social and environmental problems. It is not the task of theology to come up with such solutions, and there will sometimes be genuine differences among Christians about the practicalities of remedying various ills. It is, however, legitimate to ask: What are the stumbling blocks in human nature that make it so difficult to adopt really effective solutions, especially to major global problems such as climate change? Often the world seems caught in a vicious circle of "Why should *I* have to compromise *my* standard of living?" and the perhaps more understandable question, "Why shouldn't I have everything that people in affluent countries have already got?" There are real questions about how my attitudes and expectations need to change in order to alleviate the suffering of other people and other creatures. So we need to ask:

- How does the Orthodox Church's tradition and teaching provide the framework for the necessary changes?
- How does it shape us—if we allow it—into people able to break the vicious circle?

The Orthodox Church's vision of God's creation cannot adequately be explored by focusing on a single aspect of the tradition. Different strands of the tradition throw light on each other. Theological writings of the church fathers refer to such themes as man's "dominion" over nature; ascetic writings talk about "despising the world." It is not unknown for people to pick out a few such quotations and conclude that the Christian tradition leads us to treat nature with contempt. But if we turn to stories of holy lives, of the people who live out this theology, we discover that what it means in practice is radically different from our expectations. Then again, take the theme of the material world being transfigured, so that it speaks to us of God and conveys something of his glory, or the theme of all creatures offering praise to God in their own way. Before modern times, we find almost no theological writings discussing these ideas directly; we might be tempted to think that these are modern developments, perhaps even non-Christian in inspiration. But when we look at the Orthodox Church's worship and sacramental life, we can see these themes as a constant through the centuries.

In order to convey the broader picture, therefore, we will take various aspects of the Orthodox tradition in turn. We will start by looking at writings of the church fathers that discuss the material world and the place of man. We will also look at the ascetic tradition and its attitude to matter; the witness of lives of holiness; the cosmology of our liturgical texts; sacramental life and its implications for our life in the world. We will highlight some themes in the thinking of modern Orthodox Christian writers and theologians, some of whom are responding directly to contemporary environmental concerns and "eco-theological" thinking. In conclusion, we will look more closely at some aspects of the Orthodox vision of creation that seem particularly timely today, and some areas that should be further explored.

A central figure in Orthodox theology of creation, whose name will come up repeatedly, is the great seventh-century theologian St Maximus the Confessor. In one of his best-known passages, Maximus speaks of the human as a "bond of unity" in creation: our role is progressively to unite the disparate aspects of the created order, and ultimately to unite the whole with God. Any presentation of the Orthodox Christian vision of creation and ecology should reflect something of this purpose, in however modest a way. It should aim to bring together apparently conflicting concerns and competing "issues," pointing to common threads and suggesting how they may be complementary to each other rather than divisive. We may think of the "divisions" between recognizing Christ in our neighbor and finding him in all of his creation; between contemplation of the world around us, and use of it to serve our own and others' needs; between the theological and the scientific understanding of the material world. The Church's vision of creation will not help us much if we cannot relate it to everything else we know about the universe: to its immensity and complexity, but also its imperfections and the suffering of its creatures.

To understand our role in creation is essential, but it is only a start. In order to discover how best to fulfill that role, we need to make every effort to understand how our actions affect the world and everything living in it. And this brings us to perhaps the most important "division" that we must try to bring into unity. The scale of the problems now facing humans invites paralysis—not to mention denial. In order to get beyond the paralysis, it is necessary to hold together honest recognition of the problems, and our own complicity in them, and the Creator's power and purpose. It is necessary to accept that human beings *are* the cause of the world's plight; and that we are *also* God's chosen instruments through which all things are to be brought to fulfillment in Christ.

Let us now look to the Orthodox Church's tradition and explore how our calling may be envisioned and articulated.

chapter one

Themes in the Church Fathers

If we want to explore Christian teaching about the created world, where do we start? There is a bewildering variety of assertions about the Christian attitude to the material creation, both from those claiming to speak for Christianity and from its critics. Nearly everyone will quote Scripture: the Genesis creation stories, the Psalms and prophets with their invocations of the natural world, the "groaning of creation" in the Epistle to the Romans, to name but a few. But as we all know, what really counts is the way such texts have been understood and used. An idea may be found in Scripture, but actually have played little part in shaping the Christian world view.

This is why we begin with the church fathers—the theologians, teachers and saints whose writings encapsulate the Church's interpretation of Scripture and understanding of doctrine—and look to see what picture of Christian cosmology emerges from their writings. Does Christian tradition start from the belief that "the earth is the Lord's" and creation is "very good"—or that everything comes under man's "dominion" and exists for his sake? Does the earth "praise the Lord," or is it a fallen world needing to be "subdued" by humans? And what about the special role of humans in God's plan for the world: do scientific insights into the affinity between humans and other creatures make a mockery of this belief, or serve to deepen our understanding of it?

We cannot expect the church fathers to provide direct answers to all of the practical questions and dilemmas that arise today. Our worlds are so different: above all, perhaps, the balance of power between man and the natural world is so different. The notion that humanity could hold in its hands the fate of thousands of species and of the earth itself, or that human numbers could increase to threaten the carrying capacity of the planet, would have been beyond the imagination of anyone before modern times.

What we can hope to get from the Fathers is a sense of the Orthodox Church's basic beliefs about God's creation—the sort of beliefs that actually provide a "spiritual compass" when one faces practical choices. What is the spiritual significance of the material world? What is God's purpose for it? In what way is God present in his creation? What is man's place and purpose in the world? How far does the world as we know it reflect God's original intent, and how far does it bear the marks of a "fall"? We will not attempt a comprehensive survey of the Fathers' understanding of man and the cosmos, but rather to highlight some themes that are key to an Orthodox Christian world view.

The body and matter

In recent years, as people have started looking for the underlying world views that have contributed to damage to our environment, some have decided that the Christian attitude to the material world must be at fault. Christianity, it is suggested, separates God from the world, man from "nature," the spiritual from the physical.

There is an irony here: alone of the great monotheistic religions, Christianity proclaims a God who has entered into his own creation and become part of it. But at the same time, the distinction between what is uncreated (God) and what is created (the world) is very real, and marks a major difference between Christianity and polytheistic religions. This distinction, however, has an effect that the detractors of Christianity seem not to have noticed: it emphasizes the connections and affinities between *all* things on the "created" side of the line. And this, of course, includes humans.

The depiction of Christian belief as somehow hostile to the material world is yet more ironic when we think of the revolutionary impact of that faith on classical culture. The Christian Gospel burst in upon a world profoundly shaped by the philosophy of Platonism, in which matter is associated with imperfection, and the body is an encumbrance to the soul. The hope offered by Christians—resurrection in the body—struck pagans as a "hope fitting for earthworms." It is easy for us to overlook what a revolution this Christian perspective on materiality, and on the body specifically, represented in the understanding of matter—how different it was from views in the ancient world, whether represented by Greek philosophy with its hope of escaping from the body, or by Eastern religions with their doctrine of reincarnation.[1] What civilized person in pagan antiquity would want to be tied to their material body for all eternity? Yet Christian belief in the resurrection means that the body—our own material substance—is not some kind of tomb or prison for the spirit, the "real me." The body is an integral part of our being, and our ultimate hope is to be liberated not *from* it, but *with* it. When we affirm that eternal

[1]See Fr Georges Florovsky, *Creation and Redemption* vol. 3, *Collected Works* (Belmont, MA: Nordland, 1976), 33–34, 111.

life involves *resurrection*, we are saying that matter has an eternal significance.

This emphasis is very clear in the early Fathers who wrote in defense of Christianity against the pagans. A work attributed to St Justin, who was martyred in Rome in A.D. 165, insists on this point. The human being who was formed in the image and likeness of God is a creature of flesh: the flesh is precious in the sight of the Lord, and he will not allow it to be lost. It is unthinkable for one part of man to be saved without the rest of him.[2] Later tradition says the same. As St John Chrysostom clarifies, it is not the body as such that we have to "put off" as something alien to us; it is the corruption and death which are characteristics of the body as we know it.[3]

Does this positive attitude to the human body carry over to the rest of the material world? For some Fathers it certainly does; perhaps the best example is the third century bishop and confessor Irenaeus of Lyons, who speaks exultantly of the burgeoning and fruitfulness of creation at the resurrection.[4] But from the beginning, it seems, there was the lurking temptation to tone down the radical newness of the Christian message: to think of our own resurrection as basically a spiritual existence, to which the rest of material creation is superfluous. The great Alexandrian theologian Origen may have fallen into this trap; but the Christian tradition as a whole did not follow him. Origen's attempt to spiritualize the idea of eternal life met with a sharp reaction from another early martyr, Methodius of Olympus (died ca. 311). Methodius

[2]St Justin *On the Resurrection* 7, 8.

[3]St John Chrysostom *On the Resurrection* 6 (PG 50, 427–28).

[4]*Against Heresies* V.34.2.

insists on the full reality of our bodily resurrection: like a good craftsman, God does not throw his work away when it is damaged, but repairs it. The same goes for the whole of creation. God has not established the world just in order to see it destroyed—he has created it to continue in existence.[5] Heaven and earth "will pass away," as the Lord says (Mt 24.35)—but in the sense that they will pass into a more glorious state. And Methodius finds an affirmation of this—as do many later Fathers—in St Paul's words about the creation waiting to be set free from slavery to corruption, into the glorious liberty of the children of God (Rom 8.21). After being restored to a better and more seemly state, he says, creation will remain, rejoicing and exulting over the children of God at the resurrection. There is a definite parallel between the destiny of man and that of the rest of creation. St John Chrysostom picks up this point in commenting on the same passage of Romans. He remarks that according to Isaiah, the inhabitants of the earth will die *just like heaven and earth* ("they who dwell in it will die in like manner" [Is 51.6], according to the Septuagint version used by the Church). Now, we know that the inhabitants of the earth die so as to rise again; so something similar must be true of the cosmos.[6]

The whole of God's creation has a value, and that value is eternal: this is the truth that we need to keep hold of. It is a mistake to think that we can envisage what the restored cosmos will be like, any more than we can really understand the quality of the resurrected body which is glimpsed in the resurrection appearances of Christ. It is an expectation beyond our present experience,

[5]St Methodius *On the Resurrection* 1.6, 8.

[6]*Homily on Romans* 14.5, on vv. 19–20.

perhaps best expressed in the language of poetry. And indeed, we have an eloquent testimony to the ultimate restoration of the world from the great Syrian poet-theologian St Ephrem:

> At our resurrection, both earth and heaven will God renew,
> liberating all creatures, granting them paschal joy, along
>   with us.
> Upon our mother Earth, along with us, did he lay disgrace
> when he placed on her, with the sinner, the curse;
> so, together with the just, he will bless her too;
> this nursing mother, along with her children, shall he who
>   is Good renew.[7]

Particularly striking is Ephrem's use of the image of "mother earth"—one not unfamiliar today, but usually found in a rather different context. For the fourth century Syrian, the significance of this organic relationship is not that it links us with what is mortal and perishable; rather, that it links earth and everything belonging to it with what is imperishable, since the nature of earth's human offspring has been taken up by God himself. We may recall here the traditional icon of the Dormition of the Mother of God, in which Christ the new Adam holds the soul of his own mother like a swaddled baby, reborn into new life.

Given that our concern in this book is meant to be the world in which we live, it might seem decidedly odd that we have begun with the end—with the "resurrection of the body and the life of the age to come," as we say at the conclusion of the Nicene Creed. But then for the Church, the true reality *is* "the state of things to come," in the words of St Maximus. The Kingdom of God is actu-

[7]Hymn IX.1, Sebastian Brock, trans., *Hymns on Paradise* (Crestwood, NY: St Vladimir's Seminary Press, 1990), 136.

ally the "original"; what we see in the present world is only an image of this coming reality. This may seem thoroughly paradoxical; but it is not wholly unlike what we see in the development of a human being. When we look at a human fetus, we get only a very vague sense of what this human being will become. We see something real and not illusory; but the form that we see is not intended to remain. The "truth," the fullness of its biological existence lies in the adult, which is the goal of its development, and in its life beyond the womb.

The Christian faith, then, has an *eschatological* focus, an emphasis on how things will be *ultimately*, at the *end* (*eschaton* in Greek). This itself is sometimes seen as a negative factor, preventing a whole-hearted appreciation of the world in which we live. There is no doubt that Christian eschatology is open to distortion, and has indeed been seriously distorted by some groups and sects. In its popular and sensational form, it is turned into an emphasis on the destruction of the world as we know it and the dramatic rescue of certain "elect" human beings. Such an emphasis might well lead people to see the world around them as disposable: it would seem to replace Methodius' "good craftsman" with a shrewd businessman who believes in built-in obsolescence. But graphic popular evocations of the "end times" have little in common with the church fathers' vision of the destiny of creation. What we see in the Fathers is a recognition that the "form of this world" is indeed passing away—but the *form*, not the world itself. It "passes away" to be replaced with a reality corresponding to God's original intention; and this reality has a place for material creation, even if what this might actually look like remains a mystery. To say this is to affirm the lasting, "ultimate" value of the world that God created and "saw that it was good."

Matter and the mystery of salvation

If we affirm that the material world is of enduring value, this still leaves plenty of other questions. Most obviously, perhaps: What does this mean for our relationship with the material world here and now, this side of the eschaton? We know that it serves our bodily needs—but does it also have spiritual significance? What role does it play in our relationship with God?

Some answers to these questions came in response to specific threats facing the early Church, the first of which was the powerful and diverse movement known as Gnosticism, which came to prominence in the second century. The term "gnostic," or "one who has knowledge," refers to these sectarians' claim to be heirs to an esoteric teaching, which, they alleged, Christ had imparted only to a chosen few. In its amalgam of beliefs from different religious traditions and its elaborate array of spiritual entities involved in the creation of the world, Gnosticism had certain similarities with modern "New Age" spiritualities. A salient feature of all the Gnostic sects, however, was their low view of matter. In the Gnostic system, the material world is not the creation of the true God; matter has nothing to do with spirit, and is destined for destruction. On the Gnostic view, the choice is stark. One option is to worship the true God, the Father of Jesus Christ. The other is to recognize a spiritual aspect in material creation, and thus get embroiled with the undesirable spiritual beings responsible for its creation.

The Gnostics met their match in St Irenaeus, confessor and bishop of Lyons, that staunch defender of the goodness of God's creation, who devoted five books to refuting the various Gnostic heresies. In the course of his argument, Irenaeus lays down one of the basic principles for a Christian understanding of the created world:

the world is a mystery in which ordinary, natural events reveal something deeper—the power of the Creator and Savior at work. Why, Irenaeus asks at one point, did Jesus make wine out of water at Cana, when he could have created it out of nothing? And he offers this explanation: "In this way, he showed that the God who made the earth and commanded it to produce fruit, and who established the waters and brought forth springs, was the same God who, by his Son, bestowed on mankind the blessing of food and the favor of drink."[8] What we see God doing in Christ, in the miracles, and in the sacramental life of the Church, should open our eyes to what that very same God is doing all the time throughout the world. The source of physical life and existence for all the world is exactly the same as the source of spiritual life through Christ. It stands to reason, says Irenaeus, that the revelation of the Father through Christ, his Word, should give life to those who see God—after all, it is the manifestation of God through the created world that gives life to every living thing.[9]

Irenaeus insists that God is at work in the world that we experience all around us; and this has far-reaching implications for our view of matter. Matter is shown to be a source of spiritual gifts no less than physical. Because this world is God's own creation, it is a gift worthy to be offered back to him. And when we offer it back to him, as we do in bringing bread and wine for the Eucharist, this enables him to give it back to us again as a vehicle of sanctification. It is through his material creation that he gives us food to sustain our physical life; but then that same creation is "recycled," so to speak, to give us sustenance for eternal life. When we offer

[8]*Against Heresies* III.11.5 *Ante-Nicene Fathers* [ANF] 1, 427.

[9]*Against Heresies* IV.20.7.

products of the earth as Eucharist and receive them back from their Creator as the food of incorruption, we are recognizing that the creation of the world and its ultimate transformation are both part of the same movement, the same divine plan. We see a grain of wheat falling to earth and decomposing, and "rising with manifold increase by the Spirit of God, and serving for our use, and then receiving the Word of God and becoming the Eucharist. . . ." And because we have been fed with this "eucharisted bread," we can be confident that our own flesh will follow the same trajectory, rising again and receiving incorruption.[10]

"Our opinion is in accordance with the Eucharist," says Irenaeus.[11] The centrality of sacramental life to our appreciation of the material world has its beginnings here. On the one hand, Irenaeus firmly establishes the analogy between the way God works salvation through the gift of creation as a whole, and the way he works salvation in the sacraments. And on the other hand, he highlights the significance of the Incarnation, on which all sacramental life is based. God the Word has become part of the world created through him; and this is the crucial event that enables creation to be not only a means of physical life, but also the gift of his own life to us.

Irenaeus forcefully emphasizes a truth that the Orthodox Church has never lost sight of: we ourselves are material creatures. We are created as body-and-spirit, and it is as body-and-spirit that we are destined to be saved and transfigured. And this means that in our movement towards Christ, we cannot but bring all creation with us. The Fathers had an intuitive understanding of the interconnec-

[10]*Against Heresies* V.2.3 (ANF 1, 528).

[11]*Against Heresies* IV.18.5.

tion of all matter; only recently have we come to recognize this as literal scientific fact.

The lesson from all this is that matter can never be excluded from spiritual life. This principle would later be articulated in a powerful way by St John of Damascus, again responding to heretical teachings more than five centuries after Irenaeus. This time the threat came from iconoclasm, which racked the Eastern Church for over a hundred years. John is scathing in his attacks on those who reject icons in favor of purely spiritual forms of worship, and thus seem to deny that they themselves are embodied creatures and a part of the physical world. But above all, he is passionate in his defense of the icon as the supreme affirmation of Christian faith. In the Incarnation, God has become part of his creation: that is why "I make an image of the God whom I see . . . I worship the Creator of matter who became matter for my sake, who willed to take his abode in matter; who worked out my salvation through matter. Never will I cease honoring the matter which wrought my salvation!"[12]

Seeing God in creation: wonder, word and wisdom

The Fathers' vivid sense of God's hand constantly at work in all his creation fuels their sense of the universe as a great wonder, a continuing miracle. As St Ephrem expresses it:

> We too should wonder and give thanks,
> that from the dry stalk of wheat there comes ample bread,
> that from the vine stalk there flows wine . . .

[12]*On Divine Images* I.16; David Anderson, trans., *John of Damascus On the Divine Images: Three Apologies against those who attack the Divine Images* (Crestwood, NY: St Vladimir's Seminary Press, 1980), 23.

this too is a great wonder, as great as the miracle at
Cana.[13]

It is the same sense of wonder that moves a pastor of our own day to look at the natural world and challenge the skeptic: "*show us what is not God!*"[14]

This attitude may seem problematic to some today. If everything in the world is a miracle, where does this leave scientific inquiry? Does this approach mean that it is unnecessary, even impious, to want to explore the physical workings of the world? The interest shown by many of the Fathers in the science of their day—St Basil the Great and St John of Damascus come to mind—suggests otherwise. We need to be very clear that the essence of a "miracle" is the *wonder* that it inspires. This is the meaning both of Latin *miraculum* and the Greek *thauma*. Whether it is an aspect of nature, or an isolated event that appears to go against the laws of nature, does not make much difference—that is Ephrem's point. So a strong sense of God at work in nature should make us more, not less, eager to explore the intricacies of his handiwork, rather as we might want to explore the inspirations and techniques of a favorite author. But while the patristic approach is open to scientific inquiry, it is certainly antithetical to any form of *scientism*, to the belief that science alone provides the only knowledge of the world worthy of the name.

The Fathers' sense of *mystery* and *miracle* in the universe is based on more than a lack of data about its workings. Certainly the

[13]*Hymns on the Table* III, Sebastian Brock, trans., "World and Sacrament in the Writings of the Syrian Fathers," *Sobornost* 6.10 (Winter 1974): 695.

[14]Bishop Nicolai (Velimirovic), quoted in Michael Oleksa, *Orthodox Alaska: A Theology of Mission* (Crestwood, NY: St Vladimir's Seminary Press, 1992), 39.

Fathers do frequently point to things that we cannot explain even about the world around us—how then, they conclude, can we expect to understand the mysteries of God? The disadvantages of this approach are apparent today. Many people will draw what seems to be the logical conclusion: since we can now give a very detailed explanation of the rising of the Nile, or the behavior of migratory birds, why do we need the "God hypothesis"? The Fathers' arguments from ignorance may strike us as rather facile, but they are grounded in something more profound than the actual limits of human knowledge: they reflect a keen awareness of the "depth" of created things. An awareness of "depth" means that when we do not understand the world around us, we are reminded of our own limitations. When we look closely at the natural world and learn more about it, we perceive something more profound than the Creator's "inordinate fondness for beetles"—for a start, the abundance of insects might make us reflect that our own idea of which creatures are important and valuable may be rather superficial! And as our knowledge of the workings of nature increases, this does not *explain away* the wonder of creation; instead, it deepens our sense of awe at the intricacies of divine wisdom. We will look at some examples of this shortly in St Basil's Hexaemeron, a series of highly discursive sermons on the six days of creation.

The awe that the Fathers felt before the created world, then, did not come from ignorance about the world; what struck them was the very *intelligibility* of the world. The fact that the universe is accessible to the intellect reinforced their conclusion that it is suffused with the "word" of God—his *logos*, his intelligibility or rationality.

This perception of the universe was by no means unique to the church fathers; something like it was shared by pagans of late antiquity. For this reason, it plays an important part in St Athanasius' treatise *On the Incarnation*, an apology for Christian doctrine directed against the pagans. His concern here is to show that the Incarnation makes sense, and the way he does this is still highly relevant today.

> What is so inappropriate [he asks] about the Word manifesting himself in a body? Suppose we agree that there is a Word of God in whom the Father created all things, that by his providence the universe receives light and life and being . . . But if the Word of God has entered into every part of the universe, which is simply a great body, why is it surprising or unfitting to say that he has entered also into human nature?[15]

Here we have a picture of the universe wholly pervaded by the presence of its Creator. This presence relates to the Incarnation rather as God's work in creation relates to miracles and the mysteries of the Church: in both cases, the difference in scale hinders us from seeing the recurring pattern. In fact, the larger the scale, the harder it is for us to see any pattern at all. As Athanasius continues, "Men could not recognize him as ordering and ruling creation as a whole. So . . . he takes to himself for an instrument a part of the whole, namely a human body, and enters into that. Thus he ensured that . . . those who could not lift their eyes to his unseen power might recognize and behold him in the likeness of themselves."[16] By seeing

[15] *On the Incarnation* 41.

[16] *On the Incarnation* 43; A Religious of C.S.M.V., trans., *St Athanasius On the Incarnation* (Crestwood, NY: St Vladimir's Seminary Press, 1982), 79.

the works that God performs on earth as man, we are to recognize the same hand at work throughout the universe.

There is, however, a difference between what Athanasius understands by the Word in the world, and what his pagan contemporaries meant, and that difference rests in the clear divide between God as *uncreated,* and the world as *created.* For the Stoic philosophers of late antiquity, the *logos* or "word" was a "world soul"; something spiritual, but at the same time *wholly* part of the world. The Christian understanding, by contrast, involves a paradox: the Word is *in* the world but *not part of it,* since he is uncreated and God. The rationality of the universe does not simply connect us with "a mysterious something" or a "life force"; it connects us with a personal and loving God who has lived among us as Jesus Christ.

The Arian crisis, which brought Athanasius to prominence as a defender of orthodoxy, forced him to clarify further what is meant by saying that the divine Word is "in" the world. What the Arians meant by it was straightforward. The Word and Wisdom of God says, "The Lord created me in the beginning of his ways" (Prov 8.22, LXX): therefore, by Arian logic, the Word is simply a part of the created order. But St Athanasius absolutely resists the temptation to cut the Gordian knot of the Christian paradox. It *is* the uncreated Word of God speaking here; and he is speaking of the creation *as himself*—as he will later speak of the persecuted Church as himself, when he confronts Saul: "Why do you persecute *me*?" (Acts 9.4). He can do this because he is imaged in all that was made through him, in everything that bears the stamp of the Word and Wisdom of God.[17] The metaphors that Athanasius uses to express God's presence in the world are not always entirely adequate to

[17] *Discourse Against the Arians* II.22.77–80.

the task, but we can discern nevertheless the extraordinary boldness of his affirmation: it is the wholly transcendent Creator who is entirely united with each and all by his own power.[18]

When it is no longer a matter of arguing for the Incarnation against pagans and heretics, the emphasis on the immanence of the Creator in his creation remains. Christ, the Wisdom and Word (*Logos*) of God, is to be seen "embodied" in the wisdom and rationality, the *logos* (as in "logic"), which the Fathers see everywhere in creation. The Cappadocian brothers St Basil and St Gregory of Nyssa express this with particular eloquence. An important passage for this understanding is Ps 18.2, 4: "The heavens are telling the glory of God, and the firmament proclaims his handiwork . . . there is no speech, nor are there words; their voice is not heard." Gregory takes this to indicate that the wisdom contemplated in creation is a sort of "word" telling us about God, even though the universe does not literally speak words.[19]

St Basil sees a similar meaning in the verse from Proverbs, "the Lord created me in the beginning of his ways"; he sees this passage as referring to "certain 'words' of the original wisdom laid down in creation before the rest when it was made. This wisdom calls silently upon its Creator and Lord, so that through it you may ascend to the knowledge of him who alone is wise."[20] Not only do these passages emphasize the word and wisdom that pervades the universe, they also suggest that our primary task in our dealings with the rest of creation is to "listen" to it, and respond by praising God.

[18]See *On the Incarnation* 42.

[19]*Hexaemeron* (PG 44, 73).

[20]Hom. 12, *On the beginning of Proverbs*, 3.

One can say that "listening" to the cosmos in this way is precisely what St Basil does—and keeps urging his hearers to do—throughout his homilies on the six days of creation (*Hexaemeron*). This entire series of sermons on the days of creation can be seen as a sustained hymn to the Wisdom of God who "has filled all with the works of his creation and has left everywhere visible memorials of his wonders."[21] "I want creation to penetrate you with so much wonder," he tells his congregation, "that everywhere, wherever you may be, the least plant may bring to you the clear remembrance of the Creator."[22] In this case, he goes on to talk about drawing morals from nature: you see a field of grass, and remember that all flesh is grass. The very popularity of such analogies down the centuries might tempt us to dismiss them as cliches, but they contain an important affirmation. If creation is the book of God's words, it will not only have an objective rationality which enables us to understand how it works; it will also be a way for God to speak to us personally, regardless of how sophisticated or how primitive our scientific understanding of the world may be.

But Basil is not interested only in drawing morals: he cannot restrain his fascination with the natural world *per se*, with its wonderful manifestations of "great wisdom in small things."[23] "A single plant . . . is sufficient to occupy all your intelligence in the contemplation of the skill which produced it," he says, and proceeds to illustrate the point with a discourse on a stalk of wheat.[24] He is lost in wonder at the way water becomes oil in the olive but juice in the

[21]*Hexaemeron* VIII.8. Translations based on *Ante-Nicene Fathers*, second series, 8.

[22]*Hexaemeron* V.2.

[23]*Hexaemeron* V.9.

[24]*Hexaemeron* V.3.

vine, and how its sweetness has a different character in different fruits, and so forth. Such a reaction to the intricacy of nature is, of course, by no means exclusive to believers, but Basil would go much further: the wisdom and skill seen in creation is inseparable from providential care. God is not simply a watchmaker; he is a Father. Basil illustrates this from the case of the sea urchin. Following the received wisdom recorded by Pliny, he explains that the urchin has an unerring sense of an imminent storm, and prepares itself by clinging to the bottom of a large rock so as not to be swept away: "for the Lord of the sea and of the winds has placed a clear trace of his great wisdom even in this little creature"—since nothing is outside God's providence or neglected by him.[25]

The glory of God hidden in his creatures

The idea of the created world speaking to us of its Creator has a role in the Fathers' apologetics—it is one of the ways in which they explain and argue their faith to others. But it would be a mistake to see apologetics as the natural habitat of the Fathers' teaching on creation. What we can learn above all from the Fathers' understanding of nature is not arguments or proofs for God's existence but a *way of seeing*, a perception of the world around us that is profoundly theological. This is something rather different from a self-contained natural theology in which one reasons from created things to the existence of a "designer" (as in the classic "argument from design" or its modern variant, "intelligent design" theory). The presence of the Creator written into his creation is not a conclusion: it is a presupposition, supported by observation and experience, which then opens our eyes to reading the book of creation in a different way.

[25] *Hexaemeron* VII.5.

The way of perceiving the world exemplified so memorably by St Basil is described in quite precise terms by St Isaac the Syrian (seventh century), one of the Church's most profound spiritual teachers. Just as we have two physical eyes, says Isaac, so we have two spiritual eyes. With one of these spiritual eyes we contemplate the glory of God's nature; but with the other, we see aspects of his glory hidden in his creatures—his power, wisdom and providence.[26] The idea of creation as a theophany, a manifestation of divine power and glory, is not original to Christianity. But its Christian version is summed up in the Epistle to the Romans: "Ever since the creation of the world his invisible nature, namely, his eternal power and deity, has been clearly perceived in the things that have been made" (Rom 1.20). This passage is a basic text for the belief that there can be a natural theology, a way of coming to know something of God through his creation. For the Fathers, however, there is no thought of separating this approach from other ways in which God reveals himself to us. We can approach God through his creation; but knowledge of God in turn leads us to look at creation through different eyes. This is pointed out by another great master of the spiritual life, St Maximus the Confessor. If the invisible is seen by means of the visible, says Maximus (referring to Rom 1.20), then how much more are visible things perceived through the invisible in spiritual contemplation. For to contemplate spiritual things by means of the visible things which symbolize them is nothing other than to understand visible things, in the Spirit, by means of the invisible.[27]

Maximus is asserting here that visible, material things have their own *spiritual* reality. They are not something we relate to only

[26]Hom. 46, *The Ascetical Homilies of St Isaac the Syrian*, translated by Holy Transfiguration Monastery (Boston, 1984), 223.

[27]*Mystagogy* 2.

on a practical and utilitarian level; they too have a deeper level, accessible only through contemplation. Some have suggested that an emphasis on the symbolism of the natural world denigrates its reality; that it makes the physical world *nothing but* a set of signs pointing beyond itself. But Maximus is saying that this is far from the truth. The visible points us to the invisible; but the invisible guides us back to the visible world, revealing it to us in a new light. It teaches us how to see the physical world in its full reality.

God in the universe and the universe in God

The conviction that God is the "indwelling life of things" is fundamental to Christian cosmology (or understanding of the world). But it is perennially difficult to express this conviction in a way that is not misleading. When in the Creed we confess God as "maker of heaven and earth," we are implicitly holding together two halves of a paradox: God is absolutely distinct from the created order, but everything created is inextricably bound up with him: apart from him, it simply has no being. The challenge has always been to unpack this terse confession in ways that keep a balance between the sense in which God is outside and beyond everything (*transcendent)*, and the sense of God as *indwelling* all things (*immanent*). This balance has direct consequences for the way we perceive, and therefore treat, the world around us. Overemphasize immanence, and you end up with a pantheism which identifies God with nature; overemphasize transcendence, and you have a world alien to the sacred, irrelevant to our spiritual life and our quest for God. Fear of the latter conclusion and its consequences has led some people today to be quite suspicious of the basic Christian belief in divine transcendence.

We have already seen how, in the fourth century, Athanasius and the three great Cappadocian Fathers grappled with this balance; they express the presence in creation of the transcendent Creator in a variety of images, some more and some less successful. But later Fathers developed a much more elaborate framework for speaking of God in his creation, emphasizing both the otherness by nature and the inseparable bond between the two. Of particular note are St Maximus the Confessor in the seventh century and St Gregory Palamas in the fourteenth. Our exploration of these thinkers will at points need to be technical and complex, but our attention to their subtleties will be repaid.

St Maximus and the "words" of things

Maximus is very obviously building on his predecessors. He draws implicitly on Athanasius, and explicitly on Gregory the Theologian and Dionysius the Areopagite (sixth century?). Some of his most penetrating thought is presented in the form of commentaries on the latter two, although he actually takes their thinking much further, and sometimes modifies it.

Maximus' greatest contribution for our understanding of God's immanence is his theology of the *logoi* of things. We have talked already about the *logos* or rationality of the universe as a reflection of the divine *Logos* or Word. But what does this actually mean for created things themselves and their relationship to God? And what does it mean for our own relationship with the rest of creation? Maximus explores these questions much more extensively and in greater depth than anyone before him.

Logoi, in Maximus' thought, are the intelligible principles that define the essence of every created being, and God's will and intention for it.[28] One of the first things that strikes us here is that the "essence" or the truth of the thing itself is inseparable from God's providential guidance of it, from its origin in his will and its ultimate resting place in him.

The *logoi* can be thought of as the interface between God and his creation. In and through them, all things are in God. Not, of course, in the same sense as the divine Word, the Son of the Father who is "one in essence with him," is "in" the Father. The "words" of created things do not belong to the essence of God, but reside in his loving and creative will. From all eternity, he "thinks up" all that is to exist; he knows the principles of its being in that he knows his own will. The *logoi* of things can be thought of as exemplars in the divine will for created things, "blueprints" in accordance with which the actual creature comes into being at its appointed time. There are obvious similarities with Plato's theory of "ideas" underlying all that exists, but there are also crucial differences. In Christian thought, the *logoi,* or exemplars, or conceptions—whatever term we use—never form an autonomous realm *between* God and actual creatures. They are divine *energies*—God himself active in the world. They therefore place no restriction on God's creative freedom, or on creatures' absolute dependence on him.

Again, God is in everything that exists because everything is a realization of his *logoi*, his creative will. This means that to partake in existence *is* to partake in God, in the creative will of him who is existence itself ("I am he who is," Ex 3.14, Septuagint). Maximus can therefore say that everything participates in God

[28]See, for example, *Scholia on the Divine Names* (PG 4.353B); *Ambiguum* 7; Paul M. Blowers and Robert Louis Wilken, trans., *On the Cosmic Mystery of Jesus Christ: Selected Writings from St Maximus the Confessor* (Crestwood, NY: St Vladimir's Seminary Press, 2003), 55.

"proportionately" or "by analogy"—in the way proper to itself, within its own limits. Whether it is by rationality, or vital movement, or some other essential characteristic of the creature, it enjoys participation in God.[29]

The *logoi* are regarded as immutable—they do not change, in that God does not change his mind. But this in no way means that the things defined by them are static. It is a way of saying that the dynamism, the development and unfolding of creatures is not haphazard; it is wholly within God's plan and providence. Which is to say that it too has its *logos*, for the "*logos* of being" encompasses principles of essence, potentiality, and activity. Maximus, like the rest of his contemporaries, assumes that the "natures" to which individual things belong are a permanent fixture: as long as creation endures, there have been and always will be humans, horses, olives and so forth. Yet it is not apparent why "natures" could not include a principle of development, just as individuals do. Some modern writers have therefore explored the potential of the notion of *logoi* for understanding how evolution fits into God's providence, how we can understand the dynamism of life as grounded in God's steadfast will.

The *logoi* of created things, then, are the "interface" between each and all of those things and their Creator. But they are equally a "path" by which rational creatures can come to know God. The fact that we are *rational* beings (*logikoi*) means that we are endowed with the capacity to go beyond sense experience of the world around us so as to apprehend its rationale or *logos*. When we hear the church fathers talking about "reason" (*logos*) as a prime human characteristic, it is important to bear in mind this

[29] *Ambiguum* 7, ibid.

connection. The term "reason" in English is loaded with post-Enlightenment overtones of the autonomy of the reasoning brain. We think of those stultifying arguments about "reason" *versus* "revelation"; reason comes to mean the capacity of human beings to make sense of the world without reference to God, and then, by extension, their capacity to order it to their own liking.

The overtones of *logos* to the Greek Fathers could hardly be more different. Our *logos*, our rationality, does indeed allow us to find out about the properties of things and make use of them. But far more importantly, it allows us to see them as reflections of the Creator's loving will, and to come to know something of him through them. But even in saying this, we have to beware of the misleading presuppositions that are the legacy of centuries of rationalism. It is not that we *reason* our way from created beings to their Creator: our contemplative understanding of them draws us towards him, but knowledge of God is something that only he himself bestows. And in that knowledge, man penetrates still more deeply into the reality of created things, for he perceives their *logoi* preexisting in God.[30] Our rationality, then, does not serve to separate us from the rest of creation; it is given to us for the sake of all creation, to enable us to *make the connection* between it and its Creator.

Spelling out God in creation

Maximus' thought is notoriously difficult to follow; so it might appear that the doctrine of the *logoi* is an abstruse piece of theological theorizing. But as we make the effort to grasp what Maxi-

[30]cf. *Centuries on Theology* 1.9, 2.4; *On Various Texts*, 71. G.E.H. Palmer, Philip Sherrard and Kallistos Ware, trans., *Philokalia* 2 (London: Faber & Faber, 1981), 115–6, 138, 180.

mus wants to convey, we begin to realize that this way of looking at reality has some dramatic consequences for our entire vision of the world around us: the divine presence within it, its destiny in God, and above all the essential unity of the created order.

Maximus reveals to us that we are standing on holy ground: the "ineffable, supranatural and divine fire," God the Word, is *present in the being of everything* as in a burning bush.[31] It is passages such as these that allow us to speak of a threefold "embodiment" of God the Word: in the created world, in Scripture, and lastly and most fully "shining forth in the flesh from the burning bush that is the Holy Virgin."[32] The idea of creation as God's book, attributed to the founder of monasticism, St Anthony (among others), appears here with a new immediacy: God is "encoded" for us in everything that he has made. We are surrounded on every side by his "letters," his "analogies" in creatures, and our task as rational beings is to spell him out.[33] The implications of this are clear: just as we revere the Scriptures, treating even the physical book with respect, and (more importantly) striving not to distort the text to suit ourselves, so we are to reverence the "book" of creation.

So the divine Word does not only become personally incarnate as a human being; there is also a sense in which he is "incarnate," by virtue of the divine energies, in his entire creation. And we can say something similar when we speak about the divine image in created beings. "Image" is a term with more than one meaning, but the meanings are related. The Son and Word of God is uniquely

[31] *Ambigua*, Difficulty 10; Andrew Louth, *Maximus the Confessor* (London: Routledge, 1996), 73.

[32] Ibid.

[33] See *Ambigua* (PG 91, 1285D).

the "image of the invisible God," (Col 1.15) and we humans are *according to* the image of God. But all other created things are images, too—they image God's will, in that they are "images and similitudes" of the *logoi* in which they participate, which reside in God's will.[34] Our own creation "according to the image," therefore, does not only *distinguish us from* other creatures; it also *links us with* them. We are bearers of that image in a world which itself images God's creative will and intentions. In a later chapter, we will see this characteristic of creation reflected in the ways in which creation leads us to God through the sacramental and liturgical life of the Orthodox Church.

The idea that God is imaged in his creation also raises some difficult questions, which cannot be ignored if the Christian world view is to have credibility. The natural world has all sorts of features that suggest anything but wisdom and love. If the smallpox virus and the killer parasite have a metaphysical "principle of existence" at all, it might be argued, then that principle images cruelty and destruction. Clearly, we cannot simply look at the actual state of the world and read off the Creator's original and ultimate will for creation. It is for precisely this reason that the Fathers see a fall, a dislocation in God's original plan, as affecting the whole created order—we will return to this point at the end of this chapter. This does not mean that things cease to bear the hallmark of their Maker in any way. A wicked human testifies to free will; and a virus, however deadly to other organisms, testifies abundantly to the vibrancy and adaptability of life. But those characteristics often *function* in a way that causes conflict and destruction. Side by side with his insistence that everything is rooted in the will of God, Maximus also sees in creation a certain

[34]See Maximus *Scholia on the Divine Names* 7.3.

"random movement devoid of divine presence," which will ultimately cease to exist when God will be all in all.[35]

When we speak of created things as imaging the divine will, therefore, we are affirming that there is a rationale in God's providence for the existence even of those creatures whose "movement" appears to be purely destructive; we are reminded of the parable of the wheat and the tares which must be allowed to "grow together until the harvest" (Mt 13.30). This is not to suggest that we should do literally nothing to alter the order of nature. Quite apart from the fact that this would mean no agriculture, medicine, or plastic arts, it would be contrary to our own innate character as creative and inventive beings. But if creatures image the divine will in their very being, this does suggest that before presuming to change some aspect of nature, we will consider very carefully what providential purpose might be served by the existing arrangement. Decisions about eliminating a pest or predator, or interfering with the course of a river, for instance—not to mention uncharted realms such as genetic engineering and nanotechnology—will be significantly influenced by our view of God's presence in creation. If there is no divine will or purpose in the natural order, then there is no reason, in principle, why human beings should not be able to make a better job of it—even though experience suggests that unintended consequences are legion. But if the natural order does reflect a purpose, then our ideas for improving it have to be measured against a rationality beyond our own. The presence of a *logos* in every created thing necessitates some form of *dia-logue* in all our dealings with creation.

[35]*Ambiguum* 7 (PG 91, 1092C); Blowers, *Cosmic Mystery,* 66

"God, properly speaking, is everything"

As we read the Fathers in general, but most especially Maximus, we start to realize how different their cosmology is from other, later ideas, such as those of the deists, who envisaged the creator as a cosmic watchmaker, who winds up the "mechanism" of the universe and then lets it run on its own. Nor, indeed, is there any room for a notion of a providence somehow running parallel to the "natural" life of created things, "intervening" from some sort of "outside." There is no "outside": God's purpose for each entity is part of its *logos*, built into the reality of the thing itself. It is hard for us to grasp this, because all human activity, no matter how creative, works with some existing "given" that is exterior to us. Maximus does on occasion use the image of an artist for God's creative work, but he moves rapidly to strip it of its implications of externality. The divine artistry that remains stamped on creatures is not simply the maker's mind and intention expressed in a material; it is their very existence. A human artist creates form: God's "art" creates being.[36]

More often, however, Maximus uses much more dramatic language for God's presence in creation; he dispenses with images that give us the illusion of being able to grasp the mystery. He affirms that God is beyond everything, but can say in the same breath that "God, properly speaking, is everything."[37] How, we might wonder, does this startling statement differ from pantheism? The word to focus on here is "is." It is not a mere equals sign: "God is everything" does not mean that "everything is God." God *is* everything, because *God is*, as he declares to Moses from the

[36]*Scholia on the Divine Names* 4.25 (PG 4, 296BC).

[37]*Ambigua* (PG 91.1257A).

burning bush: "I am he who is." For anything created, to *be* at all is to participate in "the Being," in God. This affirmation is of a piece with Maximus' cosmic vision. Christ is Alpha and Omega, and everything in between.

Some of Maximus' most remarkable thinking about the destiny of creation is developed in an attempt to explain a highly pantheistic-sounding passage from Gregory the Theologian, in which the human being is described as a "particle of God." One might expect Maximus to focus on the uniqueness and high calling of human beings; but instead, he looks at the question against a much broader background. Yes, it refers to the principle of our being, which is in God; but it also has an eschatological sense, cosmic in scope. It has to do with our appointed role in bringing *the universe as a whole* to its intended goal:

As the human being becomes godlike and his body comes to share in the gift of immortality,

> The one Creator of all enters into all things, proportionately to each, through humanity, and the many things that differ from one another by nature come into one, converging around the one nature of man. And God himself becomes all things in all, encompassing all things and giving them real existence in himself, because none of the things that exist any longer has a random movement devoid of his presence.[38]

What Maximus' explanation actually points to is not the distinction between man and other creatures, but the ultimate *unity* for which the cosmos is created. And not simply a unity, but a unity in God: as he writes elsewhere, it is for the sake of deification

[38] *Ambiguum* 7 (PG 91, 1092BC); Blowers, *Cosmic Mystery*, 66.

that *all things* have been brought into being.[39] Startling as this affirmation might seem, it is entirely consistent with Maximus' insistence that the grace that deifies all things is part of the same divine work that creates and sustains all things and guides their unfolding. Even though God is said to have "rested" after the six days of creation (Gen 2.2–3), he is "working still," as Christ says (Jn 5.17), to bring all creatures into harmony with each other and with the whole. God is at work deifying the universe, so that he will be *through all and in all* (Eph 4.6).[40]

Such passages make it quite clear that the harmony and unity of all things is a work in progress. Maximus is not asking us to believe, against all the evidence to the contrary, that such a state is already in existence. But he is saying that the intended unity of the cosmos in Christ is built into its very structure. Created things in their infinite variety can also be regarded as *one*, because their various *logoi* are united by virtue of their relation to the one personal *Logos*, the Word of God. "For he is the beginning and cause of all things, in whom all things in heaven and on earth were created . . . all things were created from him and through him and for him" (cf. Col 1.15–17).[41] The tension between this vision of unity, on the one hand, and the present reality of our world on the other, presents us with our task; indeed, it provides the blueprint for our life in God's creation. We humans, like everything else around us, are defined by our own inner principle or *logos*; through this inner principle, the one cause which holds all things together is present within us, giving rise to a "loving affinity" among all things such that "they belong to each other more than to themselves, in accor-

[39]Letter 24 (PG 91.609CD).

[40]*To Thalassius* 2, Blowers, *Cosmic Mystery*, 99–100.

[41]*Ambiguum* 7, Blowers, *Cosmic Mystery*, 54.

dance with that unifying relationship."[42] As creatures endowed with free will, we are quite able to reject this "loving affinity" with other people and other creatures; but the common ground of our being means that if we want to become truly ourselves, we have no alternative but to embrace it.

The divine energies in the world

Maximus' extraordinarily profound cosmic vision shows us the depth to which the Christian tradition can go in affirming God's immanence in all creation, and the implications of this pervasive divine presence for our own relationship with all other created things. But the definitive framework for speaking of God's presence in the world is provided only in the fourteenth century, by St Gregory Palamas. It was left to Palamas to formulate explicitly the distinction, clearly recognized by Maximus and earlier Fathers, between the *essence* of God and his *uncreated energies*. The great value of this formula is that it enables us to conceptualize, and therefore live with, the paradox that God is *both* utterly unknowable *and* can be participated in. God-in-himself is indeed inaccessible to creatures; but the divine power and energy at work in the world is also God, only in this case God-in-relation-to-creatures.

Like Maximus' conception of the inner structure of creation, Palamas' theology of divine essence and energies might easily be dismissed as abstract and academic. But its continuing importance becomes clear when we see some of the modern reactions against what is perceived as the traditional Christian doctrine of God as Creator. Those influenced by process theology, for instance, understand the traditional notion of "Creator" as plac-

[42] *Mystagogy* 7.

ing God exclusively above, beyond and outside the world, so that the created world would become the realm of the non-sacred, the non-spiritual. Central to Palamas' thinking, by contrast, is a recognition of the spiritual potential of matter; after all, he first became embroiled in theological controversy in order to defend the hesychast monks, who practiced prayer involving the totality of their bodies, and maintained that the vision of divine light was accessible to their physical eyes. Any idea that matter is impervious to the divine would fly in the face of their, and his, experience. Palamas affirms that through the incarnation, the flesh itself is revealed as an "inexhaustible source of sanctification."[43] But as we have seen in earlier Fathers, the Incarnation does not take place in a vacuum. The groundwork is already there in creation: "God is in the universe and the universe in God, the one sustaining, the other being sustained by him. Thus all things participate in God's sustaining energy, but not in his essence."[44] Palamas affirms a personal God truly distinct from his creation, who is at the same time the vital principle of everything that exists.

Man's place in creation

We have focused so far on creation as a whole: but what about the human being? Our understanding of our own position and status is clearly crucial to the way we treat the rest of creation. Without attempting to give an exhaustive account of Christian anthropology, I will try to highlight a few themes of particular relevance to our relations with the world around us. How does man fit into God's plan for the whole? What images do the Fathers use for man's place in creation, and what do these images imply?

[43]Hom. 16, *On the Incarnation* (PG 151, 193B).

[44]*Natural and Theological Chapters* 104, *Philokalia* 4, 393.

Everyone knows that the Christian tradition esteems man very highly. Indeed, the charge is often made today—albeit on rather slender historical evidence—that the "anthropocentrism" of Christianity is largely responsible for human destruction of the world around us. The notion of "dominion," so the argument goes, leads directly to the fateful misapprehension that we can be in total control of our environment. To see how our tradition actually views man, we shall first turn again to St Maximus, who provides some telling insights into the question of "anthropocentricity."

When Maximus is describing man's intended state, and the effects of his fall, he starts with precisely the question of *what is at the center*: "Man did not *move around* . . . God as his own principle in the way that he was naturally created to do; but . . . in a manner contrary to nature he *moved around* the things below him, over which he had been appointed by God to rule."[45] The first thing we notice here is that "anthropocentricity," "man as center," simply does not come into the picture, either as a good thing or a bad thing. Man was created to be *God-centered*, and instead, *he* became *centered on the world*. Now, some people today might think that such a focus on the world, on creation, is a long-overdue corrective. So why do the Fathers think otherwise? It has to do with their basic understanding of what the world is and where it is going. The world is not created in order to remain closed in on itself. So the choice is not between placing creation in general at the center, and placing the human creature alone at the center. Rather, there is a choice between revolving around *anything* within creation, and opening out to God. Any "center" other than God becomes an idol: anthropocentrism is to make an idol of ourselves. Man can never be the ultimate center of creation; he is,

[45]*Ambiguum* 41 (PG 91:1308CD). Cf. Louth, *Maximus*, 158.

however, intended to be a focal point. This is a subtle but vital difference. Man is a "natural bond"[46] bringing everything into unity around himself; and because he is a also a "mid-point" between Creator and creation, he is to bring everything into unity with its Creator. To this end, man is endowed with a "natural power to unite what was divided": male with female, the world of human life with paradise, earth with heaven, the sensible world with the intelligible, and, ultimately, creation with the Uncreated. It is this power of "uniting" that causes man to function as a "focal point." To this extent he *can* be seen as a "center" of convergence, but he functions as a "center" *so as to serve a purpose beyond himself.* Man is called to draw all things together around his own nature *so that God may be all in all.*[47] This image appears "anthropocentric" only if the top half of the picture, the vertical axis, is sliced off. It cannot be emphasized too strongly that *nothing* in the Christian understanding of man and the world is going to make any sense if this vertical axis, the reference to God, is left out of the picture.

The notion of man as a mid-point goes back at least to Gregory of Nyssa, who speaks of man as the "mean" between the "extremes" of divine and incorporeal nature, on the one hand, and animal nature, on the other.[48] (It should be noted that the Fathers are well aware that we *have* an "animal nature"—they just refuse to see it as our defining characteristic.) So Gregory accepts the familiar notion of his time that man is a microcosm, a world in miniature; but he does not consider sharing the nature of a mosquito a particularly exciting distinction. Our true greatness, he says, consists

[46]*Ambiguum* 41 (PG 91:1305B); Louth, *Maximus,* 157.

[47]Ambiguum 7; Blowers, *Cosmic Mystery,* 66.

[48]*On the Making of Man* XVI.9.

in our being created in the image of God.[49] This does not mean, however, that what we have in common with other creatures is unimportant. On the contrary, it is absolutely crucial to the purpose of our creation. Spiritual and material natures are united in man "so that nothing of creation should be rejected as worthless, as the apostle says (see 1 Tim 4.4), nor deprived of a share in communion with God." Man the microcosm—made of the same stuff as the mosquito—receives the divine inbreathing *for the sake of the whole creation*: "in order that the earthy might be raised up to the Divine that the one grace might pervade the whole of creation."[50] As in Maximus, man is given a key position *in order to refer the whole to God*. It is in this sense that some Orthodox theologians will actually describe the Orthodox view of creation as "anthropocentric." We believe that the human being is "central" to God's purposes for his creation; but this is rather different from saying that everything revolves around man's interests. "Man the mediator" and "man the consumer" both occupy a crucially influential position in the natural order: but there the similarity stops.

Images of man's place in creation

The classic statement of man's place in creation is given by St Gregory the Theologian, and repeated verbatim by St John of Damascus in his treatise *On the Orthodox Faith*. St Gregory describes this "being from both natures" in the following terms:

> a great cosmos in miniature; another angel, a "hybrid" worshipper, a full initiate (or: overseer) of the visible creation and initiated also into the intelligible creation; a king of things on

[49] *Making of Man* XVI.1–2.

[50] *Great Catechism* VI.

> earth, but subject to the King above . . . A creature trained here and *en route* to somewhere else and—the ultimate mystery—deified by its tendency towards God.[51]

If we look at the images applied here to man, we find that they reveal much about how he relates to the rest of creation and its Creator. Firstly, he is a microcosm—it is essential to his mediating role that he sums up creation in himself. Secondly, and very importantly, he is a "worshipper." Gregory explains more fully what he has in mind in one of his poems, where he describes God looking in vain for a creature on earth "who could discern his wisdom, the mother of all things"; finding only dumb beasts, he creates a "mixed creature" that can delight in his works, an initiate of heavenly things who will also sing the praises of God's "wills" and mind;[52] God's "wills" are his intentions expressed in created things. The perception of God's wisdom and purposes in creation—a key theme in St Basil's Hexaemeron—is a basic element in the human calling; and we are not simply to draw moral lessons, but to respond with praise. The next passage in Gregory's sermon must be read in this light. Is man merely the "overseer" of the visible world – or a being fully initiated into its mysteries? Gregory chooses a word that can mean either. But by coupling it with the unequivocal term "mystis" ("initiate" of the intelligible creation), he gives a strong clue that the aspect of "mystery" is in his mind. Man's "oversight" of creation is not just practical management or "stewardship"; it is inextricably bound up with being aware of the *mystery* of creation, discerning God's wisdom in the depths of created things.

[51]Hom. 38 *On Theophany*, 11; Hom. 45 *On Easter*, 7.

[52]Poem 1.1.8, *On the Soul*, lines 59–69.

This human "being from both natures" is also *king* of all on earth. Such expressions are very common in the Fathers, and very alien to us; so we need to look at it all the more carefully. It is actually a key notion: if we try to ignore it, we shall fail to understand the mind of the Fathers.

What strikes us in the present passage is that human "kingship" is what we could call a "constitutional monarchy." It depends on the "constitution" of creation; man has another King above him. But it is not just that man has to exercise his power properly because God is watching. In the thinking of the Fathers, the way that man exercises his kingship is limited above all by the "constitution" of his own nature. To see how this is worked out, we shall turn again to Gregory of Nyssa, who wrote extensively on the nature of man.

In his work *On the Making of Man*, Gregory describes in glowing terms how the Lord makes the world as a palace for man, sparing no effort in making it beautiful. Finally, he introduces the king. One might expect that he would then turn everything over to man's rule; but it is not that simple. There are some things that man is meant to rule over; others, that he is meant to admire. And above all, he is to enjoy the world in such a way as to come to know the Giver.[53] So this is the first point: the "king" does not have the right to use his "realm" however he likes; he is to use it in certain ways laid down by God. But God does not lay down the proper use of the world through some external restriction on human freedom. Proper use is determined *from within* man, by his very makeup. Of course, man is perfectly capable of using the earth in a different way—that is all too obvious. But when he does so, he is not sim-

[53] *Making of Man* II.

ply disobeying a commandment: he is ceasing to be a real human being. What we are talking about here is *creation in the image and likeness of God* as the defining characteristic of man.

Divine image and dominion

What is meant by creation in the divine image, and how does it determine the way man is to relate to the rest of creation? Staying with Gregory of Nyssa, we see that for him, the image of God consists principally in man's free will, his power of "self government."[54] Not to have any other overlord—this is indeed the property of a king. This in itself might seem directly to contradict the idea of a "constitutional monarchy." But we soon discover that human autonomy is part of a larger package: to partake in the kingly dignity of the prototype, man must be arrayed in the purple of virtue and the crown of justice. These are the attributes that make the image resemble the prototype, *without which it cannot fulfill its function in creation.*

Other aspects of the image are also set out here. God is mind (or spiritual intellect), and *logos*; these are characteristics of humans too. As God sees and hears all things, so we search things out with our senses and our understanding. But most importantly, God is love—and if this is absent, then *the whole imprint of the likeness is altered.*[55] An image that no longer resembles the original—like an outdated passport photograph—fails to fulfill its function.

Our being in the image, and hence our kingly authority, is clearly not a matter of excelling other creatures in certain natural proper-

[54] *Making of Man* IV.

[55] Making of Man V.2.

ties (e.g. rational thought). It depends on the fact that God has given us certain properties of his own. As Gregory says further on, the creation of man in the image means that God has made us partakers in all goodness.[56] Within this framework, the centrality of free will becomes clear: our freedom is of ultimate significance *because virtue is voluntary*. The freedom that characterizes the image functions properly only when it leads towards the likeness of God.

The same conclusion emerges from other categories used by the Fathers in speaking of the divine image in man. According to St John of Damascus, we are in the image in that we have reason, intellect, and free will, in our ability to form concepts and articulate speech, and in our power of ruling.[57] It is important to see what John means by "reason": it is above all the faculty that enables us to *choose* how we behave—in other words, to exercise our free will.[58] Reason enables us to act freely—without constraint—because it permits us to rein in our appetites. The dumb animals, John says, are governed by their nature—or, as we might say today, by their genetic makeup. They compete for dominance, territory, food or mates; rivals must either submit or fight. Being a microcosm, we experience the same pressures, the same imperatives from our nature. The difference is that we have the option not to give in to these pressures. We do not *have* to take part in the struggle for survival: we are free to choose instead to love those who hate us and not to resist those who wrong us. To be sure, such choices run counter not only to what we think of as "primitive" animal instincts, but also to many of

[56]*Making of Man* XVI.10.

[57]*On the Two Wills in Christ* 30 (PG 95:168B).

[58]*On the Orthodox Faith* II.27 (41).

the highly sophisticated animal instincts that underlie our social and economic structures. Yet Fathers such as St John of Damascus are telling us something startling: the "unnatural" behavior commanded by the Gospel is not just an ideal that we try to live up to. It is in fact the only way to become a real human. However "natural" it might seem to react according to the pressures of our animal nature, to do so is to violate our essential self and become something less than human.

It will not escape our notice that John Damascene's idea of "freedom" in this passage is rather different from that of a modern secular society. In our society, freedom is much talked about, but often trivialized. Increasingly it is seen in economic terms, as epitomized in "consumer choice"—essentially, a freedom to *indulge* our appetites, whether for goods, food, property, or money. Against this background, the idea of achieving freedom by restraining our wants might seem positively perverse. But is it really so odd? If freedom means having no one to dictate what we must do, how can we be free so long as we feel ourselves surrounded by "must haves"?

Damascene also refers to "our power of ruling." This too has an ethical dimension, for it involves having dominion over the wild beasts within us—the passions that dominate us and constrain our inner freedom. But it does also have to do with real power over actual creatures. As we have already noted, the whole notion of man's "dominion" over other creatures is an embarrassment and a stumbling block to many Christians today. So we need to look carefully at the traditional understanding of this idea, and how it compares with the way humans exercise "dominion" in today's world.

The term "dominion" needs some demystifying. Its primary meaning is that animals recognize man as their *master* or *lord* (Latin *dominus*)—they obey him, spontaneously and instinctively. It is important to keep in mind that the setting for the saying about man "having dominion" is God's good creation, prior to the fall. The quintessential image of dominion in practice, therefore, is Adam naming the animals. That action does indeed suggest that a measure of responsibility for animals' fate has been placed in human hands. Chrysostom—who, it must be said, has rather a "low" view of the animal world—compares Adam's naming of the animals to a master changing the names of his slaves.[59] More frequently, however, we find an emphasis on the animals' tameness and lack of fear, and the harmony that prevails among the different species.[60] Adam's dominion provides the structure for an ideal Kingdom, well-ordered and harmonious.

Human dominion over other creatures was not revoked at the fall, but it was seriously modified. By no stretch of the imagination can we look at present relationships between man and other creatures and presume to read off God's original intention. Insofar as the world is still subject to man, it is so "not of its own will," as St Paul says (Rom 8.20). As Chrysostom points out, God has graciously allowed us to retain some power over animals "by certain skills, with fear and trembling."[61] Man retains the degree of control necessary for his survival; but the natural authority flowing from the divine image has gone, to be replaced by a balance of terror. Depending on the species, either animals fear us, or we fear them.

[59]*Homily on Genesis* 14.19.

[60]E.g., Ephrem, *Commentary on Genesis* II.9; Brock, *Hymns on Paradise* 203.

[61]*Commentary on Ps 8*, 7.

Dominion and use

One aspect of the theme of dominion is the notion that creation exists "for man"—a sentiment that the Fathers frequently repeat. Such language is problematic for us today, so we need to listen with all the more care to what they are actually saying. We hear it against the background of four centuries of technological domination of nature, and are inclined to flinch. The Fathers lived in a very different world. Human life was still largely dwarfed by the forces of nature, and by seemingly endless wild expanses where humans were essentially powerless. Control over nature meant such things as agriculture, the making of clothes and the construction of buildings—arts that make human survival possible. The Fathers saw no problem in recognizing such human use as part of God's providence, and neither should we. For the church fathers, however, turning nature to practical use was not the only or even the most important reason for seeking to understand it. Creation "serves man" as an instrument of God's mercy, and as a means for us to increase in knowledge of the Creator. In both cases, it should lead us to glorify him for all his works.

Such differences in attitude remind us that creation "for man" is by no means the same as creation for man's consumption, or for man to do what he likes with. There is little evidence that the Fathers see creation as being for man's benefit in any exclusive sense. They do not address this question explicitly, but such a view would be hard to reconcile with their strong and unwavering conviction that God exercises providence for *all* creatures. We may recall the verses in Genesis where God makes very similar provision for the nourishment of both man and beast, namely plants (Gen 1.29–30). Or to take another example: when Basil wonders at God's care for the hedgehog in giving it the wit to use different exits from its nest according to the wind direction, there is no suggestion that its welfare is important only so as to provide human farmers with slug control. Creation may be for the benefit of man; but that does not prevent it being for the benefit of hedgehogs too. The Lord "opens his hand and *all things* are filled with good" (Ps 103.28, Septuagint).

One can certainly find formal statements about man and his surroundings that at first sight look disturbingly utilitarian, as well as distinctly simplistic. St John of Damascus, for instance, classes animals as useful for our food, service, or enjoyment, and plants for food, enjoyment, and medicine.[62] Everything is "for man's use, as needed"; but the qualification "as needed" already suggests a certain detachment, an absence of possessiveness. Everything is freely available, thanks to God's bounty, when we need it; so it is not necessary to stake an exclusive claim to anything *in case we might* need it. Furthermore, "use"—even according to Damascene's neat categories—is not confined to consumption or some form of exploitation. Practical uses go hand in hand with enjoyment, with a delight in other creatures as they have come from the hand of God. While enjoyment can also be selfish, it can and should be a starting point for a deep appreciation of other creatures and an offering of thanks to their Creator.

When the Fathers speak in their sermons about creation being "for man," it often seems that they are actually trying to *counter* a facile utilitarianism; they are urging their flock to look and see the divine goodness and mercy in a natural world that would often have seemed frightening and hostile. It is important to keep in mind what a novelty it is for humans to be able to enjoy "nature" at a safe

[62]On the *Orthodox Faith* II:10 (24).

distance, without having to wrestle with it. Even today, it is only for a privileged minority of mankind that the wilderness, or even the countryside, is a place of recreation rather than a place to make a precarious living, or that wild animals of one sort or another pose no direct threat to life, limb, or livelihood. So it is all the more remarkable that St Basil asks his congregation, quite crossly, "should we not reflect that not everything has been created for the sake of our bellies?"[63] Concerned that people are "reproaching the Creator for things which may be harmful to our life," he underlines that "in creation nothing exists without a reason." One example of this principle is medicines derived from poisonous plants; but another, equally good "reason" for a plant poisonous to humans is to provide food for animals. Chrysostom, too, has to deal with questions such as "what good are wild animals?" One benefit from them, he replies, is that they keep us humble; the only point of being able to tame the lion or the leopard would be to show off. But basically, he says, one might as well ask, What is the point of illness? In both cases, we should do better to be grateful for the constraints and the discipline they impose on us.[64] Elsewhere, he is less in a mood for discussion. If you do not understand the purpose of some things in creation, he tells the people of Antioch, then glorify God all the more.[65] In other words, the goodness of creation is axiomatic: if we cannot see how it works for our best interests, we should look harder. The notion of creation for man, for man's benefit, turns out to be less a statement of utilitarianism than an act of faith in God's goodness, however inscrutable. In an idiom somewhat alien to us, the Fathers are in fact asserting that "man needs nature"—and for spiritual growth, no less than physical.

[63] *Hexaemeron* V.4.

[64] On Psalm 8.5.

[65] *On the Statues* XII.7.

Characteristic of the Fathers' vision of creation is the image of a hierarchy in which everything has a part to play. Hierarchy, like kingship, is an idea not well understood in modern Western cultures. We are inclined to think of hierarchies as static and restrictive. In the more ancient understanding, however, hierarchy is essentially a structure of community; it provides a framework within which widely disparate creatures, differing enormously in the sort of contribution they are able to make, function together as one whole and serve each other. A hierarchical vision suggests that interdependence rather than self-sufficiency is the order of creation. Perhaps that is another reason why hierarchy is currently an unpopular notion.

According to the patristic view, "dominion" over other creatures does not simply signify a superior position; paradoxical though this may seem, it is also a recognition of dependency. We are given "dominion" over other creatures because we cannot survive without their assistance. St Gregory of Nyssa, for instance, explains that man's physical deficiencies are designed to make him exercise his "rule" over other creatures by ensuring that he needs the cooperation of his subjects—he needs to use the horse's speed, the sheep's wool and so forth.[66] It is true that the idea of "rule" here does imply the domestication of animals to serve our practical needs; but such a relationship with our "subjects" certainly does not imply reducing them to units of production. Animal husbandry as practiced for most of human history has almost nothing in common with the mentality of modern factory farming, and we should beware of the anachronism of conflating the two. If we wonder what domestication of animals implied to earlier Christians, we might recall the many scriptural passages where

[66]*Making of Man* VII.2–3.

the relationship between shepherd and sheep is the supreme image of care and painstaking love. Gregory himself takes up the same image; he uses the human shepherd as a paradigm of God's care for us, remarking that the shepherd wants his animals to be virtually immortal. Interestingly, Chrysostom applies the scriptural image of the members of a body to our relationship with animals: the principle of each needing the others applies "with regard to irrational animals, and in all the relations of life. The king, for instance, has need of his subjects, and the subjects of the king; just as the head has need of the feet."[67] Ephrem also uses the image of a body in this connection; and he explicitly draws the conclusion, "Our need for everything binds us with a love for everything."[68] What we have here is a picture of a world where other creatures indeed serve a purpose for us, because everything is interdependent. It is a world view that invites care rather than exploitation. And it should also make us alive to the possibility that there are things in creation whose vital contribution to the functioning of the whole we are still far from understanding.

Finally, when we hear the practical aspects of human dominion routinely emphasized in the Fathers' homilies, it is important not to forget the broader context of their words. Homilies had their place in worship; and it is worship above all that provides the counterbalance to any appearance of utilitarianism. We will talk about this in more detail in a later chapter; but here we should refer to one early prayer showing very clearly that "dominion" has another side to it. This is a passage from the *Apostolic Con-*

[67]*On the Statues* XI.12.

[68]Letter to Hypatius, in Sebastian Brock, *The Luminous Eye: The Spiritual World Vision of St Ephrem the Syrian* (Kalamazoo, MI: Cistercian Publications, 1992), 167.

stitutions, a Syrian collection of liturgical and other material from the fourth or fifth century. The text speaks admiringly of the way in which the stars, trees, animals and so forth bear witness to the greatness of their Creator's power, and then goes on: "Therefore every human being, through Christ, ought to send up a hymn from his very soul to you in the name of all the rest, since you have given him power over them."[69] The sense is very clear: the responsibility that goes with our dominant position is not primarily administrative, but *doxological.* Our "power" is directly related to our responsibility to refer all creation to God, to offer conscious praise on its behalf.

The world of the fall

We are accustomed to speaking in English of "the fallen world"; but such language is becoming increasingly problematic. Objections can be raised both to the attitudes that it might encourage, and to the validity of its historical implications. There is today an (entirely appropriate) desire to emphasize the goodness of the created world, to see it as an expression of God's will. Describing it as "fallen," it is argued, has unfortunate implications. It can encourage the idea that the material world is nothing but an impediment to spiritual life, and therefore not worth bothering with. Or conversely, if the "natural" state of the world is seen as somehow tainted by sin, then "development" and "improvement" of the earth becomes a Christian duty. This idea was strongly associated with the missionary philosophy that went hand in hand with Western colonial expansion, but its drawbacks are today very apparent.

[69] *Apostolic Constitutions* VII.35.

Then there is the question of whether talking about a "fall" affecting nature makes any historical sense. We are much more aware than our forebears that features such as death, decay and predation, traditionally associated with the fall, are integral to the functioning of the world as we know it; and also that they antedate humans by millions of years. We are conscious of the fact that a world "without corruption" would be unimaginably different from anything we know. This is certainly not a reason to argue that it could never exist. But it would strain most people's credulity today to maintain that such a world was a historical reality on this earth until altered by some human action.

So what are we to make of the notion of a "fall" affecting the natural world? The traditional Orthodox Christian view has been *both* that creation is good, *and* that it is not as it was intended to be: there has been a fall, which we constantly perpetuate, and it affects nature as well as humans. But it should be noted at the outset that there is no expression in Greek—certainly not in the Fathers—corresponding to the phrase "the fallen world." In the Orthodox understanding, it would be more accurate to speak of "the world of the fall." The difference is an important one. To speak of "the world of the fall" signals that the very laws of nature have indeed been affected by the rupture in man's relationship with God; but it avoids the implication that non-human nature has itself fallen away from its relationship with its Creator. In other words, it goes far towards meeting the objection that talking about a "fallen world" leads us to despise the creation in its "natural" state.

The historical objection is more difficult to address. The Fathers saw the creation and fall stories as far more than *simply* information about origins; but in the absence of other sources of information, they could have no idea of just how widely the Genesis accounts diverge from anything that we can reconstruct from physical evidence about the history of the earth. So the question arises: what can the Fathers' understanding of the creation and fall stories still usefully say to us, across the vast gulf that separates our scientific knowledge about origins from theirs? If these stories are not literally historical, can they really tell us anything about the actual world we live in?

As we try to answer these questions, a key point to bear in mind is the strong eschatological element in the Fathers' understanding of the creation stories. Their fundamental interest is not the state *in which,* but the state *for which* the world is created. And descriptions of the "beginning" are interpreted so as to throw light on the end: "as the restoration will be, so was the original genesis," in the words of one writer.[70] This is particularly clear in reference to paradise. Some writers, such as Ephrem, consider the primordial and the eschatological paradise to be the same place, a reality clearly outside the world as we know it.[71] Others, such as St Symeon the New Theologian, see paradise as historical, but at the same time pointing forward to the age to come. Symeon points out that it is planted on the "eighth day" (symbolic of eternity), following the seven days of creation.[72] The Fathers take it for granted that existing relations between God, man and the natural world do not accord fully with God's intention; so accounts of the creation are seen as pointers towards that intention, which is to become a reality only at the end.

[70]Pseudo-Basil, *On the Making of Man* II (PG 30, 45B).

[71]See Sebastian Brock, trans., St Ephrem the Syrian, *Hymns on Paradise* (Crestwood, NY: St Vladimir's Seminary Press, 1990), 51.

[72]*First Ethical Discourses* 1, 2.

The commandments in paradise and use of the world

Before exploring the way in which the Fathers see creation itself as objectively affected by man's fall, we should consider the related question: does the fall itself have to do with man's attitude to the world around him, and if so, how?

As we have seen already, man is created as a king, and paradise is planted to be his palace; but at the same time, he is given certain commandments. The effect of this is that his rule is immediately defined as what we have called a constitutional monarchy, with the Creator writing the constitution. The commands about what to eat and what not to eat remind man that he too has a Lord, as Irenaeus makes clear.[73] Chrysostom interprets "watching over" or "keeping" the garden in a similar sense.[74] In each case, the commandment reminds man that his relationship with the created world always involves a third party—God who is the Creator of both. It would be a mistake to see the commandments primarily as a restriction on man's use of the world, or even as a charter for "stewardship" rather than "ownership." The prime function of the original commandments was to teach man what his use of creation is meant to be: a constant remembrance of God.

There is an ancient tradition that "tilling" and "keeping" have a double meaning: they represent work on ourselves as much as on the earth. The Fathers had noticed something often glossed over in popular ecotheology today: the "tilling" and "keeping" do not refer to the earth as a whole, but to life in paradise, to the God-filled existence for which man was created. So to the Fathers' mind, the description of man's "work" in paradise must amount

[73]*Demonstration of Apostolic Preaching* 15.

[74]*On Genesis* Hom. 14.3.

to something more profound than a charter for sustainable agriculture, useful though the latter might be. One of the best-known accounts of that "something more" comes from St Gregory the Theologian. Gregory describes the Lord creating Adam and placing him in paradise—"whatever that paradise might have been," he adds casually—"to till immortal plants, by which is perhaps meant the divine ideas."[75] What Adam is to "cultivate," in other words, is the intentions, notions or conceptual blueprints according to which God has created all things—what Maximus will later call their *logoi*. This does not exclude literally working the land; but the main point is that man should live in God's world in such a way as to draw closer to its Maker, learning to perceive him ever more clearly through it. It is perhaps in this light that we should understand Ephrem's interpretation: it was not the garden that needed to be "kept" or "guarded," but God's law and his commandment.[76] Adam's work in paradise was to make sure that he kept the *relationship with God*—epitomized in the commandments about what to eat and not to eat—as the structure for his use of the world.

John of Damascus gives us a useful summary of earlier patristic thought, making it plain that there is no consensus on whether paradise is physical or spiritual: he opts for both, since the human creature is both. John's interpretation is interesting, because he does not focus primarily on the prohibition of the one tree. Instead, he offers an eloquent interpretation of the positive command given to man: when God says, "let him eat of *every* tree," he alludes to himself who is *all* in *all*:

[75]Hom. 38, *On Theophany*, 12; Hom. 45, *On Easter*, 8.

[76]*On Genesis* II.7; Brock, *Hymns on Paradise* 201–2.

> Through all things [God is saying], ascend to me the Creator; from every tree harvest one fruit, namely me who am the life. Let all things bear the fruit of life for you: make participation in me the stuff of your own existence. Thus you will be immortal.[77]

John identifies this "eating of every tree" with the knowledge of God through his creatures, which Paul talks about in Romans; the way we perceive his "eternal power and deity . . . in the things that have been made" (Rom 1.20). This is the way of life for which man was created: if he had kept to it, he would have become firmly established in goodness and become incorrupt and immortal. What then does the fall consist in? The tree of knowledge, Damascene says, can be understood as "physical, hedonistic eating"[78]; it is a surrender to our "*natural* connection to things"[79] which man was intended to transcend. The fall, we might say, solidifies man in his animal nature. It makes him merely a top predator, a "consumer." The world around us is no longer a revelation of our, and its, Creator, but a resource to satisfy our appetites.

"Cursed is the earth"?

It becomes evident, then, that the fall has much to do with the way humans perceive and use the world around them. But has it had an objective effect on the rest of creation? What are we to make of the "curse" upon the earth, or the notion that non-human creation is also waiting to be "saved"?

[77]*On the Orthodox Faith* II.11 (25).

[78]Ibid., II.11 (25).

[79]Ibid., II.30 (44).

Some of the Fathers describe Adam's ignominious departure from paradise in terms that can only recall the political realities of the Byzantine empire. It has been said that the people of the empire had a "constitutional right of revolution": if an emperor became a tyrant, he forfeited his legitimacy and could expect his subjects to revolt. So it was when Adam disobeyed the King above: the whole creation rose up against him, "no longer wishing to be obedient to the transgressor." The wild beasts turned hostile, the earth was unwilling to feed him and the sky was barely persuaded not to fall and crush him.[80] At God's command, a degree of order is soon restored, sufficient for humans to survive. But the new order makes life sufficiently difficult that humans notice what they have lost. This image makes it very clear that non-human creation has never deviated from serving God. The "curse" very clearly refers to the character of the earth *in relation to man;* in the first instance, it is a curse on the soil *as man tills it.*[81] The earth does not cease to serve God faithfully; but its "obedience" now is not to make life pleasant for man, but to make it difficult. The only suggestion that other creatures somehow participate in man's disobedience has to do with predators: we sometimes meet the idea that they have joined man in transgression, taking advantage of the concession allowed to man when he was given flesh to eat after the Flood.[82] This testifies to the Fathers' very strong sense that God did not originally make living creatures in order for them to end up as food, either for us or for each other.

[80]Symeon the New Theologian, *First Ethical Discourse* 2; cf. John of Damascus, *On the Orthodox Faith* II.10 (24).

[81]See Chrysostom, *On Genesis* Hom. 17.9; Ephrem, *Commentary on Genesis* II.31; Symeon, *First Ethical Discourse* 2.

[82]e.g. Theophilus of Antioch, *To Autolycus* II.16–17.

The most far-reaching effect on the earth from man's fall is its state of corruptibility, also associated with the "curse."[83] This is the "futility" to which the creation is subject according to St Paul (Rom 8). As a historical statement, this immediately presents problems. It is problematic to us, as we have said, because we are aware that corruptibility was a fact of the created world long before man appeared. But it is evident that the Fathers, too, were often struggling to speak about an incorrupt material creation in a way that was coherent and consistent. Later patristic writers are more inclined to go down the hazardous path of speculating how things worked in paradise, and what was the state of the world as a whole prior to the fall. Symeon says categorically that the whole earth was originally material but incorruptible, as was Adam's body.[84] Gregory of Sinai (fourteenth century), aware of the problems of envisaging life under such conditions, suggests that paradise enjoyed an intermediate state: fruit would decay, for instance, but without any unpleasant smell.[85]

Earlier Fathers, however, are happier to show a prudent reticence about a putative pre-fallen state of the earth at some point in history. They were of course aware of St Paul's clear statement that "by man came death"; but this can well be understood to refer only to death among humans. From the silence on the subject from Fathers such as Irenaeus, we might guess that they see death in the non-human creation as "natural"—at least in the sense that it existed from the beginning of time. Whether that too will be abolished in the Kingdom is another question.[86] The original mortality of animals

[83]See, e.g., Chrysostom, *On Romans* Hom. 14.

[84]*First Ethical Discourse* 1.

[85]*Commandments and Doctrines* 10, *Philokalia* 4, 213.

[86]cf. John Behr, *Asceticism and Anthropology in Irenaeus and Clement* (Oxford: Oxford University Press, 2000), 51 n. 58.

would be an obvious conclusion to draw from the Fathers' consensus that even Adam was not immortal by nature: he was created *for* immortality, which is a different matter. Adam, as a creature of earth, would have returned to earth *according to his own nature;* he was offered the chance of a different destiny through keeping God's commandment.[87] So it is hard to avoid the conclusion that the animals who had not been given that option were mortal.

A few writers, Gregory of Nyssa notable among them, are quite explicit that death did already exist among animals: what happened at man's fall was that he lapsed into an animal state.[88] On this view, the moment of the fall—if one can even speak of such a thing—would have made little immediate difference to the condition of earth's other inhabitants.

Does this make nonsense of the idea that the corruptibility of the earth is somehow integrally connected with man's turning away from God? Not necessarily. Ephrem may point the way to a more profound understanding of what is going on when he suggests that the earth as we know it—the world outside paradise—was created for man *in view of the fall.*[89] It is a product of God's foreknowledge. Man's fall is the reason for its corruptible state, but does not precede it in time. This makes more sense when we realize that not all the Fathers interpret the creation stories as literally a sequence of events in history.[90] All of them feel quite

[87]Chrysostom, *On Genesis* Hom. 17.9.

[88]*Great Catechism* VIII; cf. Ephrem, *Hymns on Paradise* XIII.5, Brock 170.

[89]*Commentary on Genesis* I; cited in Seraphim Rose, *Genesis, Creation and Early Man: The Orthodox Christian Vision* (Platina, CA: St Herman of Alaska Brotherhood, 2000), 156.

[90]See further Peter C. Bouteneff, *Beginnings: Ancient Christian Readings of the Biblical Creation Narratives* (Grand Rapids, MI: Baker Academic, 2008).

at home using the pictorial language of Genesis, which may be confusing for us; but not all of them believe that there was an actual period of historical time when man existed in an unfallen state. "Man inclined towards his senses the moment he came into being," as Maximus says.[91] Significantly, this also seems to be the view of Gregory of Nyssa, who places the creation of man in the image of God *before* the "Adam of earth" ever existed.[92] In terms of physical origins, we can say that Gregory at least envisages mortal humans appearing on a corruptible earth.

This certainly does not mean that the creation stories are myths unrelated to the real world. It does mean that the weight falls heavily on their eschatological significance: they may not tell us where creation has been, but they definitely tell us where it is intended to go. In the words of a modern theologian, "the bliss of paradise was nothing more than the seed oriented towards its goal, the state of deification."[93] Corruption, with the suffering and death that go with it, is not the state for which God brought things into being. When man actually attains incorruption through Christ the second Adam, he is to take creation with him.

The fall and the abuse of creation

It turns out, then, that the fall as the Fathers interpret it is a key to understanding human abuse of the created world. The Fathers' vision of creation is one in which everything has its origin in God; it is created to reflect him, to relate us to him, and ultimately to be

[91]*To Thalassius* 61, Blowers, *Cosmic Mystery,*131.

[92]*On the Making of Man* XXII.3.

[93]Paul Evdokimov, *Orthodoxia* (Thessaloniki: Rigopoulos, 1972), 118; translation of *L'Orthodoxie* (Neuchâtel; Delachaux et Niestlé, 1965).

filled with him through our agency. The world of the fall, however, is one in which this constant reference to God is banished from the equation. Creation is there to satisfy my wants: it is "good for food," as Genesis says (Gen 3.6). Man's original fateful choice is compounded through the ages and generations, until it hardens into a world view.

To us today, perhaps the most obvious manifestation of this skewed world view would be the abiding human tendency to see the world as existing for the sake of our appetites. The Fathers are very well aware of this tendency, as we have seen. But, reflecting the realities of their time, they are inclined to deal with it as a personal moral failing. They regarded greed as a grave spiritual sickness, whether its object was money, possessions, or luxuries of various kinds. But they had no experience of an institutionalized attitude that sees all the world's goods as commodities and has difficulty appreciating the value of anything unless it can be translated into monetary terms. The abuse of nature that the Fathers see as pervading human societies is of a different kind, much less obvious to us: it takes the form of idolatry.

One patristic writer compares the fall and its consequences for nature to a king being taken captive, with the result that all his retainers follow him into slavery. Man was created to serve God and be served by other creatures; now he falls to worshipping demons, and offers the fruits and creatures of the earth to them.[94] Or worse yet, creation itself may be made into a god and worshipped in place of God. We make it complicit in our own apostasy. This, to the Fathers' mind, is the ultimate pollution of the earth.[95]

[94]*Macarian Homilies* 11.5.

[95]Symeon the New Theologian, *First Ethical Discourse* 2.

The Fathers' preoccupation with paganism might seem of limited relevance to today's problems; and the connection between reducing creation to "good for food" and worshipping it as a god may leave us puzzled. We are used to regarding consumerism and paganism as poles apart. It is easy to see a causal connection between excessive consumption and destruction of the earth; but increasing numbers of people look precisely to paganism, in one form or another, as an antidote to a utilitarian consumerism. They would see paganism as an affirmation of the earth's intrinsic value. But the Fathers give us a different perspective, much closer to St Paul's understanding of "covetousness, which is idolatry" (Col 3.5). To them, greed and paganism are opposite sides of the same coin: and the coin is counterfeit, because it lacks the image of "the King above."

According to the church fathers' vision of the world, as we have seen, matter is shot through with spirit; all things resonate with the creative Word of the God who is also beyond all things. And the human being is placed in the midst of creation as a creature who bears the divine image and is called to relate all the rest of creation to God. Rejection of this calling takes various forms. But whether we degrade nature into a collection of commodities to serve our appetites, or exalt it into a god that we then serve, there is a common thread: the Creator is shut out of the picture. Consumerism and neo-paganism are reactions against each other within a closed system. The source of value and hope in people's lives, the "good" that they aspire to—whether or not it is explicitly called "sacred"—is confined within the created order itself. The following chapters will explore some of the ways in which the Church's tradition leads us out of the closed system, enabling us to relate to God through creation and bring it to full unity with him.

For further reading

Brock, Sebastian. "World and Sacrament in the Writings of the Syrian Fathers." *Sobornost* 6:10 (Winter 1974): 685–696.

Brock, Sebastian. "Humanity and the Natural World in the Syriac Tradition." *Sobornost/ECR* 12:2 (1990): 131–142.

Louth, Andrew. *Maximus the Confessor.* London: Routledge, 1996; esp. Introd. 5, "Cosmic Theology."

Pelikan, Jaroslav. *Christianity and Classical Culture: The Metamorphosis of Natural Theology in the Christian Encounter with Hellenism.* New Haven and London: Yale University Press, 1993.

Wallace-Hadrill, D.S. *The Greek Patristic View of Nature.* Manchester: Manchester University Press, 1968.

chapter two

The Ascetic Tradition and the Use of the World

The more aware we become of the beauty of the world, the more acutely we also feel the tragedy of our life within it. If we are honest, we cannot fail to realize that there is something profoundly wrong with our relationships, both as individuals and as a species: we so often destroy what we love. It may be the over-protected child who grows up emotionally maimed, the exquisite bird or flower driven to extinction by our desire to possess it, or the idyllic retreat that ends up as a building site or a tourist trap. Love and desire, whether for people, other creatures, things or places, are constantly merging into the urge to grasp, to possess, to keep for ourselves, to consume.

Some people today consider that humans are simply a uniquely destructive species: as long as we exist on earth in substantial numbers, they believe, we shall continue to spoil and destroy in order to assuage our insatiable appetites. This is the philosophy summed up in the sardonic bumper sticker: "Help save the earth—commit suicide." The Christian tradition is also acutely aware of this flaw in human relationships, both with other people and with the world around us. But instead of seeing the flaw as built into our nature, the Christian tradition regards it as a distortion of our true nature.

And it has a radical remedy. Instead of being attached to people and things, we are called to be detached from them. Our ordinary notions of love are turned on their heads; or, more exactly, a notion of love that is upside-down to start with is turned the right way up. If we give up all attachments for the sake of God's love, only then are we able to love all of his creation in freedom, without needing to possess it or be possessed by it. The discipline by which we achieve this detachment is called *asceticism*. Many people today associate that word with stark renunciation, something that only monastics are called to do. But asceticism is bigger and broader than that: it is a process of re-ordering our relationship with the material world, and it begins with the part of that world nearest and dearest to us—our own body.

As we have seen, Christian tradition sees the fundamental flaw in our relationship with the world as summed up in the fall story. God gives man instructions about how to use the world around him, what trees he should eat and not eat (Gen 2.16–17); in other words, use of the world is set in the framework of a relationship with the Creator. By deciding to use the world as he himself sees fit, man is making the choice to bypass the Creator. So before we can restore a right relationship with the world around us, we have to set right our relationship with God. This is the movement of *repentance:* the decision of the Prodigal Son that "I will arise and go to my Father" (Lk 15.18). It is no accident that the Gospel story of the Prodigal Son is used to prepare us for the Lenten fast; for the Church's understanding of the basic problem and its remedy is presented most graphically in the Lenten period. The parable of the Prodigal Son, read three weeks before Lent begins, exemplifies the first step of restoring a relationship with God. The fall and the expulsion of Adam from Paradise are the theme of services on the eve of the great fast, so that the *fasting itself* is presented as the movement of return to Paradise. "If we had fasted, we should never have been banished from Paradise," as St Basil says crisply.[1]

Faced with a problem that is nothing less than the human condition—estrangement from God, and a propensity to abuse and destroy his creation—it might seem odd to focus on apparently petty details of physical activities. What difference does it make, to the human condition and to the created world, what we eat and when, or whether or not we make prostrations when we pray? But we can dismiss these things as mere externals only if we forget that we are creatures of soul and body: our physical state affects our spiritual state, and vice versa.

We all know from experience that the initial decision to change, the moment of "I will arise and go to my Father," is only the beginning. Making the "change of heart" a reality is a life-long process. It means a radical *change in orientation*, so that God comes first. And that involves practice, discipline, *exercise*—in Greek, *ascesis*. Ascesis is spiritual fitness training for us as embodied creatures. It tones up our faculty of free choice so that it functions as intended—in harmony with the will of God. Meeting people who are well advanced along the ascetic way, one is deeply impressed by their inner freedom. They are liberated from their own whims and appetites; instead of a morbid dependency on things around them, they have put "a wondering and respectful distance" between themselves and the world.[2] This "respectful distance" is why many Orthodox writers today speak of an "ascetic ethos" as key to a right relationship with the world around us.

[1] *On Fasting* Hom. 1.4 (PG 31, 168B).

[2] Olivier Clément, *The Roots of Christian Mysticism* (London: New City, 1993), 141.

This might come as a surprise to some, for asceticism is one of the most misunderstood aspects of Christian life. To some ears, it still conjures up images of animosity towards matter, abuse of our bodies, and a puritanical disdain for the material world in favor of the "spiritual." Because of the importance that Orthodoxy gives to the ascetic ethos, we should look in some detail at the Christian ascetic tradition so as to discover what such an ethos involves, and what it can teach us about our relationship to the created world.

Some of the misunderstanding of asceticism has to do simply with terms used in a particular sense in ascetic writing, such as "the world," "the flesh," or "nature." Ascetic writings do talk about hating the world, mortifying the flesh and overcoming nature; but the way we hear these expressions is frequently not the way that they are meant. "The world" carries an ambiguity that goes back to the New Testament: it stands for both what we must studiously avoid loving (e.g. 1 Jn 2.15–17), and what God so loved that he sent his Son to save it. This has less to do with early Christian ambivalence than with the wide range of meanings of the Greek word *kosmos*. "Cosmos" in our sense, or more narrowly the planet earth, are possible meanings but by no means the most common: the "world" that is to be hated has more to do with what we would call "*worldliness*."

Again, "the flesh" more often than not has a negative sense in Christian thought; but that sense has little to do with our embodiment, our existence as flesh and blood beings. When St Paul lists with disapproval the "works of the flesh" (Gal 5.19–21), he does not hesitate to mix the sort of evils that we would immediately think of as carnal (e.g. licentiousness, drunkenness) with others that seem very much products of the mind (idolatry, anger, dissension . . .). Indeed, we might say that "the flesh" in this usage is first and foremost a *state of mind*. It is "total humanity—soul and body together—insofar as it is separated from God and in rebellion against him . . . [It is] the *whole* person as fallen."[3]

Even more confusingly, ascetic writers sometimes speak of a "struggle against nature." But "nature" here has nothing whatsoever to do with the natural world in the modern sense, the world around us. The opponent in question is *our own* nature. Or, to speak more precisely, it is the human condition that passes for "natural"—the distorted relationships characteristic of the fall. All this is rather confusing; but it is crucial for making sense of the Christian ascetic tradition. When ascetic writers talk about human "nature," they distinguish three states: contrary to nature, in conformity with nature, and beyond nature. The "baseline" is the nature with which we were created in the divine image; the holy person whose life shows a likeness to God is acting in conformity with our true human nature. We were created to progress from this "natural" state to one above nature, in which we become "partakers of the divine nature" (2 Pet 1.4); but instead, we departed from our true nature in the opposite direction. So before we can resume that progress, we need first to get back to the starting point; our fallen "nature" needs to be stripped away.

Even if people do not have a negative image of asceticism, they may nevertheless associate it exclusively with monasticism. Yet monks and Christians in the world have the same destination and share the same nature, so it is only to be expected that their paths will be parallel at many points. Monastics are indeed the

[3]Kallistos Ware, " 'My Helper and My Enemy': The Body in Greek Christianity," in Sarah Coakley, ed., *Religion and The Body* (Cambridge: Cambridge University Press, 2000), 93.

"experts" in asceticism, in the science of training athletes of the spirit. But the heroic feats by which a few stretch the body to unimaginable limits differ in degree, not in kind, from the "everyday" ascesis of the Christian in the world: of those who use the Church's practices of prayer and fasting to transform the passions that distance us from God and from all his creatures. Asceticism is quite simply the bedrock of Christian living.

In order to illustrate more clearly what asceticism does and does not mean, we should look more closely at the paradox of the ascetic way and the place it gives to the body, and to matter more generally.

Asceticism and the Body

We have said that it is a misunderstanding to see asceticism as disdain for matter. But if this is so, what are we to make of the description of ascetic saints "despising the flesh, for it passes away; but caring for the soul, which is immortal"?[4] "Flesh" here seems to have a literal, physical sense; so is this not a classic expression of a body-soul dualism that sees only the "spiritual" part of us as truly important?

Hearing the call to "despise the flesh for it passes away," it is easy to overlook the fact that such a statement is about "the flesh," in its ordinary, physical sense, and as such is nothing more than a brutally honest statement of reality. Our bodies will decay; indeed, everything in the natural world as we know it will decay sooner or later. Whether the timescale is a few decades or billions of years, the end is the same. Toning and pampering our bodies, and whatever

[4]Troparion for an ascetic saint.

else we do simply to maintain the physical reality we are familiar with, results in nothing more than a temporary stay of execution. If our deepest longing is that we ourselves, and everything dear to us, should live forever, we have to recognize that nothing we do on the purely physical level will achieve that end.

Our belief in the ultimate resurrection of the body in no way contradicts this reality. We do indeed "look for the resurrection of the dead," as we proclaim in the Nicene Creed; but we recognize that this is a re-creation of a body that has turned to dust, not an extension into eternity of physical life as we know it. The flesh does pass away. True, we venerate relics of the saints, pieces of their actual physical bodies that may be incorrupt, undecayed. An incorrupt relic is indeed a pointer to the glorified body; but it is not the reality of that resurrected body. The relics of a saint are like the "grain of wheat" of the Gospel, which "falls to the earth and dies" only to reveal that it possesses the seed of life. They are the "dry, lifeless seed of a holy body," as Fr Pavel Florensky says.[5] But here is the paradox: a bodily relic filled with divine power, and the resurrection glory to which it points, are the fruit precisely of "care for the soul." Care for the soul *means* care for the "me" that is eternal—a process that includes, *as a central component,* the cultivation of a right relationship with the body and the material creation to which it belongs.

How does one go about cultivating that right relationship? That is the question that asceticism seeks to answer. The science of ascetic life as we know it today, with its profound insights into the human psyche, can be traced back to the pioneers of desert monasticism

[5]Fr Pavel Florensky, *The Pillar and Ground of the Truth*, B. Jakim, trans. (Princeton, NJ: Princeton University Press, 1997), 224.

beginning in the fourth century. There is much in that tradition that is hard for modern Westerners to relate to. But the more closely we look at it, the more we realize the profound importance that it gives to material creation and to our own existence as embodied creatures. As one scholar of early Christianity writes,

> To describe ascetic thought as "dualist" and as motivated by hatred of the body is to miss its most novel and its most poignant aspect. Seldom, in ancient thought, had the body been seen as more deeply implicated in the transformation of the soul; and never was it made to bear so heavy a burden.[6]

In some cases it may seem that this burden is intolerable, and mercilessly imposed; but this approach is not universal. Among the ascetic Fathers and Mothers, there have been from the beginning considerable personal differences in their chosen ways, their degree of austerity and their attitudes to their bodies. The contrast is epitomized in two Fathers of the Egyptian desert. Dorotheus torments his poor body by working through the midday heat, with the simple justification, "It kills me, so I kill it."[7] Yet the great Poemen, in some ways the archetypal Desert Father, shocks a pious visitor for the opposite reason. To a monk surprised to find him bathing his feet, in apparent contrast with the asceticism of others, the great Elder explains, "We have not been taught to be killers of our bodies, but killers of our passions."[8]

[6]Peter Brown, *The Body and Society: Men, Women and Sexual Renunciation in Early Christianity* (New York, NY: Columbia University Press, 1988), 235.

[7]Palladius, *Lausiac History*, On Dorotheus.

[8]Poemen, 184, in Benedicta Ward, trans., *The Sayings of the Desert Fathers: The Alphabetical Collection* (London: Mowbray, 1975).

When we see the results of an ascetic attitude to the body, we are likely to conclude that Poemen's way of putting it makes more sense. A well-known example of such results comes from the life of St Anthony the Great, the founder of Egyptian monasticism. Anthony taught that we should "despise the flesh so that we may preserve the soul";[9] and yet when he emerges after twenty years secluded in a cave, his body appears anything but a victim of neglect. What particularly impresses his biographer is the state of wholeness, the true normality that characterizes his whole person, body, soul and mind. His body is neither exhausted from his fasting nor flabby from lack of exercise; he is "altogether in a state of equilibrium, as one governed by reason and *in a natural state.*"[10]

So we begin to see that the body's involvement with the transformation of the soul is not simply one-way; the soul returns the favor. It is a telling reminder of the essential unity of the human person, and a reality vividly present to the ascetic Fathers. We are told of Abba Pambo, for instance, that he prayed for three years not to be glorified on earth; but the Lord had other plans for him, and his face shone like lightning so that one could not look steadily at him. He appeared "like a king on his throne," radiant with "the image of the glory of Adam."[11] In other words, he had attained the truly natural state for which mankind was created. And this in turn points forward to the eschatological state, the glory in which the whole human being is destined to partake.

The ascetic's evolving relationship with the body is described by one of the masters of the ascetic way, St John Climacus. In his clas-

[9]*Sayings*, Anthony 33.

[10]Athanasius Life of Anthony, 14.

[11]*Sayings*, Pambo 1, 12.

sic *Ladder of Divine Ascent*, the Sinaite monk charts the whole process of the person's transformation in thirty "steps." In the early stages, one is aware only of "the flesh," which is an enemy to any progress—the more you look after it, the more harm it does you (Step 9). Halfway up, the relationship becomes more ambivalent; the flesh is a "dear enemy," and the body starts to be seen in the light of the resurrection: "How can I escape from it when it is going to rise with me?" (Step 15) On the final rung, however, the tension is resolved, as the body is revealed even in this life as participating in the glorification of the entire person: "When the whole man is in some way commingled with the love of God, he displays the splendor of the soul outwardly in his body . . . so Moses who saw God was glorified." (Step 30)

And so were many other people glorified, even up to our own day. Among them was the Russian émigré priest and theologian Sergei Bulgakov (d. 1944), author of the much-quoted exhortation to "kill the flesh to acquire a body":[12] his luminous face on his death-bed testified to the "body" which he had acquired. Better known, however, is the experience of St Seraphim of Sarov. This much-loved saint of eighteenth century Russia undertook such feats as praying for 1,000 days and nights kneeling on a rock, which might well look to us like "killing the body." Yet perhaps of all the ascetic saints, Seraphim had the closest contacts with spiritual children living their lives outside the monastic realm, and he firmly counsels his disciples against extreme ascetic labors. The aim of ascesis, he insists, is to make the body a friend and helper,

[12]Fr Sergei Bulgakov, quoted in Metropolitan Anthony of Sourozh, "Body and Matter in Spiritual Life," in A.M. Allchin, ed., *Sacrament and Image*, 2nd ed. (London: Fellowship of St Alban and St Sergius, 1987), 45.

ready and able to perform virtuous deeds.[13] And the fruits of this "friendship" are evident in his famous conversation with Nicolas Motovilov, who sees the saint transfigured before his eyes, his face shining like the sun.[14] This, says Seraphim, is what it means to be in the grace of the Holy Spirit, which is nothing other than the Kingdom of God within us. The body has been sealed at chrismation so as to become a vessel of this grace. Here is a real vision by anticipation of the resurrection: the visible transfiguration of both men, the perceptible warmth and fragrance that they sense around them, all testify that the whole person is to partake in the joy that is to come. So when we think of the fruits of ascetic struggle, we should think of people such as the serene and gentle Seraphim, who could greet every visitor with the words, "Christ is risen, my joy!"

We can see, then, what a close synergy exists between our souls and bodies in the spiritual life, and how asceticism enables them to work together in harmony. We deprive our body of creature comforts in the service of the soul; but this very process reminds the body of its high calling and prepares it for its own future glory. One of the Desert Mothers, Amma Theodora, refutes the Manichaeans' contempt for the body and points us in a different direction when she says: "Give the body discipline, and you will see that the body is for him who made it."[15]

[13]*Spiritual Instructions*: "On Fasting," "On Ascetic Labors," Sergei D. Arhipov, trans., in Harry M. Boosalis, *The Joy of the Holy* (South Canaan, PA: St Tikhon's Seminary Press, 1993), 143, 136.

[14]Valentine Zander, *St Seraphim of Sarov* (London: SPCK, 1975), 87–94.

[15]*Sayings*, Theodora 4.

Right use of material things

We can think of our body as the interface between ourselves and the world around us. It is in and through the body that we show love and care for people and things, that we know others and are known by them. It is in the body that we use the things of this world; and this use in turn is an interface with other people and other creatures who are dependent on the same resources.

Between our attitude to our own body and our attitude to the rest of the material world there is a close correlation. In both cases, the key is not to shun the material, but to find the right and healthy relationship. "It is not having a thing that harms us," says Abba Zosimas, "but being attached to it. Who does not know that the body is the most precious thing we have? How then are we told on occasion to despise it? And if this applies to the body, how much more is it true of things that are external to us."[16]

"Despising" in this context is another slippery term. It is probably most useful to think of it as the opposite of "being attached." It is helpful to compare the advice in St Basil's monastic rule, where he stresses that even possessions are not evil *per se*; the problem lies in "having a wrong attitude to things or not using them well."[17] To "despise" or "think lightly of" the things around us, including those we possess, means to reduce to a minimum our demands on them; it is to *walk lightly on* the earth. This is borne out by what we see in practice: far from treating material things with contempt, the holy ascetic commonly shows them a respect and delicacy which we almost never find in "materialistic" societies—or if

[16]Abba Zosimas (PG 78,1681AB).

[17]*Short Rules* 92.

we find it, it is reserved for a few very privileged possessions. The materialistic person values things in relation to his own desire and appetite for them; detachment, by contrast, enables one to value things for themselves, as parts of God's creation.

It is certainly true that restraint of our appetites for whatever reason helps us to "walk lightly upon the earth"; but that is not the main point here. Asceticism provides the link between our relationship to the material world and our spiritual life. It reveals to us that *the way we use material things is absolutely crucial to our spiritual progress.* As Maximus the Confessor tells us bluntly: "It is according to whether we use things rightly or wrongly that we become either good or bad."[18] He also makes another very important point, and one that places right use of the world—environmental responsibility, in modern terms—firmly at the center of Christian concerns, inseparable from the commandment of love. There are three ways, he says, in which we actively manifest love for other people: "in forbearance and patience, in genuinely desiring their good, and *in the right use of material things.*"[19] When it comes to use of the material world, it becomes very clear that asceticism is not an individual matter of self-improvement, but something profoundly communal: it has to do with how we use gifts bestowed for the benefit of all.

"True fasting consists not only in overcoming the flesh," says St Seraphim, "but also in taking that piece of bread which you would like to eat yourself, and giving it instead to one who is hungry."[20]

[18]*First Century on Love*, 92; *Philokalia* II, 63.

[19]*First Century on Love,* 40; *Philokalia* II, 56.

[20]*Spiritual Instructions,* in Boosalis, *Joy,* 142.

The same principle applies not only to food, but also to all sorts of things that we are tempted to claim for ourselves at the expense of others. Attachment to *my* property, *my* social position, *my* standard of living, is a potent aspect of "the world" in its most negative sense. When St Symeon the new Theologian urges the monk "to hate and abhor the things of the world," he immediately goes on to explain that "the world" is not livestock or food or houses or gardens, but "sin, *attachment to things*, and passions."[21] Symeon was not addressing hermits in the desert, but members of substantial monastic communities that had considerable property to manage; so this would seem to be an aspect of ascetic detachment that applies no less to Christians in the world. And indeed, we find that the social dimensions of asceticism loom largest in those Fathers who had most to do with non-monastic Christians. Some obvious examples are St Basil, with his monastic brotherhoods functioning as "ideal Christian households"[22] amidst his flock in Caesarea; or St John Chrysostom, who tried tirelessly to stir his comfortably-off parishioners in Antioch and Constantinople to ascetic exertion and charitable efforts. Chrysostom never lets us forget the wider consequences of apparently "private" ascetic exercise, and he speaks to our age no less than his own. Prayer and fasting, he points out, have the effect of reducing our wants to a minimum; they free us from covetousness and dispose us to give alms.[23] Like many ascetic Fathers down the ages, he keeps reminding his flock that the outward, physical aspects of asceticism are themselves of secondary importance: what matters is the

[21]*Catechetical Orations* 5, SC 96. 438–40.

[22]Brown, *Body and Society,* 289–90.

[23]Hom. on Matthew LVII.5.

inner freedom and detachment that come through such discipline. The physical discipline qualifies as true Christian asceticism only if it enables us to despise wealth, put away anger and free ourselves from vainglory and envy.[24]

"Right use of material things," then, encompasses the sum total of our life in the world, the way we conduct our life at work and leisure, the way we spend our money and use our property. But clearly, our "use" will depend on our attitude to the things that we use. At the basis of that attitude is the understanding of the created world as *God's gift*. Not a "gift" in the sense that it is handed over to us to do what we like with; rather, in the sense that it is *never* ours by right. It entails a constant connection with a Giver, a cause of endless gratitude to one who graciously gives us the enjoyment of what is his own. The Greek Fathers would point out that the very words we use tell us as much. That is why riches are called *khremata* (from *khresthai*, "to use"), says St John Chrysostom: the term indicates that they are not our property, but merely on loan.[25] And of course he spells out the social implications of this: "Is not 'the earth God's, and the fullness thereof?' [Ps 23.2]. Our possessions, then, belong to one common Lord; and therefore they belong also to our fellow servants. The possessions of the Lord are all common."[26] As we use the things of this world, even those to which we have impeccable legal title, we are never to forget that they remain fundamentally "possessions of the Lord," a reminder of his generosity to all.

[24]see Chrysostom, Hom. on Matthew XLVI.4.

[25]Hom. on 1 Tim. XI.2

[26]Hom. on 1 Tim. XII.3; cf. Clement of Alexandria, *Stromata* IV.13, *Paidagogos* II.13.

The Fathers are principally concerned with people appropriating more than they actually need from resources common to all the human community. But their reasoning lays the foundation for a broader vision. St Gregory the Theologian reminds us that God, who should be our example, has bestowed the basic necessities of life in abundance on *all creatures*: "he stretched out ample land for all land creatures, and springs, and rivers, and woods; and air for the birds, and water for the aquatic creatures."[27] And indeed, it is the animals themselves who set the best example of respect for these common goods. Basil points out that fish are content with the region assigned to them (unless their nature calls them to migrate); whales never leave their appointed element to go and ravage coastal settlements. This stands in marked contrast to us humans, who add house to house and field to field, enriching ourselves at the expense of our neighbor.[28] Once one recognizes natural resources as aspects of God's providential care for all creatures, it makes sense to see this universal providence as the pattern for the way we ourselves use these resources. If we are to be faithful imitators of the Creator, that means taking care for the legitimate needs of all his creatures.

The key criterion for use is need; and here again, animals may show humans the way. Thus St Neilos the Ascetic points out that "the Creator has ordained the same natural way of life for both us and the animals"—and a common diet, namely, "every herb of the field" (cf. Gen. 1:29–30) (as we saw in the previous chapter, animals eating each other is not regarded as part of God's original plan for his creation). If we use our powers

[27]*On Love for the Poor* 25.

[28]Basil, *Hexaemeron* VII.3–4.

of invention to turn this basic diet into something extravagant, it is not a sign of our sophistication compared with our fellow herbivores; we are simply showing ourselves more "dumb" than they.[29] The "dumb" beasts have a concern with basic necessities and a simplicity that puts humans to shame. This fact was not lost on Clement of Alexandria, the second century scholar and catechist who wrote more systematically on Christian living than anyone before or since. As he points out to the ladies of Alexandria, animals have more sense than to try to improve their appearance with makeup. (He is similarly scathing about the acquisition of precious stones for jewelry; significantly, he makes it quite clear that the argument "For whom are these things made, if not for us?" is no excuse whatever for taking more from the earth than we need.)[30]

A right use of creation involves restraint and self-limitation, as well as a recognition that we are dealing with common resources. But it also involves an awareness that all things are created "good," and therefore have the potential to be used well. "We should use all things for the glory of God, and not refuse anything on the grounds that it is evil," according to the 11th century writer Peter of Damascus.[31] Ascetic abstinence, whether from food, sexual relations or other things, must be clearly understood in this light. Abstinence has nothing to do with denying the goodness of creation. It simply serves as a reminder that using things to the glory of God may equally involve *not* using certain good things under certain conditions, for the sake of the spiritual or physical well-

[29]*Ascetic Discourse*, *Philokalia* I, 246–7.

[30]*Paidagogos* II.13.

[31]*Seven Forms of Bodily Discipline. Philokalia* III, 90.

being of our neighbor or ourselves. This is very clear in St Paul's discussion of food offered to idols, where he concludes, "if food is a cause of my brother's falling, I will never eat meat." (1 Cor 8.13) This should throw light on some of the choices facing us today. If one decides to avoid some food or other product on principle, for instance because producing it harms other people's health and welfare or involves unacceptable cruelty to animals, that is certainly not a matter of rejecting God's gifts as evil.

If all things are recognized precisely as gifts and tokens of God's generous love, then they are never something to be taken for granted and wasted. This attitude is strikingly reflected in the monastic tradition, in the notion that everything we use is in a sense sacred and worthy of respect. We find this expressed explicitly in the Rule of St Benedict of Nursia, the founder of Western monasticism in the early 6th century: "Look upon all the tools and all the property of the monastery as if they were sacred altar vessels."[32] About a century earlier, St John Cassian—whose writings had a great influence on St Benedict's Rule—had visited the Egyptian monasteries; and he was greatly impressed to hear of a brother who was judged "careless about sacred property" and made to do public penance because he had dropped three lentils while washing them. As Cassian explains, the Egyptian monks "believe not only that they are not their own, but also that everything they possess is consecrated to the Lord. So if anything whatsoever has once been brought into the monastery, it ought to be treated with the utmost reverence as a holy thing." They therefore take great care even of things that might be regarded as common and paltry, and consider it a good work to put them in a better place, or to dust them.[33]

[32]Rule, XXI,10.

[33]*Institutes* IV.20.

This attitude toward "ordinary" things can be seen as a constant of the ascetic tradition. As St Basil writes, "the Christian ought to regard all the things given to him as being for his use, not to hold as his own or to hoard; and he should be careful of everything since it belongs to the Lord, and should not overlook any things that might be being thrown away."[34] This very practical advice from a letter entitled "On the perfection of the life of solitaries" is another reminder that the basic principles of the ascetic way make no distinction between the monk or nun and the married Christian. And one of these principles is that the way we treat material things has an ethical dimension, no less than our treatment of people: things as well as people deserve a proper respect. We find the same emphasis in that very down-to-earth ascetic writer of the sixth century, Dorotheos of Gaza. It goes against the conscience, he teaches, if for instance one has a perfectly good blanket but wants to exchange it for a new one "for the sake of prestige, or from mere thoughtlessness." It is similarly inadmissible to use things badly and damage them; he gives the example of wearing our clothes out too quickly, or leaving fabrics in the sun too long.[35]

The same spirit is still very much alive in our own day. Disciples of the Athonite Elder Joseph the Hesychast, who died in 1959, recall him bending down painfully to pick up any tiny thing that spilled on the ground. "Don't despise even the smallest of things," he would tell his disciples; "waste of these things counts, and the blessing will depart from our house."[36]

[34]Letter XXII.1

[35]*Discourse* III, "On Conscience"; Eric P. Wheeler, trans., *Dorotheos of Gaza: Discourses and Sayings* (Kalamazoo, MI: Cistercian, 1977), 107.

[36]Elder Joseph, *Elder Joseph the Hesychast: Struggles – Experiences – Teachings (1898–1959)* (Mount Athos: Vatopaidi, 1999), 138.

We have seen that "despising the flesh" in the ascetic sense prepares the body for glory. But what is the outcome of "despising" (or detaching ourselves from) things around us? On the one hand, it is to the benefit of other people, who have the opportunity to use resources that we might otherwise hoard or waste. But the ascetic attitude to the inanimate world goes far beyond seeing it simply as a resource; the beauty of any monastic garden will testify to that. The effect of such an attitude on the world around us is best expressed in the words of another contemporary Athonite, as he describes the daily work of the monastery—the sorts of chores that monks share with the rest of the world, but in a community where "there is nothing that is mine or yours, but all is in common." Things are to be used when needed; but use and contemplation become one:

> Another example of light is our work, which here [in the monastery] is not a servile labor but a *diakonia*, a service performed for the monastic community without gain, without necessity, without force; a well-pleasing sacrifice which is illumined by prayer and becomes a transfiguration of the world and of objects, a way of continuing the Divine Liturgy outside church. Because here the light is the contemplation and use of the physical world, not for pleasure but for the needs of the community; not like the destructive consumption based in technology, but in order to make nature already now a partaker of the glory of the children of God, and allow it to sing praises with them.[37]

[37]Archimandrite Aimilianos of Simonopetra, "The Experience of the Transfiguration in the Life of the Athonite Monk," in Heiromonk Alexander Golitzin, *The Living Witness of the Holy Mountain* (South Canaan, PA : St Tikhon's Press, 1996), 205; translation adapted.

Ecological asceticism today

On a very practical level, asceticism addresses one of the most intractable obstacles to dealing with environmental problems. Whether on the level of individual behavior or national policies, proposed solutions so often founder on the unspoken question: *Will we have to give something up?* And if one is thinking in terms of material "things" or benefits—standard of living, range of consumer choices—then the obvious answer is, "Of course we shall." When we are talking about large-scale problems such as climate change, technology can only take us so far. We can be confident that the affluent in today's world—which includes most of the readers of this book—will also need to fly less, drive less, and consume fewer exotic goods, *in addition* to using the most energy-efficient means for whatever they do. Often people are reluctant to admit this openly, afraid of being dismissed as killjoys. So it is not enough to point out unpopular facts: it is also necessary to challenge the lie that self-indulgence is the key to a fulfilled and happy life. It is worth noting that many environmentalists are now discovering independently what the Christian ascetic tradition has taught for almost two millennia: the joyful freedom of a simplified life, comparatively unburdened by worldly cares.

The ascetic tradition gives a radically new perspective on self-limitation, on the sort of restrictions on our range of options that a sustainable way of living is likely to demand. Such limitations are neither a way of making ourselves miserable, nor an occasion to feel self-righteous. They are opportunities and tools "to silence, with God's help, our loud-voiced will," as the Finnish author Tito Colliander puts it so aptly.[38] They are providential aids in our spiritual struggle.

[38]Tito Colliander, *The Way of the Ascetics* (London & Oxford: Mowbray, 1983),14.

Whether we are thinking of the Church's traditional disciplines such as fasting or of an "environmental asceticism" of living in a more sustainable manner, there is always the tendency to think in negative terms: "giving up" or "self-denial." But once we start thinking about the detachment that is the aim of ascetic practice, we realize that it has more to do with *giving* than with *giving up*. It is possible to use the world's resources, to buy and sell, yet to do so in a spirit of detachment. When people focus on frugality ("giving up") in order to limit the environmental harm we cause to others, they are often challenged: What about all those people whose livelihoods depend on our consumption? This is a fair question, provided it is raised in good faith; because if it is applied consistently, it means that the best interests of all those involved in the production chain should be uppermost in our minds when we go shopping. And that, of course, presents a challenge: will I make an effort to buy fairly traded coffee, local organic produce or sustainably harvested lumber—or will I chose the product cheapest for me or the one that happens to take my fancy? Detachment is that quality that enables us truly to use our wealth and purchasing power for the benefit of others; to serve our needs, without being slaves to our own tastes and fancies.

"The monk," says the great spiritual writer Evagrius, "is separated from all and united with all."[39] The non-monastic Christian may not be separated from other people and things in terms of space; but all Christian asceticism has the goal of *detachment* for love of God. And that detachment allows us to embrace all other creatures as objects and instruments of God's love, not of our own desires. Far beyond lessening our environmental impact, the ascetic way brings us to a new vision: "it renders creation personal and trans-

[39]*On Prayer* 124; *Philokalia* I, 69.

parent," as Metropolitan Kallistos writes, "so that we regain our sense of wonder before the sacredness of the earth."[40]

We cannot agree, then, with the misanthropic pessimism of "Help save the earth: commit suicide!" But if we replace "commit suicide" with "die to the world" in the traditional Christian sense of that phrase, then the slogan would be remarkably apt.

For further reading

Aimilianos, Archimandrite. "The Experience of the Transfiguration in the Life of the Athonite Monk," in Hieromonk Alexander Golitzin, trans., *The Living Witness of the Holy Mountain*. South Canaan, PA: St Tikhon's Seminary Press, 1996: 194–215.

Anthony, Metropolitan of Sourozh. "Body and Matter in Spiritual Life." A.M. Allchin, ed. *Sacrament and Image: Essays in the Christian Understanding of Man*. London: Fellowship of St Alban and St Sergius, 2nd ed. 1987: 36–46.

Boosalis, Harry M. *The Joy of the Holy: St Seraphim of Sarov and Orthodox Spiritual Life*. South Canaan, PA: St Tikhon's Seminary Press, 1993.

Brown, Peter. *The Body and Society: Men, Women and Sexual Renunciation in Early Christianity*. New York, NY: Columbia University Press, 1988.

Chryssavgis, John. *Beyond the Shattered Image*. Minneapolis, MN: Light and Life Publishing, 1999, esp. Chapter Five, "The Sacredness of Creation in the 'Sayings of the Desert Fathers' " and Chapter Six, "The Desert is Alive."

[40]Bishop Kallistos (Ware) of Diokleia, "Lent and the Consumer Society," in A. Walker and C. Carras, eds,, *Living Orthodoxy in the Modern World* (London: SPCK, 1996), 83.

Clément, Olivier. *The Roots of Christian Mysticism.* London: New City, 1993.

Colliander, Tito. *The Way of the Ascetics.* London & Oxford: Mowbray, 1983.

Makarios, Father. "The Monk and Nature in Orthodox Tradition." *So that God's Creation might Live*: Proceedings of the Inter-Orthodox Conference on Environmental Protection, the Orthodox Academy of Crete, November 1991. Ecumenical Patriarchate of Constantinople, ET 1994: 41–48.

Ware, Bishop Kallistos of Diokleia. "The Transfiguration of the Body." A.M. Allchin, ed. *Sacrament and Image: Essays in the Christian Understanding of Man.* 2nd ed. London: Fellowship of St Alban and St Sergius, 1987: 19–35.

Ware, Bishop Kallistos of Diokleia, "Lent and the Consumer Society," in A. Walker and C. Carras ed. *Living Orthodoxy in the Modern World,* London: SPCK, 1996: 64–84.

Ware, Bishop Kallistos of Diokleia. " 'My Helper and My Enemy': The Body in Greek Christianity." Sarah Coakley, ed. *Religion and The Body.* Cambridge: Cambridge University Press, 2000: 90–110.

(Zizioulas), John, Metropolitan of Pergamon. "Ecological Asceticism: A Cultural Revolution." *Sourozh* 67 (February 1997): 22–25; reprinted from *Our Planet* 7/6 (1996).

chapter three

The Saints and Their Environment

The Fathers' writings about man and the cosmos and about the ascetic way come from a world very different from the one familiar to most of us. The same may be true of ascetic writers, even when they are our contemporaries. So there is always a risk of misunderstanding what they are saying, and misjudging how their precepts would be applied in practice. Fortunately, however, the patristic and ascetical teaching is spelled out, in its practical and lived dimension, in a wealth of examples, from early centuries up to present day, of the way in which people of holiness live in God's creation.

Precisely because these examples come to us in the form of stories, they are not always taken as seriously as they deserve. Often they describe things outside the experience of most of us; but it would be rash to conclude on this account that they are fairy-tales. The relationship they depict between holy people and their surroundings is too consistent, and too well attested, to be dismissed so easily. Some of the most remarkable stories are first-hand accounts from our contemporaries. Instead of dismissing such accounts on the grounds that "things like that don't happen in the real world," it might be more prudent to suppose that our experience of reality could be incomplete.

This is not to claim that all the stories are historically accurate. The saints' *Lives* (that is, the written accounts of their lives) certainly do include stories that have grown in the telling, and in some cases also contain legendary elements. But these too can give insight into the Church's understanding of man's place in creation. Even when a story is not strictly historical, it may still graphically express the values and aspirations of the community that has transmitted and received it.

In saints' *Lives* and stories of holy people, we find many themes that throw light on humans' proper place in creation. We see the extent of human authority over other creatures, and the way in which that authority relates to our creation in God's image. We find the idea that creation is there for the benefit of humans, but it is equally evident that the benefit works both ways; the saints use both human skills and their powers of intercession for the benefit of all sorts of creatures. The extent to which all creatures on earth are interdependent is something we are only now discovering; yet a sense of this truth comes across, differently expressed, in stories of saints even from early times. We find that the transforming power of holiness extends not only to animate creatures, but to things and places too. Sometimes the transfigured world around the saint is perceptible also to others; but we also see that the holy person perceives a transfigured world, a world directed toward God, where most of us would see only the utilitarian and the ordinary. And finally, we discover that the relationship between man and the world indicated in saints' *Lives* is faithfully depicted in icons: as we "read" an icon, we meet the same themes in another form.

The restored image and human authority

The saint is a person in whom the original beauty of the divine image is being restored: "In you, Father / Mother, was preserved what is according to the divine image," in the words of the troparion to an ascetic saint. He or she is an icon of the new Adam; so it is in the environs of this "icon," if anywhere, that we should expect to glimpse a restored paradise—man and creation in the state for which they were created. As we have seen with the holy ascetics, the inner transformation of the person extends outwards to his body; and it has a ripple effect on the physical world around us, whose substance we share. In the lives of holy people we may see a restoration—albeit highly localized—of the setting in which man was originally given "dominion" over other creatures. That is why these lives provide such important insights into how human authority in creation is actually intended to function.

The first thing we notice is that the saint typically exercises the authority of love. Here is a person totally focused on God, a living example of what it means to "despise" everything else for love of him. Yet what we see as the outcome of this single-mindedness is not a rejection of other people and creatures, but an ever closer bond of love with them: "separate from all and united with all."[1] Relationship with the Creator of all things cannot, by definition, be something exclusive; it is the key to a love that embraces all creatures. "Anyone who loves God loves not only his fellow man, but the entire creation as well: trees, grass, flowers. He loves everything with the same love," according to an Athonite saying.[2]

[1]Evagrius, *On Prayer* 124; *Philokalia* I, 69.

[2]Archimandrite Ioannikios, *An Athonite Gerontikon: Saying of the Holy Fathers of Mount Athos*, translated by Maria Derpapa Mayson and Sister Theodora (Zion) (Thessaloniki: Kouphalia, 1997), 31.

And this affirmation has a corollary, neatly expressing the natural authority that flows from a right relationship with the Creator: "Love the One, and even the wild beasts will love you." The latter is a saying of Fr Amphilochios of Patmos, the much-loved twentieth-century elder well-known also for his love of trees.

The relationship between man and other creatures is mutual, but it all depends on the human being's relationship with God. Other creatures' reactions depend on the person growing into Christ, in whom the fall is undone and the proper balance in creation restored. St Isaac the Syrian describes the interaction between the "humble man" and wild animals in this way:

> The moment they catch sight of him their ferocity is tamed; they come up and cling to him as to their Master, wagging their tails and licking his hands and feet. They scent, as coming from that person, the same fragrance that came from Adam before the transgression, the time when they were gathered together before him and he gave them names in paradise. This scent was taken away from us. But Christ has renewed it and given it back to us at his coming.[3]

As another great Syrian, St Ephrem, reminds us, the harmony surrounding Adam before his transgression extended to relations between the animals themselves, who also intermingled with no fear of each other.[4] And in fact, both accounts describe faithfully

[3]Sebastian Brock, trans., in A.M. Allchin ed., *The Heart of Compassion: Daily Readings with St Isaac of Syria* (London: Darton, Longman and Todd, 1989), 41. The text comes from Hom. 77 according to the numbering of Holy Transfiguration Monastery, trans., *The Ascetic Homilies of St Isaac the Syrian* (Boston, 1984), 383.

[4]Commentary on Genesis II.9, in Brock, *Hymns on Paradise*, 203.

what is sometimes seen in the presence of the saints. Thus in the 15th century, a monk went to visit the Russian hermit Paul of Obnora, a forest-dweller who had lived for three years in a large hollow lime tree. The visitor was amazed to find the saint with birds perched all over him and feeding from his hand; next to him was a bear, waiting its turn; foxes and rabbits were running around, *without enmity between them and with no fear of the bear.*[5] There are countless such stories from all periods and all corners of the Christian world, many of them very well attested. The effects of holiness on the created world cannot readily be dismissed as pious fantasy.

Since our natural authority derives from the divine image, other creatures recognize that authority to the degree that the image is recognizable in us. Indeed, the correspondence between divine likeness and authority is so close that the behavior of animals may be used as a sort of "barometer" for a person's relationship with God. John Moschos in his *Spiritual Meadow* tells of one Abba Paul the Roman, who is burdened by a grave though involuntary sin—his carriage had run over and killed a child. Unsure whether God has accepted his repentance, he finds a lion and tries to provoke it into devouring him; and when it fails to respond, he concludes that his sin must be forgiven.[6] Even more striking is an incident in the Life of St Sava the Sanctified, one of the founders of Palestinian monasticism in the fifth century. Like several Fathers in the deserts of both Egypt and Palestine, St Sava was attended by a lion, out of whose paw he had pulled a splinter. The saint's

[5]*The Northern Thebaid: Monastic Saints of the Russian North* (Platina, CA: St Herman of Alaska Brotherhood, 1975), 39, emphasis added.

[6]*Leimonarion* 101. *Life of Abba Paul of Greece.*

disciple Flavius had a donkey; and whenever Flavius was away on an errand, it was the lion's job to look after the donkey. This worked well until one day, Flavius had to go into the city, and while he was there fell into grave sin; whereupon the lion ate the donkey. Flavius, we are told, understood immediately why this had happened, and did not dare face the Elder.[7] As with St Paul of Obnora, the interaction between the animals themselves is dictated by the spiritual state of the humans in their midst—except that in this case, the effect is negative. The pattern depicted in Genesis repeats itself: when man "falls" again, the animals too resume their fallen state.

Some accounts make it crystal clear that our authority is conditional: to misuse it is to forfeit it. This point is illustrated with some precision in another story from Palestine. A novice, nervous about the leopards in the area, was assured that there had only been one case of a monk being harmed by a leopard. The monk had encountered the animal on a narrow path and commanded it in Christ's name to give way, whereupon it obediently leapt down to another ledge. But the monk, being less God-fearing than the leopard, proceeded to throw stones at it, with the result that the leopard rushed up by another path and scratched him, but did not use its teeth at all. The ambivalence of the animal's response exactly mirrors the inconsistency of the man's behavior: he had invoked the authority of Christ, but then failed to act according to Christ's image.[8]

[7]Life of St Sava, 49; Cyril of Scythopolis, R.M. Price, trans., *Lives of the Monks of Palestine* (Kalamazoo, MI: Cistercian Publications, 1991), 148–9.

[8]Life of St George of Choziba, V.21; Tim Vivian, tr., *Journeying into God: Seven Early Monastic Lives* (Minneapolis, MN: Fortress Press, 1996), 87–8.

Paradise glimpsed

In the environs of a holy person we catch glimpses of paradise, of the created order restored to its intended state. But there is also plenty of evidence of a work in progress: a transformed human being is living in a world that has yet to be transformed. Instances of the latter sort are often easier for us to relate to; they give us more practical clues as to how to act in a world afflicted by the fall.

The part played by predators illustrates well the "work in progress" aspect. There is clear consensus that the Creator's original plan does not include animals hunting and eating each other. There are cases of predators changing their ways completely, or at least being expected to do so; one desert monk used to share his provisions with a lion until it went back to its old ways and resumed hunting, whereupon he chased it away.[9] A prime example of deliberate transformation of animal behavior is the touching story of Makarios the Egyptian and the hyena. In all versions of the story, Makarios was in possession of a fine sheepskin given him by a hyena in gratitude for healing her blind cubs. In the Coptic version, however, he is highly suspicious about how she got the skin; he does not want to accept something acquired by violence, and therefore refuses the gift until the hyena promises not to kill again.[10] If she cannot scavenge enough carrion, she is to come and ask him for bread. If Makarios places unusually severe restrictions on the animal's behavior, that is probably because the gift of the skin threatened to implicate him in the cycle of preda-

[9] *Leimonarion* 163, *Life of Abba Paul of Greece*.

[10] Helen Waddell, *Beasts and Saints* (Grand Rapids, MI: Eerdmans, repr. 1996), 12–14.

tion. Behavior that might be acceptable for a wild animal on its own is unacceptable for a human who is struggling to restore in himself the image of God.

What we see more often, however, is evidence of an intermediate state between the world of the fall and paradise. Man's authority is restored in the saint; but in a world that is not yet paradise, the animals retain the nature proper to them in the world of the fall. As an outpost of the restored creation, the holy person acts as a bulwark, protecting from the effects of the "fallen" world those who ask his intercessions. This means that predators will respect other animals belonging to or protected by the saint; they do not abandon their instincts, but submit them to the will of the holy person. On occasion, that may mean exercising those instincts to his advantage. We hear, for instance, of Kyriacos in the desert of Palestine, who enjoyed good relations with a lion. The lion protected the hermit's vegetable patch by keeping the wild goats down, and also chased off malevolent human marauders; but it thoughtfully withdrew, even in the middle of a meal, when it realized that it was making the Elder's visitors nervous.[11]

In a world that still awaits full transfiguration, ferocious animals may serve to protect the saint, and his basic needs, from other creatures that are less cooperative. The latter all too often include humans: because animals are "unfallen," part of the creation "subjected to futility not of its own will" (Rom 8.20) their response to the restored image is more intuitive and immediate than that of creatures endowed with free will. A story concerning Abba Amoun, one of the Egyptian Desert Fathers, illustrates the

[11]Cyril of Scythopolis, *Life of Cyriacus* 15–16; Price, *Monks of Palestine,* 255–6.

difference dramatically. He was being plagued by robbers stealing his meager provisions, and finally in exasperation detailed two large snakes to guard the door of his cell. When he next went out, it was to find the would-be burglars paralyzed by terror. He proceeded to contrast their behavior unfavorably with that of the snakes, rebuking them as "more ferocious than the wild beasts" who "thanks to God, obey our wishes."[12]

If animals eating each other is often tolerated, animals eating or terrorizing humans is not; indeed, it may actually be considered morally culpable. Thus we hear of another Egyptian Desert Father, Abba Helle, who commanded a crocodile to die to atone for the lives it had taken—despite the fact that it had twice obediently ferried him across the river when bidden.[13] Presumably he decided that it was unrepentant, and could not be trusted with humans who lacked his own charismatic authority. Especially in the lives of earlier saints, from times when the ravages of wild beasts were a widespread and terrible threat, the saints are frequently seen using their authority over animals to protect people from them. Yet while they use whatever means are necessary, minimum force is preferred. Another desert Father, renowned for his meekness, achieved no less satisfactory results by non-violent persuasion; he "spoke gently" to a gigantic hippopotamus and commanded it in Christ's name to leave the farmers' land alone, and applied the same technique successfully to a crocodile.[14]

[12]*History of the Monks in Egypt* IX, 5–7; Norman Russell, trans., *The Lives of the Desert Fathers* (Oxford:Mowbray and Kalamazoo, MI: Cistercian Publications, 1981), 80–81.

[13]*History of the Monks* XII, 6–9; Russell, *Lives*, 91.

[14]*History of the Monks* IV.3; Russell, *Lives*, 66.

Usually, it seems to be the animal's choice whether it accepts peaceful coexistence, or remains unregenerate and takes the consequences. Abba Amoun, who had enlisted the help of snakes to such good effect, was asked on another occasion to protect the local peasants against a giant snake that was terrorizing them and destroying their livestock. This one showed no reverence, however, and tried to attack the elder; so he confronted it and said, "Christ who will destroy Leviathan will destroy you too," whereupon it burst open and died.[15] The formula he uses is noteworthy; so is the fact that snakes (or dragons) seem more likely than other animals to end up being killed as thoroughly incorrigible. It makes us wonder whether these stories are actually about authority over natural animals, or about "serpents and scorpions and all the power of the enemy" (see Lk 10.19). We should note, furthermore, that more recent ascetics have often taken pains to counter the idea that actual snakes are accursed and automatically deserve destruction. A striking example was the Elder Theoktistos of Patmos (died 1917), who shared his cave with a dozen or so vipers and tried to teach the local boys not to kill them. People remembered him in his old age going out every noontime with a saucer of milk for a snake that lived in a nearby rock.[16] The saints show us that an individual animal may sometimes need to be destroyed, but there is no warrant for stereotyping an entire species as evil. Symbolism is one thing; God's living creature, even a serpent or scorpion, is another.

[15]*History of the Monks* IX.8–10; Russell, *Lives*, 81.

[16]Irina Gorainoff, "Holy Men of Patmos," *Sobornost* 6:5 (Spring 1972): 341.

One of the most remarkable features of the "restored paradise" around the saints is that human authority extends beyond sentient creatures to the inanimate world. "Not only beasts, but the elements themselves obey such a man," as Cyril of Scythopolis writes of the great Euthymius, desert-dweller and monastic founder in fifth-century Palestine.[17] Obviously in the case of inanimate nature, there is no question of direct communication. So this authority above all reminds us that in the saint, we are not looking at certain natural human qualities that other creatures appreciate, but at a relationship with God through which the entire order is restored. The state of affairs in Eden, before the earth was subject to any curse, is clearly recalled in a story of the desert Father Copres. Abba Copres had told the newly-baptized peasants in the vicinity that if they had faith in God, even the desert sand would bear much fruit for them. So every year they would bring him a spadeful of sand to bless, and their fields became the envy of Egypt.[18]

A natural authority over the elements, unaided by technology, may not be easy for the modern mind to accept; but the evidence for it is by no means confined to ancient times and distant places. The following story is told of a saintly priest's wife in Alaska, Olga Michael, who died just a few years ago and is already said to have worked miracles. The night of Matushka Olga's death, in November, a strong southerly wind blew forcefully and continuously, melting the snow and river ice—this enabled neighbors to arrive by boat, normally quite impossible at that time of year. The day of her funeral was like spring; the procession was even joined by a flock of birds, although by that time of year, all birds have

[17]*Life of Euthymius*, 13; Price, *Monks of Palestine*, 18.

[18]*History of the Monks* X.26–9, Russell, *Lives,* 86.

long since flown south. The birds circled overhead, and accompanied the coffin to the grave-site. Because of the unprecedented thaw, the usually frozen soil had been easy to dig. That night, the ground re-froze, ice covered the river, winter returned. As Fr Michael Oleksa comments in recounting this story: "the cosmos still cooperates and participates in the worship the Real People offer to God."[19] Matushka Olga was a Real Person—not only according to the name of her tribe (Yup'ik), but according to the image of her Creator restored in her.

It is always a temptation to romanticize the relationship between holy people and other creatures, and the message it gives us about humans' place in nature. We are certainly to conclude that the intended state of creation is one of harmony, where creatures cooperate in love and without fear. But we must also recognize that the route towards that state involves compassion, indeed, but no sentimentality. The saints' relationship with other creatures is one in which man has authority, and even, in extreme cases, power of life and death. On the other hand, the stories of the saints constantly remind us how far this "authority" is from being arbitrary. And indeed, how far it is from much of the behavior that we usually associate with the idea of being in authority. "The rulers of the gentiles lord it over them, and their great men exercise authority over them: it shall not be so among you," Christ tells his disciples (Mt 20.25–6). The example of the saints suggests to us very strongly is that the "lordship" over the earth and dominion over the animals to which we are appointed is equally to be exercised in the spirit of "it shall not be so among you." If we want to become masters of ourselves and of creation, says the Athonite

[19]Michael J. Oleksa, *Orthodox Alaska: A Theology of Mission* (Crestwood, NY: St Vladimir's Seminary Press, 1992), 205.

elder Archimandrite Vasileios of Iviron, we will achieve this by becoming servants of all.[20]

Creation "for man": Coexistence and interdependence

In accounts of holy lives, we sometimes encounter the idea that everything exists "for man's benefit." But we also discover that what this means to the saint is very different from what it means to someone who does not see himself as the servant of the Creator of all things. Certainly, the world around us is to be used as necessary to serve man's basic physical needs. But there is also another "benefit" to be derived from other creatures, less obvious but vitally important: we grow spiritually by perceiving how God's beauty and wisdom is reflected in them, and adjusting our own lives accordingly. This particular way of seeing creation as a "gift" to us is frequently implicit, but it is made explicit by St Maximus, when he says that man receives the natural laws of things as gifts *when he imitates them in the way he lives*. By this imitation, man "reveals in himself all the majesty of the divine wisdom which is invisibly present in existent things."[21] Creation is "given" to us, not as a commodity to use at whim, but as a pattern for our own relationship to its Creator.

This nuanced understanding of creation given "for man's benefit" translates into a strong sense of interdependence and mutual respect between humans and other created beings. The saint is one who is prepared to *share space* with other creatures—sometimes literally. There is more than one story of a desert anchorite taking

[20] *Ecology and Monasticism* (Montreal: Alexander Press, 1996), 10.

[21] *To Thalassius* LI (PG 90, 476C–481C).

refuge in a cave during the midday heat, only to find a lion already in occupation. When the lion starts roaring and snarling at him, the monk points out that there is plenty of room for both of them. If the lion does not like the arrangement, it can go away. In the version of this story told of St Savas the Sanctified, it is worth noting that the saint reminds the animal that "*we both have one Creator;* I myself was fashioned by the hand of God and privileged to receive his image." The starting point for coexistence is a basic equivalence between earth-dwellers, precisely as creatures. The privileged status of the human being justifies him in resisting the other creature's wishes; but it does not mean that he can simply order the previous occupant out when it is possible for the needs of both to be accommodated.[22]

A paradoxical picture emerges: the saints have authority to kill animals by a word if required, and yet they consider they have no right to disrupt other creatures' lives—let alone harm them—more than absolutely necessary for human survival. There is a measure of "moral equivalency" between the needs of humans and those of other creatures, and all parties are expected to play fair. So we are told that St Anthony, finding his vegetable patch depredated by wild asses, "playfully" took hold of one of them and asked it, "Why do you hurt me *when I do you no injury?*"[23] He then commanded them in the name of the Lord to go and graze elsewhere. The human appeals to the animal on the basis of the fact that he is impinging only minimally on its territory; the aim is to find a solution that will give access to the necessities of life

[22]*Life of Sabas,* 33; Price, *Monks of Palestine,* 128. Cf. the similar story of "a certain old man" cited in Waddell, *Beasts and Saints*, 22.

[23]Athanasius, *Life of Anthony*, 50.

to all concerned. In a much more recent incident, we hear of a wild boar that was ravaging the vegetables at one of the smaller communities on Mount Athos. Finally, it was caught and brought to the Elder of the community. Rather than killing or transporting it, the Elder had a special stall made for it in the stables. He gave the animal strict instructions to leave the vegetable garden alone; if it was hungry, it was to come to the stable and ask for food.[24] Wild boars need to eat too.

Animals in the service of man

Particularly with holy hermits, we see a relationship with animals that precludes the need for domestication: wild animals are simply summoned to serve as needed, and they readily comply. There is another story told of Abba Helle, that bane of man-eating crocodiles: once as he was returning to his cell laden with provisions, he noticed some wild asses grazing and commanded in Christ's name that one of them should come and carry his burden. Immediately a she-ass trotted over and allowed herself to be saddled and loaded up;[25] it seems that she fared better than the similarly obedient crocodile. This was an isolated act, but St Mamas—known as a friend of animals, and often depicted riding on a lion—gathered quite a flock of wild animals which came to him to be milked, so that he even had enough cheese to distribute to the poor.[26]

[24] *Athonite Gerontikon* XLVII, 455.

[25] *History of the Monks* XII.5; Russell, *Lives*, 90.

[26] Cited in Joanne Stefanatos, *Animals and Man: A State of Blessedness* (Minneapolis, MN: Light and Life, 1992), 229.

These examples suggest that humans should be able to call on animals to serve their needs; there is no implication that domestication is illegitimate. On the other hand, it is clear that animals, whether domestic or wild, have their own legitimate needs, which humans must respect. Domestication does not reduce the animal to chattel, to be used or abused at will. One early monk, as we hear, was expelled from his monastery because he had struck a mule in the face and killed it; he was sent to St Savas to be guided to repentance.[27] Our responsibility for other creatures goes beyond avoiding gross cruelty, however. An Athonite story relates how a former Patriarch of Constantinople, retired to the Holy Mountain, learned this the hard way. Once when the Patriarch was taking his loaded donkey up a steep path, he saw two monks, radiant with light, wiping the sweat from the animal's face. Already an old man, he was no doubt hot and tired himself, and was quite put out that the donkey should be receiving this care rather than he. But when he complained to the two luminous figures, they replied rather sharply that he deserved no such solicitude, since he was not carrying the load; the donkey had done all the work.[28]

The ultimate service rendered by animals to man is to become food for him; and the saints seem to accept the eating of meat as a fact of the fallen world, even though many of them, as monks, do not participate in it. St Gregory the Theologian recounts how a genteel Christian family, driven into the mountains by the last great wave of imperial persecutions and quite unused to living by their wits far from civilization, called on the Lord to help them in their predicament. He describes the sequel in terms reminiscent

[27]Sabas, 44; Price, *Monks of Palestine,* 143–4.

[28]*Athonite Gerontikon* XL, 384–5.

of subsistence hunting cultures even today, where "the food on which your life depends, you harvest successfully only because that animal has sacrificed itself to feed you."[29] No sooner had the family prayed than a herd of fine, plump stags emerged from cover, "prisoners of prayer and righteous petition." The animals in front urged forward those following, seeming almost annoyed that they had not been summoned sooner.[30] Even in the world of the fall, animals serve the Lord by giving their lives for humans at his bidding.

But there is equally a sense that the life of another creature is not to be taken lightly. In a culture where hunting was a matter of subsistence rather than profit or even sport, we nevertheless hear of hunters deprived of a particular victim because the Lord wills to save its life; often a holy person is involved in ensuring its sanctuary. The balance between hunter and hunted is further illuminated by a story from Anastasius of Sinai. A monk was approached by Saracen tribesmen who had nothing to eat; the monk instructed them to shoot one wild goat, but not to attempt a second. Having brought down the first goat with ease, one Saracen decided to ignore the latter part of the monk's instruction—whereupon his bow snapped.[31]

[29]Father Michael Oleksa, "The Confluence of Church and Culture" in Constance J. Tarasar, ed., *Perspectives on Orthodox Education* (Syosset, NY: Syndesmos/ Department of Religious Education of the Orthodox Church in America, 1983), 11. The reference is to a Yup'ik whale hunt.

[30]*Panegyric on St Basil,* 7.

[31]*Récits* X, ed. Nau, *Oriens Christianus* II (1902): 66.

Man in the service of animals

Service in the created order is not all in one direction, then: and one of the ways in which humans serve animals is by protecting them. A particularly dramatic example comes from the life of St David of Garesja, a Syrian hermit living in Georgia around 500. As he was praying in the mountains one day, a hunted partridge took refuge at his feet. Challenged aggressively by the irate falconer, David replied by making a parallel between the Lord's providential care for David himself in the wilderness and for the hunted bird: "He whom I believe in and worship looks after all his creatures. . . . By him are brought up all men and all animals and all plants, the birds of the sky and the fish of the sea. . . . Now go away and hunt other game, for today this partridge has found a haven with me, so that it may be saved from death." The hunter scoffs at the idea that any power can protect either man or bird from his anger; he realizes his mistake only when he raises his arm to strike David a deathblow, and it withers.[32]

Here we see another sense in which all earthly creatures are on an equal footing. The man is the means of the animal's protection, but he is not the ultimate source of it. Unlike the typical modern city-dweller, the citizen of the desert is acutely aware that man, no less than other creatures, is absolutely dependent on God's mercy. We are reminded of St Savas the Sanctified, guided to a remote and highly inaccessible cave by an angel who reassures him, "he who gives food to the animals and to the young ravens that invoke him will himself take care of you."[33] The ultimate Giver is God: but

[32]David Marshall Lang, *Lives and Legends of the Georgian Saints* (Oxford: Mowbray, 2*nd* revised ed. 1976), 88–9.

[33]*Life of Sabas* 15; Price, *Monks of Palestine*, 106–7.

in various ways, both man and animals may be called on to serve each other as instruments of his merciful purposes. This fits well with the image of creation as an interdependent *body*, such as we have seen for instance in Ephrem and Chrysostom (see p. 78). No single creature can afford to forget its need for all the rest.

Provision of food and healing are among the more obvious ways in which humans serve other creatures. There are innumerable accounts of animals turning to holy people for healing, whether it is lions in the Near East, roe deer on Mount Athos or bald eagles in Alaska. Often the saint simply administers basic first aid; in these cases, the remarkable element in the story is the animal's trust. Intuitively it recognizes that here the "fear and dread" of man (see Gen 9.2), which came in the wake of the fall, no longer applies.

But man is not only in a position to serve other creatures' needs through his knowledge and skill; it is also his role to intercede for them. St Mamas' prayer for domestic animals, that no "diabolical catastrophe or any other malady" should come upon them, shows how he repaid the service of the deer who gave him milk.[34] Examples of individual animals saved from harm by the prayers of a saint span the Christian world. We learn that the intercessions of St Savas the Sanctified—after his death—protected a camel which had lost its footing, in response to the entreaties of its Saracen driver.[35] And many centuries later, we find Fr John of Kronstadt beseeching the Lord on behalf of a horse that was being swept away by the river, and not ceasing until, to the amazement of the helpless onlookers, the animal made it safely to the bank.[36] But

[34]cited in Stefanatos, *Animals and Man*, 236.

[35]*Life of Sabas* 81; Price, *Monks of Palestine*, 195.

[36]Abbess Thaisia of Leushino, *The Autobiography of a Spiritual Daughter*

it is David of Garesja once again who gives us one of the most dramatic examples of a human using his spiritual authority on behalf of an animal—or trying to. On one occasion, the saint was confronted with a dragon that was terrorizing his companion deer, not to mention his disciple. At first the hermit threatened to "turn it into food for the mice" by the power of Christ. In response to the creature's entreaties, however, he relented and promised it safe passage out of the area instead; and was indignant when the Lord struck it with a thunderbolt despite David's assurances.[37] One does not have to believe in dragons to appreciate the profound sense of responsibility towards other creatures, including those inconvenient to us, that this story implies.

The compassionate heart

When we consider the holy person's relationship with other creatures, it would be anachronistic and misleading to think in terms of "animal rights"—just as Christian love cannot be reduced to "human rights." People, let alone other creatures, are not invited to exercise direct claims over each other: the imperatives come from the Lord. Rather than a recognition of rights in the modern sense, what we see in the saints is freely-given compassion, in the image of God's compassion and mercy towards all his creation. This is summed up in the well-known passage from St Isaac the Syrian, where he speaks of the "compassionate heart" which burns "for the sake of the entire creation, for men, for birds, for animals, for demons, and for every created thing"; the humbled

of St John of Kronstadt (Platina, CA: St Herman of Alaska Brotherhood Press, 1989), 287.

[37]Lang, *Georgian Saints,* 85–6.

heart that "cannot bear to hear or to see any injury or slight sorrow in creation," and "even prays for the race of reptiles because of the great compassion that burns without measure in his heart in the likeness of God."[38] It is notable that this compassion is by no means focused specifically on non-human creatures—it is an all-encompassing love. It extends to all that God has made, irrespective of our own convenience.

Typically, this compassion is most marked in the most severe ascetics. The Ethiopian anchorite Abba Yafkerena-Egzie, known for his monumental asceticism, would weep for worms;[39] Fr Pavel Florensky describes his spiritual Father, the Elder Isidore, rescuing uprooted weeds and putting them in water;[40] St Silouan of Mt Athos was pained to see leaves or grasses broken without good reason.[41] It is important not to think of this compassion for all creatures as in any way sentimental. Nor, on the other hand, is it an optional extra in spiritual life; it is an essential part of acquiring likeness to God. Another story of Yafkerena-Egzie illustrates this graphically. The ascetic had agreed one day to meet a fellow hermit who lived on an island, and together they walked across the lake on the water. On arrival, the other hermit shook dust of his shoes, but Yafkerena-Egzie discovered some moisture on his. Some might consider this a modest price to pay for walking over

[38]Homily 71, *Ascetical Homilies* 344–5.

[39]Florensky, *Pillar and Ground*, 221.

[40]Florensky, *Salt of the Earth* (Platina, CA: St Herman of Alaska Brotherhood, 1987), 71.

[41]Archimandrite Sophrony, *Saint Silouan the Athonite* (Maldon: Monastery of St John the Baptist, 1991; Crestwood, NY: St Vladimir's Seminary Press, 1999), 94.

a lake; but Yafkerena-Egzie recognized it as a sign of imperfection, so the two monks prayed to be told the reason. The answer was this: Yafkerena-Egzie had hidden some seed barley so that the birds did not eat it, whereas God in his mercy provides for all creatures alike. This is a story about priorities in spiritual life: this anchorite would fast from food and water for 40 days at a time and do 7,000 prostrations an hour, but he could not attain perfection without sharing his meager food with God's other creatures.[42]

Side by side with this all-embracing compassion, we may also discern in the saints a recognition that all creatures enjoy, not "rights" precisely, but a "rightful place" in the created order. Whether they are hungry birds, rapacious dragons, or tiresome weeds, their role is determined by God's purposes, not our preferences. The recognition of their rightful place goes hand in hand with the absence of sentimentality. There is no attempt to engulf another creature in possessive love, to anthropomorphize it, to violate its otherness. The integrity and unique quality of other creatures, animate and inanimate, must be respected: it is precisely through this unique quality that we glimpse "the divine wisdom invisibly present" in them, to refer again to Maximus' understanding of creation as "gift." It seems that something of this understanding underlies the ascetic's sheer delight in other creatures. In a striking instance of this, St Savvas of Vatopedi describes his amiable strolls with the lions while he was living in a cave near the Jordan. The lions would let him observe them carefully and in great detail, "standing near [him] in a quiet and friendly manner, never wanting [him] to stop." From this, he "gained as never before a wonderful

[42]Florensky, *Pillar and Ground*, 221.

knowledge of God's creation." His "soul was pierced by a powerful sense of God's glory and love"; he recalled David inviting all creation to praise the Lord, and sang with him, "How exalted are your works, O Lord; in wisdom have you made them all."[43]

Unrivalled in his appreciation of nature was a much-revered elder of our own day, Elder Porphyrios of Athens (1906–1991), who would ask eagerly after the spring flowers and drew great inspiration from the nightingale singing in the wilderness. His affirmation of delight in God's creation was whole-hearted; he would urge his spiritual children to admire the sea and the beauties of nature, to delight in fields and flowers. All these things, he would say, are the "little loves" that draw us to the great love that is Christ.[44]

Such an appreciation of other creatures and their rightful place is far removed from any morbid attachment to animals as a substitute for human relationships. It is also sharply distinguished from the notion that humanity is the blot on the pure natural world, and therefore less worthy of consideration than other species. Not for nothing does the Athonite saying insist that the lover of God loves everything with *the same* love. We see this exemplified in the Egyptian anchorite Theon. We are told that he appeared "with the face of an angel" as he healed the crowds of sick people who thronged to him every day; he compelled an outraged mob to release unharmed the robbers who had come to his cell intending to attack him; and he would spend his nights with the antelope and wild asses and gazelles, sharing with them his supplies of water and enjoying their company, since "these creatures

[43] *Athonite Gerontikon* XLVII, 446–7.

[44] Sisters of the Holy Convent of Chrysopigi ed., *Wounded by Love: The Life and Wisdom of Elder Porphyrios* (Limni, Evia: Denise Harvey, 2005), 218.

delighted him always."[45] And centuries later, Elder Theoktistos on Patmos did not befriend only vipers; he also took mentally disturbed people into his care, returning them to their families much improved.[46]

In the stories of the saints' interactions with animals, there are many details that we are not going to follow to the letter. But on a broader view, their relationship to animals shows us a sobriety and compassion that modern urban societies have largely lost. Most of us actually have very little sense of *coexisting with* other creatures: they are either engulfed in our world, or out of sight and out of mind. The dog is treated as a member of the family, and the cartoon cow or pig makes a cheery kitchen decoration; but the unseen cow, pig or chicken that supplies our food is treated as a machine. With the detachment that comes through ascetic discipline, the saints give us an example of *distance from* other creatures, and of *responsibility for* them. Other creatures have their own unique place in God's creation, and are not to be re-created in our image. But this places a burden of responsibility on us, because in many ways—and today more than ever—other creatures are in our power. The saints set us an example of how to exercise that "power" in the image of our Master who came to serve.

Holiness and place

The interdependence between man and other creatures is very evident in the relationship between the holiness of a person and the *place* in which he or she lives. The interaction between the saint and the place works both ways. Holiness transforms places,

[45] *Monks in Egypt* VI.4, Russell, *Lives*, 68.

[46] Gorainoff, "Holy Men," 341.

certainly; but it also seems that sometimes a particular place is appointed to nurture the saint. In the classic instance, St Anthony hears a voice from heaven telling him to go to "the inner mountain"; when he gets there, he sees the place and "as it were moved by God, loves it."[47] Still more dramatic is the experience of St Savas, who one night sees a pillar of fire reaching from earth to heaven. He reacts with Jacob's words, "How awesome is this place." (Gen 28.17); and on investigating the spot at first light, he finds a wonderful cave perfectly shaped for a church.[48]

Sometimes the reciprocal relationship between man and place, working together for God's glory, is especially clear. Euthymius and Theoctistus were "guided by God" to a highly inaccessible cave, and "overjoyed as if that cave had been prepared for them by God"; they in turn cultivated this place, which was formerly a den for wild animals, so that it acquired the character of a church of God.[49]

Probably the most striking contemporary example of synergy between people and place is Mount Athos. One of the great figures of contemporary Athonite monasticism, Archimandrite Aimilianos of Simonopetra, speaks of the "holy peak" of Athos as "the axis of the world uniting heaven and earth, the column by which [the Athonites'] prayers ascend to God, God's footstool, the dwelling-place chosen by the All-holy Queen." He sees Athos as a sort of summary of all the mountains where God has chosen to reveal himself; of all the "holy mountains" of the Christian world where God has rested in his saints.[50]

[47]St Athanasius, *Life of Anthony,* 50; cf. *Life of Euthymius*, 14.

[48]*Sabas*, 18; Price, *Monks of Palestine*, 1101.

[49]*Life of Euthymius*, 8; Price, *Monks of Palestine,* 11.

[50]"Experience of the Transfiguration," in Golitzin, *Living Witness*, 195, 197.

Certainly it is true—and this too is an Athonite saying—that it is the *way* you live that saves you, not the place.[51] The ascetic is reminded not to put his confidence in any place as a substitute for his own effort; one does not attain holiness by osmosis. But none of this alters the fact most important for us here: it is possible for places in this world to be transformed through a human being filled with the Holy Spirit. The very rocks and earth and plants are capable of being suffused with holiness, and may then in turn further God's purposes by bringing people close to him. In this cooperative process, the human being receives the place as God's gift, apprehending its God-given inner reality and making his own life accord with that reality. Another pioneer of the contemporary Athonite revival describes the synergy of person and place in very concrete terms:

> Like the chestnuts and cherry trees that used to thrive at the Skete without fertilizers or pesticides, its monks, simple and natural as they were, were spiritually nourished by the tradition of the holy place . . . Theirs was a life of coexistence with the Saints and with the creation. When Fr Andreas sang in church, it reminded me of the moaning of the wind in the chestnut forests. When the bells rang, the jackals in the woods answered with their cries. When old Metrophanis was digging, he used to talk to the birds and the trees . . . He would come to my hut sometimes and ask me, "What are you doing, Papa-Vasilis? Painting icons? I do calligraphy too—I draw on the soil with my mattock."[52]

[51]*Athonite Gerontikon* XIII, 130.

[52]Archimandrite Vasileios, "Reminiscences of Iviron Skete," in *Beauty and Hesychia in the Athonite Way of Life* [in Greek] (Iviron Monastery, 1999), 75–6.

It is a profound comparison: the earth itself becomes the canvas on which the image of God is depicted, by the daily work of those who bear this image in themselves; of people whose every activity is part of a struggle to restore that image. These humble, unassuming elders "made the Skete a Holy Mountain, a paradise." While they lived, they were "a blessing to everyone and friends to the snakes"; and now their relics "remain in that place as a sacred compost."[53] With these earthy images, Archimandrite Vasileios captures the vital significance for the cosmos of the human being, as a creature of earth in process of being deified. If the human unity of body and soul can receive the holiness of God, that holiness cannot but spread to the material surroundings whose substance we share. The material world is not impervious to the divine; and this means that its value cannot be reduced to the utilitarian. It is destined to become, as Bishop Kallistos of Diokleia says of the Holy Mountain, "a sacrament of the divine presence"; and he elaborates: "The monks, the monasteries and the icons are enfolded . . . within an all-embracing context of sacred space . . . The very rocks and earth of the Mountain, with all its flowers, shrubs and trees, possess an intrinsic sacredness."[54] If this is the ultimate calling of the world around us, we cannot but look at every place with different eyes.

Creation transfigured

Looking at the lives of holy people, a final thing that strikes us is that their whole *perception* of the created world changes. Or

[53]Ibid., 83.

[54]"Gerald Palmer, the Philokalia and the Holy Mountain," *Friends of Mount Athos Annual Report* 1994, 26–7.

to put it better, perhaps, they perceive in it a reality that most of us do not. When the Scriptures, or the Fathers, or the liturgical texts speak of creation praising God, it is easy to regard this as a literary device, or perhaps a metaphorical expression of a theological truth. But judging from the lives of the saints, it seems more probable that this way of speaking is quite simply an expression of experience. Anastasios of Sinai relates how one year at Pentecost, when the Liturgy was celebrated on the peak of Mt Sinai, the mountains responded with "Holy, Holy, Holy" and kept it up for half an hour; he goes on to explain that "it was audible only to those with ears to hear."[55] Was it the praise from the mountains that was the remarkable event—or the fact that humans were able to hear it? Experiences of this sort recur with remarkable consistency through the ages. The anonymous 19th century "Russian pilgrim" describes how the Jesus Prayer opened to him "the knowledge of the speech of all creatures" so that he could actually hear everything praising God.[56] Others have been led by the Psalms to a direct apprehension of that praise from all creation which the psalmist invokes. It is said of a contemporary Athonite hermit that as he was reading the psalter one day, his mind was transported, and his spirit embraced the trees and flowers and fish and mountains and seas; and then he saw heaven and earth united and the entire universe praising God.[57]

To speak of a "transfiguration of creation" in such cases is clearly to speak from the viewpoint of human experience. Just as the

[55]Anastasius of Sinai, *Récits* III, *Oriens Christianus* II, 61–2.

[56]R.M. French, trans., *The Way of a Pilgrim* (London: SPCK, reprinted 1973), 31–2.

[57]Archimandrite Aimilianos, "Mount Athos: Sacred Vessel," in Golitzin, *Living Witness*, 191.

transfigured Christ does not change in himself, but simply allows his disciples briefly to perceive him as he is, so it is with creation's praise of God: it becomes perceptible only when humans have ears to hear.

What the Athonite hermit experienced in his vision, his Elder, Joseph the Hesychast, hints at in his writings. In one of his letters, he urges a spiritual son to visit and enjoy the beauty of spring and summer on the Holy Mountain, where the rocks and the whole of nature are "voiceless theologians speaking theology" and "unfolding profound depths of meaning and leading your heart and mind to the Creator."[58] Here we see how closely such a perception is related to "natural contemplation," the contemplation of the Creator through his creation, on which many of the Fathers are so insistent. And we start to realize that this contemplation underlies a work such as St Basil's *Hexaemeron*. It is far from being a merely intellectual exercise, reducing the things around us to instructive allegories. Properly practiced, such contemplation is inseparable from a profound appreciation of things in themselves. One can, indeed, speak of a relationship with them, as fellow creatures and worshippers of a common Maker. We recall the 18th century Siberian hermit Zosima; like the Elder Joseph, he experienced all creation as leading our spirit to unite with its Creator, and during Easter he would wander through the woods singing "Christ is Risen," "as if announcing to all creation the Resurrection of its Creator."[59] Such people perceive the hid-

[58]Letter 57, *Expression of Monastic Experience* [in Greek] (Holy Mountain: Philotheou Monastery, 4th ed. 1992), 315.

[59]Abbess Vera Verkhovsky, *Elder Zosima: Hesychast of Siberia* (Platina, CA: St Herman of Alaska Brotherhood, 1990), 128, 131.

den reality of a world created to praise God simply by being, and to lead us to him. And it is as though their perception frees that reality to be manifest to other people.

The transfigured world of the icon

What a saint's *Life* describes in words, the icon depicts visually and practically. Visually, in that its purpose is to depict a deified human being, and the transformed world around him or her; and practically, because the very fact that matter can be used to depict such a world tells us something about the nature of matter itself: that it is not a barrier between us and God, but a suitable medium for conveying his glory to us.

The basis for the icon and for the saint's transformed relationship with his environment is one and the same: it is the fact that God has entered into his creation, and the divine image in man has been restored in Jesus Christ. This is the reality glimpsed by the disciples when Christ was transfigured on the mountain, for the glory he radiates is not only that of his divinity; it is also the original beauty of his human nature, the glory for which humanity was created. It is the Greek custom that the first subject attempted by an iconographer should be the Transfiguration; and this reminds us of the profound truth that *every* icon is an icon of transfiguration. Every icon depicts its subject matter, not as it appears to our earthly senses, but as it is created to be—as a window to God. It depicts a world in which matter is filled with light, as Christ's clothing was on Mount Tabor.

The icon does not depict people or events with all the cluttered detail that the observer or the camera would see; neither does it try to make figures as lifelike as possible. It employs abstraction and avoids naturalism, and by these visual means points us to a vision accessible only to the eye of the soul. In place of the outward appearance of creatures as we know them, we are led to see the inner principles of their being; their "intelligible words" which echo God the Word. According to the distinguished twentieth-century iconographer L. Ouspensky, the manner in which creatures are depicted in the icon alludes to "the mystery of paradise";[60] for paradise is not only a state of harmony, but also a state in which everything around humans connects them with the Creator. The natural world as depicted in the icon suggests the "immortal plants" or divine conceptions of created things, which, according to St Gregory the Theologian, Adam was meant to cultivate in paradise.[61]

To the spiritual eye, the eye of contemplation, all creatures are grounded in God's conception of them; that is why the iconographer cannot simply paint the subject according to his or her own conception. In the visual language of the icon, light plays a key role in conveying this grounding of creation in its Creator. The saint and the things around him do not cast any shadow. There is nothing to suggest an external light source; everything is illumined from within by the divine light. For the illumination of God's energies does not shine on the world from outside, but is the ground of its very being; in some traditions, this is indicated also by the use of gold as the background for the icon.

[60]Leonid Ouspensky, *Theology of the Icon*, vol. 1 (Crestwood, NY: St Vladimir's Seminary Press, 1992), 189.

[61]Hom. 38, *On Theophany*, 12; Hom. 45, *On Easter*, 8.

The icon of the Transfiguration illustrates the relationship between the divine energies and created things. The light from the divine Word does not throw his surroundings into relief, but gives them transparency. As Metropolitan Anthony of Sourozh writes,

> One has the impression that these rays of divine light touch things and sink into them, penetrate, touch something within them so that from the core of . . . all things created, the same light reflects and shines back[;] as though the divine life quickens the capabilities, the potentialities of all things and makes all reach out towards itself. At that moment the eschatological situation is realized, and . . . "God is all in all."[62]

What is the icon telling us about relationships within the created order? Looking at it superficially, it might seem to convey a quintessentially anthropocentric vision of the world. Many icons show only the human figure; when other creatures are depicted, the human figure is still central, and usually proportionately larger than other creatures. But no icon can be properly understood in isolation; it requires a context, and this context is provided by the iconographic scheme of the church building as a whole. Nothing in that scheme corresponds to the fallen relationship between man and his environment, according to which everything revolves around man and his desires. The iconography of the church represents the new heavens and new earth. And in this re-ordered and transfigured cosmos, the central place belongs not to mere humanity but to the human face of God. In the church dome, we find Christ *Pantokrator* (the Almighty), in and through and for whom all things are created. It is his likeness that the saints below

[62]"Body and Matter," 45.

him on the walls have acquired; it is to his image in the saint that all creation responds. That is why, in the icon, birds, animals and plants take on a different aspect and a new radiance in the presence of the saint; the mountains incline towards him; the natural and the man-made environment become a harmonious whole. This is to show that man is the focal point *through* whom all things are led beyond the confines of their createdness. This is why "everything that surrounds a saint *bows with him* to a rhythmic order. Everything reflects the divine presence, and is drawn—and also draws us—*towards God.*"[63]

The harmony depicted in the icon is certainly a direct challenge to the portrayals of harmony and tranquility familiar to us from secular art, those landscapes and glories of nature apparently untouched by human hand. The Church would not see such landscapes as an end in themselves, but we can perhaps see them as a starting point—and if that is the beauty of the starting point, what will its ultimate fulfillment be like? These unpeopled landscapes speak to us of the place appointed to us to grow into Christ; we think of St Anthony, who set eyes on his desert retreat "and loved it." One might say that nature is sparsely represented in iconography; but the converse of this is that when it does appear, it is never merely decorative. It is not simply scenery for the human drama: it is the environment in and with which the human being, a creature of body as well as soul, is called to deification. The icon and the saint's *Life* challenge us with a vision of the relationship between man and nature that aspires to something more than damage limitation. Man in his fallenness might be well advised to "leave no trace" on the landscapes he passes through. But man restored to

[63]Ouspensky, Ibid., emphasis added.

Godlikeness cannot leave his surroundings unchanged. As bearer of the image of Christ, he conveys to it "in place of things corruptible, things incorruptible."[64]

Man's engagement with the environment in which he lives is expressed in the icon when elements of nature—a river, the sun or moon—are given as it were animate features or depicted with a face. This should not be taken to mean that other creatures are swallowed up in human identity, deprived of their own reality. Rather it indicates, in a visual language accessible to humans, that the elements of this world are not forever inert and impersonal. They too bear the stamp of the divine Word, in whose image we ourselves are created. In some way, mysterious to us, they too participate in relationship, serving God and praising him.

We have said that iconography depicts the transfigured world not only visually, but practically. The very fact that an icon can be made, that it can serve as a channel of communication between us and its holy prototype, is itself a testimony to the eschatological reality of the world; it demonstrates the reality of the world as perceived by the saints. All realms of the material world are represented in the raw material for an icon: minerals, animal products from mammals, birds and fish, vegetable matter. If all this can be formed into an icon of God incarnate, it is because the created world *is already* an icon. As Fr Paisios of the Holy Mountain used to say, the grass and stones are also icons, filled with God's grace.[65] Most of us are unable to perceive the iconic quality of the world around us in its natural state. It recalls the problem identified

[64]Liturgy of St Basil, Anaphora.

[65]Alexander Belopopsky and Dimitri Oikonomou, ed., *Orthodoxy and Ecology Resource Book* (Bialystok: Syndesmos, 1996), 55.

by St Athanasius: we fail to see the divine Word at work in the universe as a whole because of the immense scale. So that same Word reveals himself in a human body, to enable us to see him face to face; and in this way, we are able to recognize that face when we turn back again to the created world. So it is with the icon. In order to form the likeness of God's human face, rocks are ground into pigment, a wooden panel is cut from a tree. To the physical eye, the result is unrecognizably different from the original rock or tree in its natural state. But we are invited to see beyond the superficial dissimilarity, to understand that these created things have not been diverted from their true nature; they have fulfilled it. The icon reveals to all of us what the holy person perceives intuitively: every rock and every tree is a "voiceless theologian," speaking to us of God and pointing us to him.

Transfigured world and daily life

It is not always easy—to say the least—to relate the world of the saints to our own everyday life, where harmony is rarely the dominant characteristic of our environment or our relations with other creatures. A hermit in the desert might co-exist with local fauna; but the population of a city is bound to displace many, many other creatures. And then there are the creatures whose interests seem to be in direct conflict with our own: does "loving everything with the same love" really extend to the mosquito or the deer tick?

To this last question, the holy ascetic might well answer "Yes." But what does that mean in practice? It defines such a person's own relationship with unattractive and dangerous creatures; but there is always a difference between what one may accept for oneself and what one expects others to bear. The saints show us clearly that genuine love for God spills over into loving compassion for all his creatures, just as it is inseparable from love for our brother and sister. In the world of the fall, an all-embracing love does not exclude the possibility that animals may need to be deliberately killed if they threaten human life, like Abba Helle's crocodile. Yet the saints teach us that the life of even an insect should not be taken thoughtlessly, and that our power over other creatures gives us a responsibility for their welfare. The stories of how holy people have lived inspire us to look hard at the possibilities for coexistence before taking more drastic action; and if we want to avoid outright conflict with other creatures today, ecological understanding is one of our most valuable tools. To return, for instance, to the aforementioned deer tick: we discover too late how the explosion in tick populations is linked with the extinction of the passenger pigeon, whose flocks would strip the oaks of acorns. With the birds gone, a wealth of acorns fed a growing population of mice, hosts for the ticks. There *was* a world in which we could coexist more easily with the tick, and we destroyed that world—not in the days of Adam, but in the twentieth century.

When we think about the displacement of other creatures and habitat destruction as a result of human activities, or the uses to which we put domestic and experimental animals, the approach will be similar. If we can discern a principle, it would be that human *needs* prevail—but not human whims or human greed. If I am harming other creatures by serving interests of my own, I must consider honestly whether my "need" is real or frivolous, and whether it can be fulfilled in some other way.

The way we interact with other creatures cannot, however, be reduced simply to a set of ethical principles. Fundamental to our attitude, and therefore our behavior, is the way we perceive the world around us. Much modern thinking is dominated by ways of perceiving that are based on "nature red in tooth and claw": the world is an arena of cutthroat competition, a battleground of selfish genes. It is important to recognize that these are not objective descriptions, but frameworks for an interpretation of the facts—lenses through which we perceive reality. And the Church offers us a different lens, that of the icon. An icon of the transfigured human being, and in some cases the environment around him or her, *does* speak to us of the actual world around us, but in its spiritual reality. It is the world with its potentials fulfilled. This is a vision of the world for us to hold onto as we decide how to share space with the creatures around us and how to treat the land in which we live. The ultimate contrast is not between shaping our environment or preserving it in a pristine state. The choice before us is whether or not we will embrace its potential, as the saints have done, so that natural and manmade features alike become a sacrament of divine presence.

For further reading

On the lives of saints:

Chitty, Derwas J. *The Desert a City.* Oxford: Blackwell, 1977; Crestwood, NY: St Vladimir's Seminary Press, 1999.

Chryssavgis, John. "Sacredness of Creation in the Sayings of the Desert Fathers." *Studia Patristica* XXV (1991): 346–51.

French, R.M., trans. *The Way of a Pilgrim.* London: SPCK, 1973.

Golitzin, Hieromonk Alexander. *The Living Witness of the Holy Mountain.* South Canaan, PA: St Tikhon's Seminary Press, 1996.

Gorainoff, Irina. "Holy Men of Patmos." *Sobornost* 6:5 (Spring 1972): 337–344.

Lang, D.M. "A Forerunner of St Francis: David of Garesja." *Lives and Legends of the Georgian Saints.* Oxford, Mowbrays, 1956, 1976: 83–91.

Russell, Norman, trans. *The Lives of the Desert Fathers.* Oxford: Mowbray and Kalamazoo, MI: Cistercian Publications, 1981.

Makarios, Father. "The Monk and Nature in Orthodox Tradition." *So that God's Creation might Live.* Proceedings of the Inter-Orthodox Conference on Environmental Protection, the Orthodox Academy of Crete, November 1991. Ecumenical Patriarchate of Constantinople, English trans. 1994: 41–48.

Stefanatos, Joanne. *Animals and Man: A State of Blessedness.* Minneapolis, MN: Light and Life, 1992.

Waddell, Helen. *Beasts and Saints.* Grand Rapids, MI: Eerdmans, repr. 1996.

On the icon:

Evdokimov, Paul. *The Art of the Icon: A Theology of Beauty.* Fr Steven Bigham, trans. Oakwood, 1990.

Hart, Aidan. "Transfiguring Matter: The Icon as Paradigm of Christian Ecology." ‹http://www.aidanharticons.com›

Oleksa, Michael. "Icons and the Cosmos: The missionary significance." *Sourozh* 16 (May 1984): 34–45; reprinted from *Sacred Art Journal* 5.1 (1984): 5–13.

Ouspensky, Leonid. *Theology of the Icon*, vol. 1. Crestwood, NY: St Vladimir's Seminary Press, 1992, esp. Chapter 10, "The Meaning and Content of the Icon."

Quenot, Michel. *The Icon: Window on the Kingdom.* Crestwood, NY: St Vladimir's Seminary Press, 1991.

chapter four

God's Creation in Orthodox Worship

One of the most basic, natural responses to the world around us is a sense of wonder. This is common ground: such a sense of awe is shared by believers and unbelievers alike. People will sometimes say, "How can you look at the night sky (or a flower, or whatever) and not believe in a Creator?" But the answer is, of course, "Very easily." One can just as readily get lost in the fascinating complexity of the created world in itself, and never look beyond it. Wonder at the creation does indeed lead many people to God. For others, however, it provides a substitute for him. Nor is the problem a new one. St Gregory Palamas remarks that Christians respond with praise and wonder when we contemplate the masterpiece of God's visible creation; and then he goes on: "The learned men among the pagans also praise creation and respond with wonder when they investigate it. But in our case it is to the glory of the Creator, while in theirs it is to the detriment of the Creator's glory."[1]

It is often said that a sense of wonder is essential if we are to respect the natural world and take proper care of it. So we might

[1]Homily 34, *On the Transfiguration.*

want to ask if the Church's tradition contributes to this wonder and respect. Does it have something distinctive to add to our natural and spontaneous reaction?

It has long been an important principle in Christian theology that "the rule of prayer is the rule of faith" (*lex orandi lex est credendi*). We express what we believe in the way that we pray, especially in the words and actions of our liturgical prayer. It is not hard to see how this applies to the Orthodox Church, where the liturgical texts contain a wealth of theology and are regarded as an authoritative source of theological understanding. This is especially true when we consider the Church's understanding of the created world: worship gives us insights into the relationship between all creation and its Creator that are hard to find in other theological writings. We will therefore look first at Orthodox worship in general, especially at the texts of our liturgical hymnography: Stikhera, Troparia, Kontakia, Kanons. Then in the following chapter, we will look specifically at sacramental life, and its implications for our daily lives.

"Let every breath praise the Lord"

When we look at the worship of the Orthodox Church, one of the first things we notice is that it affirms our sense of wonder as a proper response to creation. But it goes further: it teaches us how this wonder should be *focused,* as an offering of praise to the Creator.

Wonder and praise are themes that reverberate through the daily cycle of worship, above all in the words of the Psalms:

> Bless, the Lord, O my soul . . . You have set the earth on its foundations . . . The trees of the Lord are watered abundantly . . . The high mountains are for the wild goats; the rocks are a refuge for the badgers . . . These all look to you, to give them their meat in due season . . . O Lord, how manifold are your works! In wisdom have you made them all (Ps 103).

These words belong to the Psalm with which the Church begins every Vespers, and which brings before our minds the rich diversity of the created world, its interconnectedness and the dependence of all on its Creator. Since the Church reckons the day from evening to evening, this means that we end our working day and begin our liturgical day by meditating on the wonders of God's creation; and this meditation is an offering to his glory. When we move from night into dawn in the service of Matins, it is a similar story. In the Six Psalms at the beginning of Matins, there is a reminder that we are not alone in offering praise to God: "Praise the Lord, O my soul . . . Bless the Lord, all his works . . ." (Ps 102, Septuagint). But this cannot compare with the vision of cosmic praise expressed at the Praise Psalms at the end of the service, enhanced with liturgical additions to the text:

> Let every breath praise the Lord; praise the Lord from the heavens; to you is due praise, O Lord. Praise him, sun and moon . . . you waters above the heavens . . . fire and hail, snow and frost, stormy wind fulfilling his command . . . beasts and all cattle, creeping things and flying birds . . . [for] his glory is above earth and heaven. (Ps 148).

If we look more closely at this offering of praise, which is so fundamental to worship, we see that it has three aspects. We praise God *for* all creation, as in Psalm 103; but we equally praise him *with* all creation, animate or inanimate. And in a certain sense we offer praise also *on behalf of* all creation.

"Accept our praises which together with all your creatures we offer according to our strength," the priest prays at Matins.[2] Sometimes we are given the impression that the "creatures" with whom we join in praising God are exclusively reason-endowed, i.e. the various ranks of angels. This is the impression given by the eucharistic Liturgies used today, those of St John Chrysostom and St Basil. But if we look at the Liturgy of St James—the early Jerusalem rite—a broader picture emerges:

> It is truly right and fitting, proper and our bounden duty to praise you, you, to bless you, to worship you, to glorify you, to give thanks to you . . . who are hymned by the heavens and the heavens of heavens and all their powers, the sun and moon and all the choir of stars, the earth, the sea and all that is in them.[3]

And only then come the heavenly Jerusalem, the saints and angels. The ancient Liturgy of St Gregory the Theologian seems to have the same breadth of vision, saying more laconically, "Things visible worship you, all of them fulfilling your word."[4] Clearly, there are different ways of "worshipping"; other earthly creatures do not worship consciously. Yet there is a sense in which they are "offering worship" simply by being as God has made them, by

[2]Matins, prayer xi; I.F. Hapgood trans., *Service Book of the Holy Orthodox-Catholic Apostolic Church,* 4th ed. (Brooklyn, NY: Syrian Antiochian Orthodox Archdiocese, 1965), 25.

[3]Anaphora prayer, Liturgy of St James.

[4]Alexandrian Liturgy of St Gregory the Theologian.

reflecting his glory. Our own thanksgiving is a characteristically human, conscious activity; but it also makes us part of a greater movement, a cosmic hymn of praise from all created things.

This awareness of the entire created order praising its Lord is something that the early Church inherited from the Old Testament. As we have seen, cosmic praise has also been experienced at first hand by people of holiness throughout the centuries. But it is principally through liturgical texts that the Church affirms this as objective reality, albeit a reality concealed from most of us most of the time. An early church order, ascribed to the third-century Bishop Hippolytus of Rome, includes this striking passage explaining why the Christian should pray at midnight:

> The elders who passed on the tradition to us taught us thus because at this hour all creation pauses for a moment in order to praise the Lord; the stars and forests and waters stop in their tracks, and at this hour the whole host of angels that minister to him join with the spirits of the righteous in praising God. For this reason, believers should hasten to pray at this hour.[5]

Here, humans are called to follow the example of other creatures: it is only proper that we should participate in the praise that the cosmos is already offering. But when a somewhat later text returns to the idea of cosmic praise, it gives it a different twist:

> The choir of stars moves us to wonder, declaring him that numbers them, and showing him that names them. The ani-

[5]Apostolic Tradition 36; Gregory Dix and Henry Chadwick, eds., *The Treatise on the Apostolic Tradition of St Hippolytus of Rome,* (London: Alban Press and Ridgefield, CT: Morehouse, 1992), 66–7. The translation is our own.

> mals declare him that puts life into them; the trees show him that makes them grow. All these creatures, being made by your word, show forth the greatness of your power. Therefore every human being, through Christ, ought to send up a hymn from his very soul to you in the name of all the rest, since you have given him power over them.[6]

As we mentioned in an earlier chapter, this text is striking for the way it understands man's dominion: our "power over" other creatures has to do with *offering praise on their behalf.* Man is uniquely placed. Unlike the angels, he is a part of the material creation; but unlike other material creatures, he is an articulate creature capable of conscious awareness of God. So when he fulfils his nature by offering praise consciously, he is to do so "in the name of all the rest." Clearly, our "power" over other creatures is not a power to mould them to our own desires. As in Hippolytus, it is their own given relationship to their Creator that dictates what we are to do in their name.

There is, however, a paradox in human nature. Man is uniquely able to articulate praise; but he is also unique in his freedom to refuse to do so. We may reflect on this as we listen to one of the greatest hymns of cosmic praise, the Song of the Three Children. The Hebrew youths were cast into the fiery furnace for refusing to bow before Nebuchadnezzar's idol and "worship the creation in place of the Creator"; so as they stand amidst the flames, preserved unharmed through God's power, they call on every rank of creature to join them in praising the true God and "exalting him above all for ever": the heavens, the angels, the sun and moon, showers and dew, mountains and hills, whales and monsters.

[6] *Apostolic Constitutions* VII.35.

Various categories of humans are mentioned at the end, after all the others. This canticle is sung with great solemnity at the Easter Vigil (Holy Saturday morning), as the climax of a long series of readings. The readings all relate in one way or another to the "Passover" from death to life which we experience personally through baptism, and communally in the paschal feast; and they date from a period when Holy Saturday was the prime occasion in the year for adult baptisms. The recitation of the Song of the Three Children would originally have coincided with the moment when the newly-baptized processed from the baptistery into the church—the latest group of humans to *rejoin the ranks of creatures offering praise to God.*

Creation and salvation

So the daily prayer of the Church affirms our natural wonder at the created world and transforms it into praise for the Creator. The yearly cycle of worship, especially as we celebrate our salvation at the great feasts of Christ, features a somewhat different emphasis. Our liturgical celebration of the feasts give us insights into the process of our salvation that make us turn back to creation with a redoubled sense of awe. For the more we learn about God's work of salvation, the more we recognize the truth that St Irenaeus insisted on so vehemently against the Gnostics: creation and salvation are part of the same plan. They follow recognizably similar patterns; they bear the signature of the same Craftsman. They can in fact be understood as one continuous act.

We may note one liturgical detail that illustrates this connection. When we celebrate the three great feasts of our salvation—Easter, Christmas and Theophany—the long series of Old Testament readings at Vespers begins in exactly the same way at each feast: "In the beginning God created the heavens and the earth." God's work of salvation begins with his work of creation; and the salvation accomplished in Christ brings his work of creation to its appointed goal. In order to explore this interconnection, we will look at the way the natural world responds to its Lord and the ways in which it sets man an example, before examining in more detail how the created order serves as a pattern for salvation.

Creation responds to its Lord

There are the many texts that speak to us of *creation as a whole responding to its Lord at his coming*. Here, for example, are some of the Psalm verses chosen for the Liturgy on Christmas Day: "Let all the earth worship you and sing praises to you: let them sing praises to your Name, O Most High" (Ps 65.4, Septuagint); and "The heavens are telling the glory of God and the firmament proclaims his handiwork" (Ps 18.2). "All the earth" evidently refers to a community, not literally the planet. But does it mean simply the human community? Comparison with other texts suggests a broader meaning. A hymn for the forefeast of Christmas is typical: "Mountains and hills, valleys and plains, rivers and all creation, magnify the Creator now being born."[7] And as for the heavens declaring the glory of God, we are invited to see a literal example of this at Christ's birth: "Using a great star as its mouth, heaven proclaims the presence on earth of him who has ineffably become poor for our sake."[8]

[7]December 22, Vespers; Apostikha 3.

[8]December 23, Matins; 1 Kanon 7.2.

All creation rejoices at the coming of the Savior because it is an event of cosmic significance. But this does not contradict the idea that everything hinges on the salvation of man. On the contrary, this is often explicitly the cause of the rejoicing:

> Make ready, O cave . . . rejoice, Bethlehem, land of Judah, for our Lord has arisen from you. Hear, O mountains and hills, and the lands round about Judea: for Christ is coming to save man whom he fashioned.[9]

These sentiments echo a passage from Isaiah read at Theophany to celebrate the manifestation of God in the flesh: "sing for joy, O heavens, and exult, O earth; break forth, O mountains, into singing: for the Lord has comforted his people." (Is 49.13). Are texts such as these simply a literary device to emphasize human joy? There is reason to believe that they are something more. This way of speaking about the non-human creation relates quite closely to St Paul's image in the Epistle to the Romans, where he describes the groaning of all creation as it awaits the "revealing of the sons of God" in order to be set free from "bondage to decay" (Rom 8.19–21). This liberation is connected precisely with "the redemption of our body" (Rom 8.23); and at the Nativity, all creation is receiving its first glimpse of that very redemption through the high honor now accorded to the flesh: "The King comes forth from your loins, Daughter of peace, clothed now in the flesh as in royal purple."[10]

It is appropriate, therefore, that humans and non-human creatures stand side-by-side to greet the incarnate Lord, each respond-

[9]Sunday before Nativity, Vespers; Forefeast Apostikha.

[10]December 23, Matins; 2 Kanon 7.3.

ing to his gift of salvation in its own way. We see this in one of the most frequently quoted Christmas hymns:

> What shall we offer you, O Christ, who for our sakes have appeared on earth as man? Every creature made by you offers you thanks. The angels offer you a hymn; the heavens, a star; the Magi, gifts, the shepherds, their wonder; the earth, its cave; the wilderness, the manger: and we offer you a Virgin Mother.[11]

In a hymn for the Theophany apparently modeled on this, Christ receives "ministers" from all parts of creation in order to fulfill the mystery of his manifestation on earth: " . . . Gabriel from among the angels, the Virgin from among men, the star from among the heavens, Jordan from among the waters."[12]

We see how this pattern, of humans and other creatures responding to Christ side-by-side, continues to accompany Christ's saving work. It is very clearly present when the Church speaks of Christ's Passion. According to the "Praises," the lamentations sung at the Burial Service of Christ on the evening of Holy Friday, the Virgin Mother stands sorrowing at the foot of the Cross and calls on the entire creation: "O hills and valleys, the multitude of men, and all creation, weep and lament with me, the Mother of our God" (Stasis I). And creation responds accordingly, each element "lamenting" in its own fashion:

[11]Nativity, Vespers; on "Lord I call," 4. Most of the liturgical texts cited here can be found in Mother Mary and Kallistos Ware, trans., *The Festal Menaion* (London: Faber and Faber, 1969; South Canaan, Pa: St Tikhon's Seminary Press, 1990); *The Lenten Triodion* (London: Faber and Faber, 1978). Translations have been adapted.

[12]Compline, Lity 6.

> The whole creation was changed by fear, when it saw you, O Christ, hanging on the Cross. The sun was darkened and the foundations of the earth were shaken; all things suffered with the Creator of all.[13]

Surely it is here, if anywhere, that we might begin to make sense of the suffering of the world, animal as well as human, and its relationship to a loving God. It is traditional Christian teaching that God *as God* cannot suffer. The divine nature is not changeable; it does not experience emotions. To some people today, this suggests that God is distant and indifferent. But the earthly life, and above all the earthly death of God incarnate tell a different story: here is "the changeless God, who suffering in the flesh was changed." And the entire world resonates with the suffering of God clothed in his own creation. In the words of a Greek poet, "Golgotha raises up to heaven the suffering of the earth"; and we may perhaps see this as the suffering not only of humans, but also of all earth's creatures.

It might be tempting to dismiss the Gospels' description of the sun being darkened, and other phenomena, as no more than a conventional literary device—a way to underline the importance of an event that actually concerns humans alone. But in fact, these descriptions speak of something much more profound: the bond between Creator and creation. *All things suffer with the Creator of all.* Cosmic "disintegration" is evident at the Crucifixion, because the one who dies is the same one *in whom all things hold together.* Another verse from the Praises on Holy Friday (Saturday Matins) makes this explicit: "The whole creation was altered by your Passion: for all things suffered with you, know-

[13]Holy Friday Vespers; on "Lord, I call" 1.

ing, O Word, that you hold all in unity"(Stasis I). We notice here the resonance of another scriptural passage fundamental to our understanding of all creation's response to Christ: Colossians 1.15–20, which speaks of Christ as the first-born of all creation, in whom, through whom and for whom all things were created, and in whom all things "consist" or hold together. This is one of the classic passages showing the inextricable connection of creation and salvation. It is the first-born of creation who is revealed as first-born from the dead. It is only natural, therefore, that all creation responds to his resurrection as one: the Myrrh-bearing Women greet him as the first fruits of humanity, and "all things are filled with light; heaven and earth, and the nether regions" (Easter Kanon).

Creation as an example to humanity

So we stand side by side with other creatures in our response to our salvation, just as we join with them in offering praise. And again, as the created world may set us an example of praise, so other creatures may serve to guide us towards salvation. Here, too, the idea of creation drawing us to God takes on a new dimension in some of the liturgical texts.

All creation comes together to greet the Creator; but in several notable instances, it is the non-human element that takes the lead. The star brings the magi to Christ; the ox and ass appear beside him in the icon of the Nativity because "The ox knows its owner and the ass its master's crib"—in contrast to his people, who "do not understand" as Isaiah says (Is 1.3). Even more striking are some of the liturgical texts for Theophany. The words of Psalm 113.3 ("The sea looked and fled: Jordan turned back") are often applied to Christ's baptism. But it seems that they are not so used primarily in order to point to baptism as a new Exodus; they serve to indicate that here, too, the river recognizes "the presence of the Lord," as the same Psalm says (Ps 113.7). There is thus a close parallel between the reaction of the waters and that of the Baptist, who fears to lay his hand on Christ's head. In some texts, the Jordan actually addresses John:

> John cries out in fear: "The Jordan and the sea fled, O Savior, and turned back; and how shall I place my hand upon your head, before which the seraphim tremble . . . ?" "Why, Baptist, do you delay baptizing my Lord?" the Jordan cries to John; "Why do you prevent the cleansing of many? He has sanctified all creation; let him sanctify me also and the nature of the waters, since for this he has been made manifest."[14]

It is Jordan's example that makes John draw back in fear; and again, it is the river that persuades "the greatest among those born of women" to overcome his fear, and explains to him why Christ's baptism is necessary for the salvation of the world. Of course, dialogue such as this is not meant to be a factual record of events; but this does not mean that its function is purely decorative. We can see it as a poetic way of making the point stressed by St Athanasius: that out of all creation, only man has strayed from God's purpose. The elements have never ceased to recognize the Word as their Maker and their King.[15] It is therefore only to be expected that other creatures, animate and inanimate, should sometimes set humans an example in recognizing and serving the Lord.

[14]January 2, Vespers; Apostikha. For similar texts, see January 5, Matins and Sixth Hour, Stikheron.

[15]*On the Incarnation* 43.

The Creator imaged in his creatures

God comes into his world through one particular creature—the human being, formed in the beginning according to his image and likeness. So at Christ's coming, members of the human race immediately recognize the affinity: here is "God with us." He is not just among us, like an ancient Greek deity paying a visit to earth; he is part of our nature. And the beauty that he reveals in that nature is our own *archetypal* beauty, the "original" in whose image the human being was formed.

Some of the liturgical texts suggest to us, however, that man is not the only creature to find in God incarnate some "affinity" to itself. The heavens recognize him as the sun: "The Sun comes to be born, hidden in a bright cloud, and is made manifest in a cave; for a brilliant star brought kings from Persia to worship him."[16] The earth recognizes him as a flower: "A rod from the root of Jesse, the Virgin, has budded, putting forth an unfading flower, the Creator of all, who as God adorns with flowers the whole earth that cries to him: Glory to your power, O Lord."[17] The waters receive him as the River of Delight (Ps 35.9, LXX): "O earth and things upon the earth, dance and rejoice exceedingly. The River of Delight is baptized in the stream."[18] The Incarnation does not do away with the infinite distance of nature between God, who is the uncreated, and the world, which he has made. But it does show us that this infinite distance is only part of the story. We can equally speak of a mysterious connection between Creator and creation, stemming

[16] December 23, Matins; Forefeast Kanon 6.2.

[17] Sunday before Nativity, Matins; Forefeast Kanon 4.1.

[18] January 5, Vespers; Apostikha 1.

from the fact that God's creative energies are echoed and reflected in all that he has made. We may therefore say that the Incarnation builds on an existing connection—not only between God and his image in man, but also between God and all of his creation.

We recognize this connection in the way God uses his creation to relate to us. Christ comes to give us life; and in the process, he reveals himself as the archetype of all God's natural gifts, which sustain our earthly life. He comes to bring us knowledge of God, and so shows himself the archetype of creation as it is intended to be—a gift through which we come to know the Giver. It is no coincidence that he calls himself Bread (Jn 6.35, etc.), the basic foodstuff on which our life depends. We also find him described as the water of life,[19] or myrrh poured out.[20] He comes to us as a flower on a shoot (Is 11.1, Septuagint), as dew or refreshing rain (Judg 6.37, Ps 71.6). He hangs on the Cross like a cluster of grapes, in the words of a hymn for the cross,[21] pouring out his lifeblood so that it can become life for us.

Now, of course this is not literal language. In literal terms, Jesus Christ is a human being, and is not a loaf or a bunch of grapes. Such metaphors can be applied to God only because he condescends to "clothe himself in our language," as St Ephrem memorably puts it.[22] But the remarkable thing is that he has prepared for this condescension by filling his creation with potential metaphors, with

[19]January 3, Matins; Kanon 3.1.

[20]Song of Songs 1.3; cf. Holy Unction, Kanon 4.1.

[21]Exaltation of the Cross, Matins; Lauds 2.

[22]*Hymns on Faith* 31; Sebastian Brock, trans., *A Garland of Hymns from the Early Church* (McLean, VA: St Athanasius' Coptic Publishing Center, 1989), 64.

signs that point to himself because they were created to do so. He has deliberately created a world that is "God-friendly."

Creation and salvation: discerning the pattern

So God becomes part of his creation using created forms designed to receive him: his image in the human being, and his imagery in other creatures. And no less strikingly, his work of salvation follows in various ways the patterns he has already established for the *salvation*—the safety and wholeness—of his material creation.

As a good example of this, we may look at the language in which the Church's tradition speaks of the fall of man and its reversal. The fall of man is marked by a disruption in relationships within the created world. Man decides to use God's creation without reference to God—a decision symbolized by eating of the one tree God has forbidden. And the consequences fall not only on the man and woman and their descendants, but also on the earth: "Cursed is the ground because of you." The relationship between God and man is ruptured, and in consequence the earth is degraded; it brings forth only thorns and thistles (Gen 3.17–18). The disruption in relationships also extends into human society: Adam and Eve's first action after the fall is an attempt to shift the blame for their own actions, and this is followed within a generation by the first murder.

The disruption in the intended order of creation affects other elements besides the soil. A prominent feature of the Old Testament world is the fact that the waters are a lair of dragons, the "natural" stronghold of evil powers (cf. Ps 73.13—"You broke the heads of the dragons on the water"). This view of water is very evident in some of our liturgical texts, particularly those celebrating the Baptism of Christ. Many of the texts for the feast of Theophany speak of Christ's baptism as cleansing the waters and crushing the "dragons" lurking there. If the element essential for our life is portrayed as a death-trap, the clear message is that something has gone wrong in the natural order. In modern terms, the results of the fall may be characterized as a form of pollution.

Pollution in the physical sense means that an element is in some way perverted from its natural function: it "falls sick." Earth or air or water—the essentials for our life—become instead sources of sickness or even death to us and other creatures. And this is precisely what happens when our proper relationship with the material world and its Creator breaks down. Material creation and the senses with which we interact with it cease to nourish us as gifts of God's love and care; instead of aiding us to grow towards God, they provoke greed, envy, and all the other negative impulses known to Christian tradition as passions. And when we act on those impulses, we usually end up passing on the damage, often in physical ways, to other people and other creatures. We ourselves become "a pollution to air and earth and water," in the somber words of one hymn.[23]

Analogies between physical and spiritual pollution continue as the story of salvation unfolds. When the Creator sees his world polluted through human sin, how does he respond? *He plants a tree.* "One tree in Eden brought death to man, but another on Golgotha granted eternal life to the world."[24] The remedy has precedents in the natural world, in the way he has appointed

[23]Tone 7, Monday Vespers; on "Lord, I call" 2.

[24]Thursday of the First Week of Lent, Vespers.

ordinary trees to function for the health of his creation. It also has precedents in signs he has performed in human history. At the feast of the Exaltation of the Cross, we are reminded of the occasion when God's people were complaining about the undrinkable waters of Marah; so he showed Moses a tree, which was to be thrown into the bitter waters to make them sweet (Ex 15.25). In a similar way, the Lord plants the tree of the Cross, which puts down roots deep into the earth, drawing out the bitterness of the earth and transforming its fruit.[25] Hymns for the feasts of the Cross tell us more about how this Tree functions. Taking up polluted waters through its roots, it offers us instead "waters that shall never fail . . . flowing from its grace."[26] And it brings to ripeness a fruit, an antidote to that other fruit which Adam and Eve once tasted: partaking of this new fruit, "we have gained incorruption and are restored once more to Eden."[27] As with a "natural" tree which counteracts physical pollution, the air, too, sees the benefit of its cleansing power: the branches extend high above the earth, so that the powers from beneath the earth tremble when they see it displayed in the air in which they dwell (cf. Eph 2.2).[28]

Humanity misused a tree and polluted the world: God cleanses his world by the tree of the Cross. The misuse culminates in the instrument of torture and execution, the quintessential tree of death: God's use of the tree reveals it as the tree of life.

[25]Cf. Romanos, 'On the Victory of the Cross' 15; Archimandrite Ephrem Lash, ed. and trans., *St Romanos the Melodist: On the Life of Christ: Kontakia*, (London/San Francisco,CA: Harper Collins, 1995), 162.

[26]Sunday of the Veneration of the Cross, Lauds 2.

[27]Sunday of the Veneration of the Cross, Vespers, on "Lord, I call" 4.

[28]Exaltation of the Cross, Kanon 5.2.

But the texts for the Cross have something more to say. The use of a cross and not some other instrument to bring about Christ's death does not simply provide a wealth of tree metaphors for salvation; we are told that it has implications for actual growing trees. Listen to the Kanon for the Exaltation of the Cross:

> Let all the trees of the wood rejoice, for *their nature is made holy by Christ, who planted them in the beginning* and was outstretched upon the Tree.[29]

When humans impair their relationship with God, the land and all that is in it mourns; when Christ restores that relationship, the very landscape rejoices.

But why does the use God makes of one particular wooden object affect the whole "nature of trees"? Surely it is because the One who makes the tree an instrument of his saving work is the same One "who planted [it] in the beginning" for the physical life and survival of his material world. The new use of the tree does not ignore the purpose for which it was originally created; it builds on that purpose, developing the creature's potential to the highest degree. The tree's natural functions—providing food and shelter, purifying water, enriching and stabilizing the soil—are thus revealed to have a spiritual counterpart, cosmic in scope.

We have come full circle: human misuse of a tree resulted in a curse upon the earth, and now the life-giving tree revokes that curse. At the Great Blessing of the Waters at Theophany, we hear this renewal of the earth prophesied by Isaiah in these terms: "Instead of the thorn shall come up the cypress" (Is 55.13). Why the cypress? It is not simply that it is considered a finer and more

[29]Exaltation of the Cross, Kanon 9.1.

useful tree than scrubby bushes; it is the foremost of the trees traditionally associated with the Cross: "The glory of Lebanon shall come to you with the cypress, the pine and the cedar together to glorify my holy place, and I will make the place of my feet glorious" (Is 60.13, Septuagint). These words of Isaiah, interpreted as a prophecy of the Cross, are heard at the Easter Vigil and again at the Exaltation of the Cross. They are a graphic expression of the way God calls his creation to serve his saving work.

Creation restored

We have seen that creation recognizes its Lord and rejoices in his coming; and also that it guides us in greeting him. But now the image of the tree of the cross and its meaning for "all the trees of the wood" brings us to another question: how is non-human creation affected by the coming of the Creator? To put it another way, what does salvation mean for the world that has not "erred from the path of God's purpose for it," as St Athanasius says, but is nevertheless a victim of the fall? The answers that we find can be summed up under two headings: *renewal* and *sanctification.*

Renewal is a theme associated particularly with Christ's appearance on earth: "Christ has appeared, desiring to make new the whole creation," in the words of the Forefeast troparion for Theophany. There is an obvious connection at Christmas between newness and the celebration of the Creator as a *newborn.* The birth of Christ does not mark only "the birthday of mankind," as St Basil says; it can also be seen as the birthday of all creation. A verse for Christmas Eve is more explicit about what "newness" for creation entails: "O creation, cast away now all your decrepitude, seeing the Creator become a creature; becoming a child, he makes you new, restoring you to your original beauty."[30] "The original beauty" (*kalos*) of creation is nothing other than the state in which it was first made, when "God saw that it was good" (*kalon*). It is only natural that creation is restored to the state described at the opening of the book of Genesis, since at the coming of Christ "Bethlehem has opened Eden," as St Romanos says. The "delights of paradise are to be found in the cave" where Christ lies (Christmas Kontakion). The "decrepitude" which creation throws off is elsewhere termed "corruption from the transgression";[31] it is the "bondage to decay" (Rom 8) whose end comes in sight when God enters into his world.

The language of sanctification is especially prominent at Theophany—not surprisingly, since the blessing of water is a prominent part of that feast. Some texts for the feast make an explicit connection between the blessing of water accomplished by Christ's baptism, and our own baptism in water. "You have accepted to be baptized . . . that having sanctified the nature of the waters, you might lead us to a new birth through water and the Spirit" (Great Blessing of Waters).[32] But it would be a mistake to conclude that "sanctification of the world" is simply a poetic way of referring to the institution of sacraments. Apart from anything else, several texts are quite explicit about a "sanctification" extending far beyond elements that are used sacramentally in any direct way. The forefeast Kanon tells us: "The voice of one crying in the wilderness was heard . . . Be sanctified, all the sea, the springs and rivers, valleys and wooded glens, all that is under the sun."[33] Other Kanons take up

[30]December 24, Matins; Forefeast Kanon 4.1.

[31]December 24, Compline; Kanon 9.1 (Greek use).

[32]*Festal Menaion*, 353.

[33]January 2, Matins; Kanon 9.5. Cf. January 5, Compline, K.4.1: "At your appearing in the body, the earth was sanctified, the waters blessed."

the idea that the earth was blessed at Christ's birth and the water at his baptism: "The earth was sanctified, O Word, at your holy birth, and the heavens with a star declared your glory; and now the nature of waters is blessed by your baptism in the flesh, and mankind is restored to its former nobility."[34] What we are hearing about is not the sacraments in any exclusive sense, but the fundamental change in nature that makes sacramental life possible.

What is this fundamental change? We spoke just now of the "pollution" of the material world as a result of man's fall; and this image is reflected in verses that talk about Christ "cleansing" the water by descending into it. But there is another metaphor that is also illuminating: creation had become enemy occupied territory. Having ruptured their relationship with God, humans then went on to evict him from his creation, declaring it sacred to various substitute gods. Only in a few isolated enclaves was God acknowledged as Lord. Christ's coming into the world begins the reversal of this process. He "evicts" the evil powers which had usurped authority over his creation: "Of old the ruler of this world [cf. Jn 12.31] was named king also of all that was in the waters . . . but by Christ's cleansing he is choked and destroyed, like legion in the lake . . . "[35]

The process culminates in Christ's Passion: "Of old the lamb was sacrificed in secret; but you, longsuffering Savior, were sacrificed beneath the open sky and have cleansed the whole creation."[36] St John Chrysostom sets out in more detail what is happening here: Christ was raised up on the Cross to purify the atmosphere, and

[34]January 5, Compline; Kanon 9.2.

[35]Forefeast of Theophany, Compline; Kanon 6.3.

[36]Holy Saturday matins; Praises, Stasis I.

the drops of his Blood purified the earth. Before Christ, Chrysostom explains, the Jews were commanded to leave the earth alone and to offer sacrifices and pray in one place only, because the earth as a whole was defiled by pagan sacrifices. But since Christ has come and cleansed the whole inhabited earth, every place has become a place of prayer for us; the whole earth is now more holy than the Holy of Holies.[37]

We still build houses of prayer; we still consecrate certain material objects specifically for the worship of God. But the relationship between the "holy place" and the rest of the earth has changed fundamentally. The place of worship, and whatever belongs to it, is no longer an embattled enclave. It is now a revelation of the earth as it truly is, transparent to its Creator. Since Christ came into the world, his creation has become "secretly sacramental."[38] When we consecrate a place or an object , when we dedicate it to sacred use, we are showing our readiness to lift the veil of secrecy.

The earth—holy or polluted?

This understanding of "cleansing the earth" brings us to the heart of Christianity's challenge to paganism, whether ancient or modern. The growing popularity of paganism today has much to do with the idea that it celebrates the sacredness of the earth; that it is a "spiritual" antidote to the vision of a cold, disenchanted universe governed by impersonal forces. The Church sees it differently: paganism and scientism are seen as two sides of the same coin. In each case, our proper wonder at the universe is diverted to

[37]*On The Cross and the Thief* Hom. 2.1.

[38]Cf. Olivier Clément, *On Human Being: A Spiritual Anthropology* (London: New City, 2000), 115.

the wrong object. Scientism sees natural forces *per se* as the ultimate object of respect and awe; paganism goes one step further and declares them to be gods. Created things are thus turned in on themselves, alienated from their true allegiance.

There are several stories from early church history describing the contest between Christianity and paganism. Often they show an uncompromising directness: the Christian evangelist may topple an idol or fell a sacred tree. Such stories may be unappealing to modern sensibilities, but we should try to understand what is happening here. The Church was not declaring war either on sculpture or on trees: but it needed to make a point about the locus of spiritual authority, the power to which the created world responds. An object that was considered to have spiritual power in itself turns out to be powerless when its true Creator is invoked.

In the Christian view, then, nothing in nature possesses divine power and holiness *in itself*. But nor is anything devoid of the Creator's power and energy. All is created to be sanctified, to be made holy in Christ; and our calling is to recognize and manifest this holiness. But the liturgical texts remind us also of the shadow side of this intersection of the material and the spiritual. From the very beginning, our sin—our estrangement from God—is seen as leaving scars also on the natural world. The breakdown of natural systems that we are seeing today cannot therefore be seen simply as a set of physical problems to be addressed by technological solutions, or even by changes in outward behavior: it also carries a spiritual message.

One of the most striking expressions of the notion of human sin as in itself a pollution of the earth is to be found in the kanon for October 26, commemorating the earthquake that struck Constantinople in 740. "See how we all have erred; and the earth which has done no wrong is terribly punished," we sing; and again, "The earth voicelessly cries out, groaning: Why do you all pollute me with many evils? Sparing you, the Master scourges me all over. Perceive this, and by repentance propitiate God." Pre-scientific ideas about the causes of earthquakes, we might say. But are these verses not also telling us something more profound? They remind us that the well-being of the world around us cannot be separated from our relationship with God. This is an insight well known to the prophets of the Old Testament:

> There is no faithfulness or kindness, and no knowledge of God in the land . . . Therefore the land mourns, and all who dwell in it languish, and also the beasts of the field, and the birds of the air, and even the fish of the sea are taken away. (Hos 4.1,3)

As we look at some of the trends in today's world, elements of this description may seem alarmingly familiar. Often there is a clear connection between human activities and the malaise of the earth: it turns out that beasts, birds and fish are "taken away" because we have destroyed their habitat, hunted them to extinction or unwittingly triggered some chain reaction that leads to their destruction. Some might want to argue that this is purely a matter of physical cause and effect, implying no judgment on the justice or injustice of our activities. Yet if our forebears could recognize God's "righteous chastisement" even in purely "natural" disasters such as earthquakes, should we not recognize that he might be telling us something through environmental disasters in which we have an obvious hand?

Worship gives us no blueprints for what we must do and avoid doing to keep the land from "mourning." Instead, it gives us a powerful and profound vision of the sort of world we live in and use every day. Everything in the natural world praises God, speaks of him, and draws us to him as the star drew the magi. And as we look at the natural processes of the world, the work of water in the environment or the growth of trees, we see more than marvels of physics and chemistry on which our lives too depend: we perceive the patterns of God's work of salvation. It becomes hard to use such a world wastefully or thoughtlessly.

For further reading

Mary, Mother and Kallistos Ware, trans. *The Festal Menaion*. London: Faber and Faber, 1969; South Canaan, PA: St Tikhon's Seminary Press, 1990.

Mary, Mother and Kallistos Ware, trans. *The Lenten Triodion*. London: Faber and Faber, 1978.

Schmemann, Alexander. "The World as Sacrament." *Church, World, Mission*. Crestwood, NY: St Vladimir's Seminary Press, 1979: 217–227.

Schmemann, Alexander. *For the Life of the World*. Crestwood, NY: St Vladimir's Seminary Press, 1973.

Schmemann, Alexander. *Great Lent*. Crestwood, NY: St Vladimir's Seminary Press, 1974.

Theokritoff, Elizabeth. "Creation and Salvation in Orthodox Worship." *Ecotheology* 10 (Jan. 2001): 97–108.

Ware, Archimandrite Kallistos (Metropolitan Kallistos of Diokleia). "The Value of the Material Creation." *Sobornost* 6:3 (1971): 154–165.

chapter five

Sacramental Life and Sacramental Living

The liturgical texts introduce us to the idea of an "original beauty" in creation, a state to which it is restored at the coming of Christ. It is a beauty glimpsed in holy people, and even in their natural surroundings. For those of us who have not been blessed to meet such people in person, the icon conveys something of this transformation. But our principal introduction to the original beauty of the world comes through the sacramental life of the Church. The bread and wine of the Eucharist, the water used for a baptism or to bless our homes and other objects, the oil for anointing the sick, are revealing something fundamental about the world in which we go about our daily lives. As Fr Alexander Schmemann never tired of emphasizing, to consecrate any object is to refer it back to its own "original" meaning, to God's conception of it—which is also its "ultimate" meaning.[1] Matter used in a sacrament is not a separate category of matter, sacred as opposed to profane; it could better be described as matter unveiled, revealing to us the true Godwardness—the *sacramental quality*—of things we use and handle every day. The Orthodox understanding of the world as a whole may be described as a *sacramental cosmology.*

[1] *The Eucharist* (Crestwood, NY: St Vladimir's Seminary Press, 1987), 61.

This is why the sacramental life of the Church is key to the way we live in this world.

We will look first at the meaning of matter and of the human being according to this sacramental cosmology; then we will say something about the ethos that goes with this world view, and the way in which a sacramental vision colors our attitudes to other people, to matter and to time.

The original meaning of creation

When an object or a substance, such as oil or water, is consecrated in the Church for sacramental use, it is obviously being dedicated to a particular function. Its new role may or may not be an extension of its everyday use or its natural symbolism. Holy unction for healing reflects the ancient therapeutic use of olive oil—in the sacrament of anointing, the Lord reveals himself as the One who "makes glad the souls and also the bodies of mortals" (Kanon at Holy Unction, Ode 1). Water is used for washing: baptism in water is a spiritual cleansing, but it is also, even more importantly, a passage through death to life. The symbolism of matter in a sacrament usually has direct precedents in Scripture, and so it is here: God drowned sin in the Flood, and brought his people to a new life through the Red Sea, harnessing the destructive power of water to destroy their enemies. Frequently the scriptural record shows God using created things for his work of salvation in a way that reflects the natural use of his gifts, but not always: as a precedent for holy unction, the Kanon for the anointing service cites not only the emollient properties of oil, but also the olive branch that indicated the abating of the Flood (Kanon Ode 3). But there is no rigid distinction to be made between God's action in human history and his action in the rest of his creation; either way, we are seeing a history of God's engagement with the material world. The sacraments, or mysteries of the Church (the Greek word for sacrament is *mysterion*), are various ways in which God reaches out to us through matter; they all have their basis in what St Paul calls the "great mystery of our religion," God manifest in the flesh (1 Tim 3.16). So both scriptural and natural precedents for the way matter is used sacramentally remind us of the "groundwork" for the Incarnation; the fact that God reveals himself in a world shaped from the beginning to serve his purposes and to receive him.

We can see the basis for sacramental use of matter set out in one of the prayers for the Blessing of Waters:

> You by your own will have brought all things from nothingness into being . . . The fountains are your servants . . . you have sanctified the streams of Jordan . . . Do you yourself be present now as then through the descent of your Holy Spirit, and sanctify this water.

The prayer then goes on to cite Old Testament examples of works of salvation through water—the drowning of sin in the Flood, liberation through the Red Sea, water from the rock in the wilderness—and to pray for the water here to be endowed with various properties. But we can say that all these instances of God working through water, Old Testament and contemporary, are simply aspects of the one central fact: "the fountains are your servants." And the service performed by these creatures of the Lord includes the preservation of physical life, no less than spiritual. We come back to the analogy between nature and sacrament which St Irenaeus insists on: One cannot consistently maintain that the Eucharist is the Body and Blood of the Lord without also accepting that the Lord himself is the Word through whom the world is created, whose power gives us the wheat and grapes in the first place.[2]

In most sacramental services, matter is converted from the purely "natural" usefulness that we are familiar with into a vehicle for divine power: bread maintains physical life, the Eucharist nourishes us for eternal life. At baptism, however, the transformation is more dramatic. The prayer for the blessing of water depicts the transition of the water from its "polluted" to its "sacramental" state; and what strikes us is the very different ways in which evil powers and divine power relate to the element itself. Firstly, this is what is said of the power of evil:

> We pray you, O God, that every aerial and obscure phantom may *withdraw* itself from us; and that no demon of darkness may *conceal* itself in this water; and that no evil spirit ... may *descend into* it with him (her) who is about to be baptized.

This relates to the Old Testament idea of water as a lair of destructive forces ("dragons"): but that does not alter the fact that the power of evil is something *external* to creation. Water may be its preferred "cover," but it has no "right" to be there. Earlier, in the prayers for the exorcism of the person being baptized, the power of evil has been reminded that its operation anywhere in the material world is only temporary, and by God's concession. In a reference to the humiliating incident in the land of the Gadarenes (Lk 8.31–3), the demons are reminded that they "have no power even over swine." As one of the desert fathers said when demons

[2]See *Against Heresies* IV.18.4.

demanded that he should leave a pagan temple since it "belonged to them": "No place belongs to you."[3]

When, however, we come to the *blessing* of the water—its transformation into a channel of grace—this does not involve adding some alien element into its nature. To be sure, the Holy Spirit is invoked upon it—but, then, it is he who already "fills all things." As we sing at Matins, "It is of the Holy Spirit to reign over creation, to sanctify it, *to set it in motion*," (Song of Degrees, Tone 2). Or to quote another antiphon from the Songs of Degrees, "By the Holy Spirit the whole creation is made new, *restored to its original state*" (Tone 1). When the Holy Spirit comes upon the water—or upon any part of his creation—it is as if he unveils a potential inseparable from its deepest nature:

> But do you *declare* this water to be the water of regeneration, the water of sanctification . . . the fountain of life.[4]

The verb in this prayer of St Basil's (*anadeixon*) is the same one that he uses in his eucharistic prayer for the consecration of the eucharistic elements: the root of the word in the verb "to show" (*deiknynai*) suggests a change of function rather than of nature. The water is not "turned into" something unrelated to its God-given nature. Rather, it is "promoted" to doing the Holy Spirit's work of sanctifying and giving life; this shows its most mundane functions in a new light. All around us, water is already serving as the chosen vehicle for the Giver of Life. As the holy water sprinkles our homes, so the rain sprinkles the earth and kindles new growth, greening the branches of the trees. It is this life-giving

[3]Elias 7; *Sayings of the Desert Fathers*, 61.

[4]Hapgood, *Service Book*, 278.

work that we acknowledge at the feast of Pentecost, when we decorate the church with green branches in honor of the coming of the Holy Spirit.

God's sacramental and natural blessings are constantly echoing each other: beneath the veil of the ordinary lies the sacramental hiddenness of the natural world. This is graphically illustrated in a story from a communist prison camp in Yugoslavia. It was the feast of Theophany, but of course the believers in the camp were forbidden to hold any services. A group of them gathered during exercise time around Fr Vladimir Rodzianko (later Bishop Basil of San Francisco). As they walked, "he recited the service and, pointing to the falling snow, said that [this] was the holy water and it blessed the whole camp."[5] Against the backdrop of human evil, the elements reveal their ultimate meaning as ministers of God's blessing.

The meaning of man

Through sacramental life, then, we begin to experience the natural world as a whole as a "sacrament and gift of God's love," in the words of Fr Dumitru Staniloae.[6] When we call something a gift, we are not describing its nature but its function—specifically, the part it plays in a relationship. "The world as gift of God's love," therefore, is best seen as a statement not about the rest of creation *in itself*, but about *our relationship to* it. When we make use of the world, this is not because we own it, or because it is ours by

[5]Anon. "In Memory of His Grace, Bishop Basil (Rodzianko)," *Orthodox Vision* 5.1 (Spring 2000), 7.

[6]"The World as Gift and Sacrament of God's Love," *Sobornost* 5:9 (Summer 1969), 662–673.

right: it is due entirely to the generosity of its sole Lord, who generously allows us to share in its benefits. We cannot use or enjoy it, or interact with it in any way, without recognizing that we are beholden to a Giver. We humans are by no means unique in being recipients of God's bounty: he opens his hand and "all things are filled with good" (Ps 103.28, Septuagint). What *is* unique about us is our ability to perceive the relationship between God, ourselves and other material creatures, and to respond accordingly. If matter in relation to us is a divine gift, then our proper role in relation to matter is to offer it back to God in thanksgiving. To quote Fr Alexander Schmemann again, it is in the act of thanksgiving that man *becomes himself*.[7]

It is no coincidence that at the heart of the Church's sacramental life we have the mystery of *thanksgiving—eucharistia* in Greek, the Eucharist. If we look at the early Fathers and the oldest eucharistic texts, it is clear that for them, thanksgiving for creation is central to the Divine Liturgy. Insofar as the Liturgy is a sacrifice, it is a sacrifice of praise (which is actually still how we characterize it in the text of the Liturgy itself: "Mercy, peace, a sacrifice of praise"). We do not know exactly what eucharistic prayers St Irenaeus was familiar with as a layman in Smyrna or a bishop in Lyons, but his writings leave us in no doubt about the essence of the eucharistic offering: we offer the firstfruits of God's own creation as a token of our own thankfulness. Christ instructs humans to offer the Eucharist in order to teach them gratitude, and it is this thank-offering that sanctifies the created world.[8] This is why the Anaphora prayer, the prayer of eucharistic offering, develops

[7]*For the Life of the World* (Crestwood, NY: St Vladimir's Seminary Press, 1973), 60.

[8]*Against Heresies* IV.17.5, 18.6.

over the centuries into a grand recitation of thanks to God "in all things and for all things"[9] (Liturgy of St John Chrysostom). Perhaps the most comprehensive example of this is the Anaphora prayer ascribed to James the son of Zebedee in the *Apostolic Constitutions*. This does not actually date from apostolic times, and may not ever have been in regular use in the form given (though it has occasionally been used in modern times); but it undoubtedly reflects the Church's understanding of what such a prayer should consist of. At prodigious length, the prayer offers thanks for the entire created order, from the angelic powers and the four "elements" of earth, water, fire and air, to flowers, animals tame and wild, and birdsong; only after that does it recount the creation and fall of man and God's plan for salvation, culminating in the coming of Christ.[10]

Over the centuries, additional layers of interpretation and symbolism have complicated our perception of what the Eucharist is all about. In the Byzantine tradition the Liturgy came to be seen primarily as a symbolic re-presentation of the entire life of Christ, while Western Christianity was increasingly preoccupied with the sense and manner in which Christ is present in the consecrated elements. The symbolic interpretation is losing its dominance today; but what tends to replace it is not a rediscovery of the Eucharist as thank-offering, but an emphasis on receiving Holy Communion as part of the individual's spiritual life. In communities divorced from agriculture, where few in the congregation have ever made bread, let alone grown and harvested wheat, it is perhaps not surprising that the Eucharist is regarded less as something we

[9]Sometimes translated "on behalf of all and for all."

[10]*Apostolic Constitutions* VIII.2.12.

offer than as something we receive. Yet the essence of the service has not changed. True, the recitation of God's benefactions now begins only with the creation of man. But our response to the remembrance of these benefactions is the same. We *offer back* to God his own gifts (since nothing in the world is our own), accompanied by the only thing that is properly ours: our praise, blessing, and *thanksgiving*. In the eucharistic Gifts, our gratitude is given tangible form. And in return, we receive God's Gift of himself in tangible form. A creation transformed into thankfulness is one able to receive the Holy Spirit: "send down your Holy Spirit upon us and upon these Gifts."

The profound significance of the Eucharist as the action in which humans give thanks for creation leads many contemporary Orthodox theologians to speak of man's "priestly" role in the world, a theme to which we shall return in Chapter 6. This image is intended to underline man's unique responsibility for bringing the material creation of which he is a part to its fulfillment in Christ. We think of understanding and creativity as fundamental elements of being human, and so indeed they are. But the human being finds his true meaning not simply in understanding how the world works, nor in transforming it through his own creativity, but in making all his use of it an offering to God.

A eucharistic ethos

The life of the Church is not readily distilled into ethical principles, but it undoubtedly fosters a certain *ethos*—an atmosphere or mode of living. If we believe that we become our true selves only when we give thanks to God, it is not surprising that the idea of a "eucharistic ethos" should loom large. Contemporary

Orthodox often speak of a "eucharistic and ascetic ethos" as an antidote to a way of living that is environmentally destructive. The two epithets illuminate each other. The ascetic aspect indicates that we walk lightly on the earth as we learn to distinguish need from greed. But the eucharistic aspect shows how this differs from a joyless puritanism: the emphasis is not on *giving up*, but on *giving thanks*. A eucharistic ethos starts from the recognition of everything created as "God's own," so that all our use of the world is a cause for thankfulness to him. We may offer creation back to God by using it creatively, transforming it to suit human needs; but we can equally "offer" all that we incorporate into our own mental world through knowledge and understanding. But whether we are dealing with the land on which we live, the produce of the earth, raw materials and other "natural resources," or distant corners of the universe, we can see our work, our research and our study in terms of an offering to God's glory.

If the Eucharist speaks to us of man's priestly role, it also reminds us that such a role is never exercised in isolation. The eucharistic Anaphora is not a priestly monologue, but a *dialogue* between priest and people. The priest *commemorates* God's works of loving-kindness and *offers up* the gifts, whereupon the laity takes up the offering of praise and blessing:

> Priest: .. *offering you your own gifts of your own gifts, in all things and for all things*
>
> People: *we praise you, we bless you, we worship you, we give thanks . . .*

And similarly with our daily life in God's creation. If we are to make our life and work an offering to the Creator, we need to do so in dialogue with all the rest of creation, which has never ceased to do God's will. In the words of a contemporary Athonite Elder, we find ourselves "part of the Liturgy concelebrated by the entire universe . . . Everyone who has entered into the Liturgy sees the 'words' the inner principles of existent things, *concelebrating* with the One incarnate Word . . ."[11] The expression of *gratitude*, in recognition that all comes from God, may be seen as the conscious, human counterpart of the *praise* that all created things offer simply by being what they are, by unfolding and functioning in accordance with God's will.

The "eucharistic ethos," might also be described more broadly as a "sacramental ethos." Our attitude to the material world draws on the totality of our sacramental experience—the totality of our experience as part of the *mystery of the Church*. All our dealings with the "ordinary" world around us have a sacramental *hiddenness* about them: beneath the surface lies a mystery of relationship with the Creator.

What might such an ethos look like in practice? A remarkable story from sixth-century Syria gives us one insight. The writer John of Ephesus describes a meeting with a wandering monk once when he was visiting a monastery. As they sat in the refectory for a meal, John noticed that the monk was eating so slowly, and with such deliberation, that finally he decided to ask him what he was doing. This is what the monk replied:

> I hope that God will not judge me for having opened my mouth over food which is derived from God's gift with-

[11]Archimandrite Vasileios of Iviron, "*The Light of Christ Shines upon All" through All the Saints* (Montreal: Alexander Press, 2001), 24, 23; italics added.

> out stretching my thoughts to give praise for his bounty. I hope in his name that I shall not be condemned for having stretched forth my hand to my mouth without every time . . . similarly stretching forth my tongue to praise and my mind to prayer on behalf of those who labor and sweat and toil to supply my need.[12]

In this anonymous monk's approach to the very ordinary business of eating a meal, we see three principles at work. First, in everything the monk praises God for his generous gifts. Secondly—and this should be noted, because it is not so often emphasized—his gratitude extends to *other people.* His every mouthful connects him not only to the ultimate Giver, but also to everyone who has been involved in the process of conveying those gifts to him in a form that he can use. And lastly, the process *takes time.* If the monk's behavior was odd enough to excite curiosity in an early Syrian monastery, it would be still more unusual at a modern fast food counter.

Reflecting on this story, we might say that sacramental life has three aspects that are of direct relevance to how we live our daily life:

- it involves use of God's material gifts;
- it is inseparable from relationship to other people;
- it entails a particular attitude to time.

We will explore each of these in more detail.

[12]*Lives of the Eastern Saints, Patrologia Orientalis* 17: 256; quoted in S.P. Brock, "World and Sacrament in the Writings of the Syrian Fathers," *Sobornost* 6:10 (Winter 1974), 695.

Sacramental life and matter

Sacramental life connects us with the material world. This might seem to be putting things the wrong way round: surely the point of the sacraments is to connect us to God? And indeed it is; but the way in which they do this is highly significant. They reveal a pathway to God that is not simply "spiritual": it runs through bread, through water, through the love of a married couple. The sacraments remind us that we relate to God as bodily creatures, so that the physical world surrounding and sustaining us is essential to that relationship. The role of matter in sacramental life speaks to us both of our dependence on material creation, and of our responsibility towards it.

It is often pointed out that our offering at the Eucharist is not "raw nature," but matter shaped by human hands and minds: we offer bread and wine, not wild grains and grapes. Much the same can be said of almost all matter used sacramentally (with a significant exception, which we will return to shortly). What is less often noted, however, is that there is no such thing as a purely human product. And this is not just because we shape things out of existing "raw material," unlike God who creates out of nothing; even the shaping is not entirely our doing. Our human capacity to shape the world into new forms is often seen as contrasting us with the rest of nature; but does it not also reveal some continuity? From one point of view, our transformation of the natural world—as in breeding and growing grains, grinding flour and making bread—is only the tip of an iceberg of transformations going on all the time in nature. The eucharistic bread, which is a human offering, is totally dependent on the activity of yeasts, the physical and chemical processes that provide nutrients to the soil, and the unremitting labor of microorganisms that create humus, to name but a few essential contributors. On a purely physical level, the Eucharist is a cosmic celebration on an awe-inspiring scale. We are the ones who literally make the "offering," since offering is a conscious activity. But by analogy, we could see the bread and wine as also being the "offering" of all the creatures involved in their making: of the rocks and plants and bacteria without which there would be no soil, and indeed the cosmic dust of which the earth is composed. Without us, the product of these creatures' activity would not be offered to God in thankfulness; but without them, there would be nothing for us to offer. This too is part of the humbling message of the Eucharist. It turns out that in all our dealings with the world around us, we are handling "matter through which our salvation has been brought to pass," in John Damascene's phrase.

Once we become aware of the cosmic prehistory of "our" offering, it is easier to remember that God's action in the world is prior to ours; he does not require our action in order to be present in his own creation. This is clearly illustrated in the sequence of events in our sacramental life. We enter the Church through a spiritual birth accomplished through matter; and the matter in question, water, is the one exception to the rule mentioned above. The water of baptism is consecrated by the descent of the Holy Spirit, but it is completely unmodified by human activity. In the early Church, the practice was to baptize in "living," that is, flowing, water; it did not even require the human labor of pouring it into a font. So the sacramental starting point for Christian life is that element original to creation in the symbolic language of Genesis—the Spirit "moved over the waters"—and essential to physical life as we know it. "Water and the Spirit" precede all other sacraments in our church life. And water, through which the Spirit gives physical life, is also an absolute prerequisite for all the organic matter used in other sacraments.

All this gives an important insight into the context within which we go about our characteristically human business of shaping the world. It suggests that we are not spiritual alchemists, charged with "improving" the world so *that* it can serve as God's instrument; we are something closer to "gardeners," charged with "working *and keeping*"[13] a world which *is already* his instrument.

Creativity, the propensity to change and shape our surroundings in a free and conscious way, is undoubtedly a key human characteristic. It is sometimes identified with the "kingly" vocation of the human being; it is to be seen as an aspect of the divine image in us, and that means that it has the potential to be developed in a way that is Godlike. Sacramental life provides examples of such a development—examples of matter shaped so as to serve and reflect God in new and different ways. It is obvious how this applies to the bread and wine of the Eucharist, or to oil for anointing or holy chrism. But we also see at baptism, for instance, how the clothing of the newly baptized person is accompanied with the words "the servant of God is clothed with the robe of righteousness" and the hymn "Grant unto me a robe of light." The very act of putting on a man-made article of clothing becomes an image of "putting on Christ" and his righteousness. This is even more clearly illustrated in the vestments of the clergy. Each item indicates some aspect of God's power and grace at work in the celebrant, and appropriate verses are recited as it is put on.

[13]Gen 2.15, LXX.

It is thus quite reasonable to see the sacramental life of the Church as affirming human "working" of the world in principle. But how much practical guidance can it give us? It would clearly be a mistake to think that, just because human products can have a sacramental use, anything that we might do with the world is thereby given blanket legitimacy.

If we are looking for a criterion for proper "working" of the world, we might start with the one given us when we first come into the Church and prepare for baptism:

> Make him (her) rejoice in the works of his (her) hands and in all his (her) generation; *that he (she) may render praise unto you, and sing and worship and glorify your great and exalted name.*[14]

It is revealing to compare this prayer for "the works of our hands" with the prayer for the blessing of waters quoted above: "Great are you, O Lord, and marvelous are your works: no words suffice to sing the praise of your wonders!" The way that we work in the world should bear a clear likeness to the way God works in the world: as his works inspire praise of him, so likewise should ours.

To be legitimate, then, our use of the world and its materials must be in one way or another an offering for God's glory. Perhaps the clearest example of such use is the icon. Here is a work of human craftsmanship that takes representatives of the animal, vegetable and mineral worlds and forms them into a visible image of God's transfigured creation—a creation through which we worship him

[14]Prayer "at the reception of a catechumen," preceding the service of Baptism; Hapgood, *Service Book*, 271.

and he pours out his grace on us. As St Leontios of Cyprus writes, with the icon in mind:

> It is through me that the heavens declare the glory of God: . . . through me the waters and showers of rain, the dew and all creation, venerate God and give him glory.[15]

Insofar as Leontios speaks of creation's praise being channeled *solely* through us, his statement needs to be balanced by other insights concerning non-human creation; there is a real, though obviously metaphorical, sense in which the created world does speak for itself. But that is simply not Leontios' concern; his purpose is to defend the making of icons against the iconoclasts, who considered it idolatrous to worship God through his material creation. This is why Leontios emphasized so strongly that when we use uniquely human skills to make matter articulate in praise of God, we are fulfilling the words of the Psalmist who calls on all creation to praise the Lord.

In reminding us that man is the one earthly creature who can literally articulate praise, Leontios is making an important point about our crucial role. There is no arrogance about claiming such a role for humanity. It is a statement of fact, too often proved by its converse—the unparalleled ability of human beings to *obscure* the voice of creation's praise. It is in our nature to use the world around us as an extension of our own articulacy—to "make a statement" with it. And that human propensity brings with it a weighty responsibility. Will our "statement" accord with creation's own non-articulate "voice," forming it into new and

[15]*Fifth Homily of Christian Apologetic against the Jews, and on the Icons* (PG 93,1604B).

varied images of God's beauty? Or will we deform creation into a mirror of our own twistedness?

If we want to use God's creation to his glory, there is no *a priori* rule for how this is to be done. As the icon shows us, it does not necessarily mean leaving things as nearly as possible in their natural state: the wooden board requires trees to be felled, rocks have to be cut or quarried and then ground to produce pigments. The natural destiny of an egg is to produce a chicken, not to provide a medium for the iconographer's traditional egg tempera paint. On the other hand, we certainly cannot conclude that all "unnatural" uses of created things are equally legitimate, just because they fall within the scope of our ingenuity. In affirming our use of the world, the Church is not giving us clear answers to ethical dilemmas, or even easily-followed guidelines. The important point is rather that our *use* of the world, no less than our contemplation of it, can be an occasion to discern God's wisdom and decode his "words" inscribed in all created things.

This is, of course, easier said than done. We see all around us the results of an excessively activist, meddlesome interpretation of man's role in the world; an implicit assumption that everything is there for us to consume or to turn into something for our use and convenience. So in reaction to this, it is hardly surprising that many people should emphasize a more contemplative approach: "Don't just do something—stand there!" But this is only a partial solution. A large part of our lives is necessarily spent in "doing something," in activities that inevitably leave a mark on the world around us: we cannot afford to give up hope of glorifying God in this whole area of life. If God can be glorified only in a few peaceful enclaves of contemplation, the world of our daily work will speedily fill up with altars to rival deities such as wealth, power, or convenience.

The sacramental use of human products does not suggest that the world is simply raw material, or that everything needs to be "processed" by human before it is worthy of God. It does not contradict the intuition that nature untouched by man is already a mystery of divine presence. But the sacramental use of our handiwork does contradict the sort of misanthropic pessimism that sees humans as the arch-destroyers, capable only of polluting and distorting the pristine beauty of nature. To the Christian, such a view of man represents a tragic confusion. As we saw earlier (Chapter 4), there is indeed a sense in which humans are a "pollution" of the earth: but this is not simply, as misanthropes would claim, "the nature of the beast." We pollute the earth, spiritually and physically, when we fail to fulfill our God-given nature; when we fail to exercise dominion over the "beasts" within us. The misanthropic view is dangerous because, like all low expectations, it risks becoming a self-fulfilling prophecy. By contrast, the Church's use of matter stands as a witness to human potential. If affirms that our creativity is not forever doomed to be in discord with the beauty of God's earth.

Sacramental life and persons

The second aspect of sacramental life suggested above is the interpersonal. We may begin by recalling what is said in the Divine Liturgy when we invoke the Holy Spirit: we pray for the descent of the Holy Spirit "*upon us* and upon these gifts." It is not only the offering of bread, but also the gathered Church that is made the Body of Christ. This effect is particularly clear again in the Liturgy of St Basil, for after the invocation of the Spirit, the prayer continues: "And unite all of us who partake of the one Bread and the one Cup one to another in the communion of the Holy Spirit . . ."

One of the fruits of the Eucharist, then, is the oneness and interdependence of the body of the Church. This is reflected again in St Basil's Liturgy in the commemoration of the living, with its extraordinary breadth embracing all conditions of human life: those who offer the gifts and those for whom they are offered; hermits, ascetics, rulers, married people, infants, children, old people, those who have strayed from the Church, travelers, prisoners, the sick, those condemned to labor in the mines. . . . Being "united in the Holy Spirit" means that unity with God and unity with other people are inseparable. One cannot partake in the Body of Christ and be blind to the needs of the other members of that Body. This too is part of the message of the Syrian monk, who could never eat a mouthful without thinking of everyone through whom the gift of food had come to him. If we think of all the people who have "labored and toiled" to produce the things we use in any one day of our lives, and what it might mean to pray for the well-being of them all, and to act in a way that did not contradict our prayers, we begin to realize how a truly eucharistic and sacramental ethos would totally transform the way Christians handle material goods.

So the offering of thanksgiving to God unites us with other people and makes us aware of their needs. But it is equally true that sharing God's gifts with other people is one of the principle ways in which we fulfill the imperative of offering them back to him. Fr Dumitru Staniloae has pointed out how this is indicated liturgically in the distribution of unconsecrated bread (*antidoron*) at the end of the Divine Liturgy; he speaks of "the custom of the Orthodox faith of distributing to the people also from the gifts which are offered to God; for faith declares that what is given to the neighbor is truly given to God."[16] There is an echo here, too, of St John Chrysostom's image of offering not only at the altar in Church, but equally at the altar of the poor person.[17] Perhaps it is not coincidental that the saints associated with the two main Liturgies that we use, St Basil and St John Chrysostom, are also among the best known for their practical works of mercy and championing of the poor.

The Eucharist further reminds us that sharing with other people is not simply something we do out of the kindness of our hearts, a gratuitous act of generosity: it is actually a matter of putting our own goods to their *proper use*. We offer in the Eucharist things that in ordinary human terms would be considered "ours." They are the products of skills unique to our kind, and were made by us personally or bought with money we had worked to earn—yet it is these very products that we declare to belong wholly to God ("Offering you your own of your own . . ."). But if our own products and property turn out in reality to be God's rather than ours, that means that they are given for the benefit of all: "The property of the King belongs to all in common," as Chrysostom underlines. The fact that they are in our hands simply means that we have the responsibility of ensuring that they serve God's purposes. No legal or social conventions of ownership can override our obligation to administer that portion of God's gifts that we "own" for the good of all his creatures.

[16]"World as gift," 672–3.

[17]Cf. *Homilies on 2 Corinthians* 20.3.

There is one sacramental service where we are reminded in a particularly explicit way that whatever we have over and above our basic needs is actually given to us for the benefit of others. In the wedding service, the priest prays for the couple: "Fill their houses with wheat, wine and oil, and with every beneficence, *that they may bestow in turn upon the needy*." In a certain sense, marriage may be thought of as an ordination to Christian life "in the world," as opposed to monastic life. Whereas the monastic has given up all possessions, the Christian in the world characteristically "owns" money and material goods—in other words, he or she is not called to eschew these things altogether, but to administer them for the good of others. It is here that the overused notion of "stewardship" has a legitimate place: it applies precisely to those things that in legal terms we "own," and to the way we use "our" money, goods, and land. Because financial stewardship is often associated with ideas such as tithing, it may be useful to remind ourselves that we are stewards primarily not of what we give away, but of what we keep to use for our own purposes. In today's complex society, "bestowing upon the needy" will mean not only charitable giving but also consumer choices—choices such as passing over the product cheapest and most convenient for me, in favor of one more conducive to the health and welfare of "those who labor and sweat and toil to supply my needs."

As we saw in the baptismal prayer quoted earlier, sacramental life makes manifest the "de-pollution" of the earth effected by Christ's coming. It reminds the "demons of darkness" that they have no place in the material world to call their own. Correspondingly, the inter-personal and social implications of the Eucharist extend this same process of "de-pollution" into human society. The Church's worship frequently reminds us that right treatment of our fellow human beings and of the material world go together, and neither one can be separated from the other. We think, for instance, of the link between fasting, almsgiving and "tearing up all unjust agreements" which we hear about in hymns for the first week of Lent. Note too that at Theophany, the feast perhaps most strongly associated with the sanctification of the material world, we also hear an uncompromising call to justice from the Prophet Isaiah:

> Wash yourselves; make yourselves clean; remove the evil of your doings from before my eyes; cease to do evil, learn to do good; seek judgment, correct oppression . . . (Is 1.16–18).

Our liturgical and sacramental life delivers an important message. Wonder at creation, celebration of the earth restored and sanctified, praise for God's gifts—these are all important aspects of recovering our true role in creation. But rediscovering our connection with the non-human world will not lead us to its Creator unless we also rediscover our connection with our own kind—unless we "cease to do evil" and "relieve the oppressed." When we think about proper treatment of God's creation, therefore, we need to realize that this is first and foremost a *social* imperative; it is a sign of our connectedness with other people in a union of love.

Sacramental life and time

It is not so hard to see that sacramental life could have something to say to us about the use of matter, and about relationships with other people. But perhaps less obviously, it also has something to teach us about another important aspect of modern life, our attitude toward time.

We know that the Church has developed daily, weekly, and annual cycles of services, which reflect the time of this world, but may be seen as sanctifying it. But we also know that the Eucharist and other sacraments have never been subsumed into these cycles. The Eucharist is a regular part of our worship: but it does not belong to any particular time of day. Vespers and Matins, or the services of the Hours, may in practice be celebrated at anomalous times of day—Matins tacked onto Vespers in the evening, for instance, at the "all-night" Vigil, or Vespers in the morning during Lent and Holy Week. But it never ceases to be evident that their *raison d'être* lies in one particular time of day; when a Lenten Vespers is celebrated in the morning, we still sing psalms about an "evening sacrifice." The Divine Liturgy, on the other hand, is not tied to a particular time of day. It is not associated with time as we experience it in this world: it is *a "time for the Lord to act."*

It is these words from Ps 118.26, "it is time for the Lord to act," that preface the celebration of the Divine Liturgy. So far from belonging to a two-hour slot on Sunday morning, the Liturgy offers the key to escaping the domination of time; it opens the way to experiencing in every moment the working out of God's eternal Kingdom.

What does this mean in practice? To help us understand, we may reflect that there are two very different possible attitudes to time. One is to focus on an "end product," setting our own private agenda for what *we* want to accomplish at a given time. Unless we are working specifically on our own agenda, the present moment and its activity have no value. In effect, every waking hour becomes a time for *me* to act.

The alternative is to see our time as a series of potential moments for God to reveal himself; and this means that *every* activity that occupies our time, whether or not it is according to our own plans, is a "time for the Lord to act." This approach means that one will be concerned less with *saving* time (in order to spend it elsewhere) than with *redeeming* time—turning to spiritual profit whatever activity or inactivity circumstances may impose. This is how time can be used to point us towards the Kingdom.

Time is undeniably an aspect of the created world; but what does it have to do with the way we treat the material world around us? The cliché "time is money" gives us a clue: it reminds us that time can be bought. Once upon a time, the "cost" would have been employing other people's labor: one could "buy time" by paying a washerwoman to do the laundry. Nowadays, time is more often purchased at the cost of natural resources: we pay for a washing machine, for the copious amounts of water it uses, and for the energy used to manufacture and to run it. From private cars and their fuel to air travel, from energy-hungry appliances to heavily-packaged "convenience foods" eaten off disposable plates, our consumption of the goods of creation is closely correlated with our desire to "save time," to do things "in our own time"—to make time serve our own agenda. Our willingness to wait for a bus or wash up dishes depends to a great extent on whether our priority is to *save* time or to *redeem* it. I recall a talk on prayer in which a nun was responding to a questioner who lamented that she had no time to pray because nobody ever helped her with the household chores: the nun pointed out how the two problems—no time to pray, and doing mindless chores alone—could in fact be fused into one solution. To fill the hours spent on housework with the Jesus Prayer is to redeem that time, turning it to our gain.

Sacramental life does much more than to show us how to use time prudently, however. It cuts right across time as we know it, giving us a radically new perspective on all that is subject to time. When we begin a Liturgy, or other sacramental service, with the solemn blessing of "the Kingdom of the Father and of the Son and of the Holy Spirit," we are entering upon a present reality that is grounded in the future. Fr Georges Florovsky expresses this emphatically when he says, " 'sacramental' means no less than 'eschatological.' What is 'not of this world' is here 'in this world'; not abolishing this world, but giving it a new meaning and a new value, 'transvaluating' the world, as it were."[18]

Does not an eschatological emphasis lead us to despise or dismiss the actual, present world in its fallen and corruptible state? Many people today—even many Christians—assume that it does. But it rather depends on what one means by eschatology. The "end times" genre of popular theology has not made a positive contribution to understanding the subject. If eschatology is simply the "final page" of history when true believers can look forward to leaving the world behind, this could well encourage contempt for creation as we know it. But if the eschaton is indeed the dynamic reality which "transvaluates" everything around us, then nothing can be despised as ephemeral. And the sacramental life of the Church is precisely the experience of eschatological reality breaking through into the world, so that creation, humanity included, is caught up into it.

[18]"The Church: Her Nature and Task," reprinted in Florovsky, *Bible, Church, Tradition: An Eastern Orthodox View* (Belmont, MA: Notable and Academic Books, 1987), 68.

It is the eschatological quality of the Church's life that is reflected when we bring perishable fruits, flowers and branches into the church for blessing or decoration, and then dispose of them carefully and reverently as things that have partaken in the holy. It is a supreme affirmation of our eschatological vision that we bring into the church the very fruits of corruption and decay and then receive them back as Eucharist, as God's gift of his own life. For the bread and wine, which we offer, are not the fruits of Paradise. They are the product of soil and compost and its rich population of organisms, and this is nothing other than the process of corruption. The elements of the Eucharist are the supreme example of a body "sown in corruption and raised in incorruption" (1 Cor 15.42, translated literally from the Greek).

So the eschatological perspective means recognizing that all creation is destined ultimately to be liberated from futility—and this will hardly lead to contempt for material creation. But the other side of eschatology is an acute awareness that this liberation is still a work in progress; and this certainly will lessen our demands on the world around us, here and now. Indeed, it is likely to lead us into direct conflict with the idea that all problems are there to be solved through hard work and diligent research. An eschatological perspective reminds us that many of life's irritants, and even its tragedies, are simply not soluble this side of the resurrection: "In the world there is struggle," as St Ephrem says. This sober assessment of earthly life may be unfashionable, but it gains a certain credence from the growing number of problems to have been caused by solutions. We eliminate the "struggle" at our peril.

When we apply the sacramental vision of time to our relationship with the rest of God's material creation, then, it does not lead us to devalue the world in which God has placed us. It does not encourage us to sit passively waiting for the "end times" when everything will be destroyed anyway. On the contrary: it should inspire us to bring our treatment of the world around us into ever greater convergence with the sacramental pattern. Our eschatological vision does, however, reveal how the purpose of the Church's work in the world differs from the aims of any secular organization, any movement whose horizons are limited to this age. A sacramental approach to the world does not try to take us either *forward* or *back* to an earthly paradise. It invites us to place our hope neither in technological advances, nor in return to a "golden age" of harmony with nature. The Church looks to the ultimate transfiguration of all things; and we serve this end by conforming ourselves to God's will.

Sacramental life points us to the underlying reality of humanity and the rest of creation; and it turns out to be a reality of interrelation. Humans and all other creatures *need each other* for their relationship to their Creator. This sheds new light on the social and physical interconnections which are becoming ever more obvious in today's world. We can hardly ignore the ripple (or tsunami?) effect of social and economic upheavals in a globalized world, and are rapidly discovering the environmental ramifications of damage to habitats or organisms in distant corners of the planet (destroy the southern forests where songbirds winter, and northern forests will suffer insect infestations). In such cases, we are learning that the adage "if one suffers, all suffer" (cf. 1 Cor 12.26) is hard fact.

So sacramental life does not only highlight the role of the material world in humanity's relationship to God. It equally draws our attention to a sometimes neglected aspect of environmental problems: humans' responsibility for each other. The sacramental life of the Church, and the Eucharist especially, points to sharing with others. This is not presented to us as a moral imperative, something that we do because it is "the right thing." We do it because we are members of one another; we cannot truly live in any other way.

Armed with this vision, we are better able to confront one aspect of the environmental crisis that no one wants to talk about: the prospects for our own standard of living. While some environmental problems are directly related to individual over-consumption, many others are associated with poverty—in other words, unequal distribution of resources. Much environmental damage—we might think of deforestation or over-fishing—comes about because people have no alternative but to destroy their future in order to survive today. The response is often to talk brightly about "win-win solutions" in which everyone enjoys economic benefits; and such arrangements can of course exist. But people are less often prepared to acknowledge the obvious: where we are dealing with resources that are limited, whether by shortage of supply or by the damaging consequences of exploiting them, not everyone can "win," in material terms, all the time. Those currently enjoying the largest share must also be prepared to give something up. This has never been a popular message, as many sermons by St Basil, St John Chrysostom and others testify, but it is fundamental to a union of love. If we can truly see ourselves as members of one body, we may learn to see personal sacrifice as gain rather than loss: for in this way the whole body can truly "win."

For further reading:

Brock, Sebastian. "World and Sacrament in the Writings of the Syrian Fathers." *Sobornost* 6:10 (Winter 1974): 685–696.

Osborne, Bishop Basil. "Sermon on the Sunday of Orthodoxy." *The Light of Christ*. Oxford: St Stephen's Press, 2nd ed. 1996:, 45–53.

Staniloae, Fr Dumitru. "The World as Gift and Sacrament of God's Love." *Sobornost* 5:9 (Summer 1969): 662–673.

Staniloae, Fr Dumitru, "Christian responsibility in the world." A.M. Allchin, ed. *The Tradition of Life*. London: Fellowship of St Alban and St Sergius, 1971: 53–73.

Theokritoff, George, "The Cosmology of the Eucharist," in Lukas Vischer, ed., *Spirituality, Creation and the Ecology of the Eucharist*. Geneva: John Knox Centre, 2007: 72–77.

(Ware), Bishop Kallistos of Diokleia. *Through the Creation to the Creator*. London: Friends of the Centre, 1996.

______. "Lent and the Consumer Society." A. Walker and C. Carras, eds. *Living Orthodoxy in the Modern World*. London: SPCK, 1996: 64–84.

Zizioulas, Metropolitan John of Pergamon. "Proprietors or Priests of Creation?" (Keynote address, Baltic Symposium, June 2003). ‹http://www.rsesymposia.org/themedia/File/1151679350-Pergamon.pdf.›

Zizioulas, Metropolitan John of Pergamon. "Man the Priest of Creation." A. Walker and C. Carras, eds. *Living Orthodoxy in the Modern World*. London: SPCK, 1996: 178–188.

chapter six

THEMES IN CONTEMPORARY ORTHODOX THEOLOGY

In articulating a theology of creation, contemporary Orthodox theologians naturally take up many themes that we have already talked about. But there are also certain areas where traditional material is developed in new ways, and used to address new challenges. This chapter, then, will revisit several of the themes we have already explored, but through the eyes of modern Orthodox theologians, who will give fresh articulation to their content and uncover latent insights.

Some contemporary thinking is responding directly to the environmental crisis, the physical consequences of our actions or inaction. But interestingly, many of the most valuable insights into our place in God's creation date from a time when there was little or no awareness of these consequences. These are insights that address underlying problems, of which environmental destruction is now widely recognized as a symptom: the consumer's-eye view of the world, contempt for the bodily aspect of human nature, a mechanistic view of the universe which sees it as devoid of divine presence.

Broadly speaking, modern Orthodox thinking about creation is dominated by two overarching themes, which we have already encountered in this book: a *eucharistic* view of the cosmos, and the doctrine of the *logoi* of things, as developed by St Maximus. Usually, the two are thoroughly intertwined. Explicitly or implicitly, they provide the framework for addressing fundamental questions of humans' proper role in the world and the value of non-human creation. They provide a non-pantheistic basis for that sense of the sacred in creation, which so many people are rediscovering. And in some quite unexpected ways, these themes help us make theological sense of the world presented to us by modern science. This is of fundamental importance: if our theological vision is to have any effect on the way people treat the physical world around them, it has to be apparent that we are all talking about the same world.

Creation as Eucharist and human priesthood

When modern Orthodox writers speak of the relationship of creation to its Creator, the imagery many of them choose is that of the Eucharist, in which the world is a great cosmic Eucharist, and man is its priest. A sacramental cosmology of this sort has increasingly found favor also among Anglican and Roman Catholic theologians, but it is an area where Orthodox have a particularly rich tradition on which to draw.

The person perhaps most responsible for developing an Orthodox sacramental cosmology was Fr Alexander Schmemann. It is of a piece with his whole emphasis on the centrality of the Eucharist in Christian life; and this connection is important, because it underlines the fact that the way we treat the world around us is inseparable from the total expression of our faith. If we participate in the Mysteries of the Church and then abuse the created world in our everyday life, we are living a contradiction. The sacramental life of the Church, culminating in the Eucharist, is the supreme revelation of the nature of creation in itself. The Eucharist is a "moment of truth" in which we see the world in Christ; the blessing of waters makes the world and all creation what it was in the beginning. Hence Schmemann's vitally important insistence, to which we have already referred, that blessing and consecration do not create a separate class of "sacred objects" opposed to all the other "profane objects"; they reveal the "sacramentality" of creation itself.[1] One might translate this into practical terms by saying that if we receive Holy Communion reverently and with prayers of thanksgiving, it makes no sense then to throw away, uneaten, half of God's gift of Sunday lunch.

Schmemann takes up the connection that we have already seen in the Fathers: he characterizes the fall as marking a change and distortion in the relationship between man and God, and in the way material creation functions within that relationship:

> The world was given to man by God as "food"—as means of life; yet life was meant to be communion with God; it had not only its end but its full content in Him . . . The world and food were thus created as means of communion with God, and only if accepted for God's sake were to give life . . . Thus to eat, to be alive, to know God and be in communion with Him were one and the same thing. The unfathomable tragedy of Adam was that he ate for its own sake. More than that, he ate "apart" from God in order to be independent of

[1]See, e.g., *For the Life of the World*, 44, 73, 132; *Eucharist*, 61, 33.

> Him. And if he did it, it is because he believed that food had life in itself and that he, by partaking of that food, could be like God, i.e. have life in himself. To put it very simply, he *believed in food* . . . World, food, became his gods, the sources and principles of his life. He became their slave.[2]

In other words, matter is meant to be a means of communion with God; but we have made it an idol. We can see the clear connection here with St Maximus' notion of the fall as a shift from being centered on God to being centered on creation.

If this is the meaning of the fall, then the way back from the fall is a Eucharistic use of the world—an attitude of referring everything in the world back to God. This attitude is defined by another great eucharistic theologian, Metropolitan John Zizioulas, "It is precisely the reversal of Adam's attitude, who took the world as his own and referred it to himself."[3] On this reading, the sin of Adam is in its essence the aberration of "anthropocentricity." And the way out of this dead end is to view man not as the center, but as the agent by whom the world is offered back to God in thanksgiving: "the priest of the cosmic sacrament," in Schmemann's words.[4] This priesthood belongs to all human beings. The sacramental priesthood does not in any way diminish this universal "cosmic" priesthood; rather, it serves to highlight the priestly essence of *every* vocation.[5] Whatever we do in life, we are offering our work and the material we use as a sacrifice

[2]*Great Lent* (Crestwood, NY: St Vladimir's Seminary Press, 1973), 94–5.

[3]"Man the Priest of Creation," in A. Walker and C. Carras, eds., *Living Orthodoxy*, 185.

[4]*Life of the World*, 15.

[5]Ibid., 93–4.

of thanksgiving. "In the immense cathedral which is the universe of God," writes the French theologian Paul Evdokimov, "each person, whether scholar or manual laborer, is called to act as the priest of his whole life—to take all that is human, and to turn it into an offering, a hymn of glory."[6]

The language of human "priesthood" in creation enjoys considerable popularity among contemporary Orthodox. It serves as a useful counterbalance to the Protestant language of "stewardship" which has gained wide currency even in secular circles, but which ties us too closely to notions of property and economics. The language of "priesthood" underlines the Godwardness of creation as a whole: it leads us to see our habitat as an "immense cathedral" and our daily life as a Eucharist.

The language of cosmic Eucharist and human celebrant emphasizes the responsibility of humans for how they use the world, but without implying that the world is "property" to be managed. Just as the priest is part of the Church body, so man as "cosmic priest" is part of the body of creation—a key part, certainly, but still a member of an organic whole. This means that the relationship with all the rest of creation is absolutely crucial to him. We all know that, on a purely physical level, man is absolutely dependent on his environment for survival; but what we are saying here goes far beyond the level of mere physical survival. "By being priest of creation," says Metropolitan John, man "relates to nature by what he *is*." This means that damaging the rest of creation is not simply a moral transgression: "in destroying nature we simply

[6]"Le sacerdoce universel des laïcs dans la tradition orientale," in L.A. Elchinger, *L'Eglise en Dialogue* (Paris, 1962), 39–40; quoted in Bishop Kallistos Ware, *The Orthodox Way*, revised ed., (Crestwood, NY: St Vladimir's Seminary Press, 2002), 65.

cease to be." Ecology is not a matter of our well-being; it is a matter of our being.[7]

The image of human "priesthood" is not found explicitly in patristic times—though, as we have seen, the Fathers do speak of man's role being to offer praise and thanks on behalf of all creation. They also speak of man as a *link* between the rest of creation and the Creator, and the idea of man as priest can well be seen as a development of that notion. Metropolitan John, the most systematic exponent of "man as priest of creation," sees human priesthood as the product of man's drive to unite what is divided (the "natural power" given to man, according to St Maximus), combined with his freedom, his power of self-determination (*autexousion)*; for this freedom is an impulse to transcend created nature. This drive to go beyond created nature is given to man *for the sake of all creation*, because all creation needs to go beyond itself in order to survive; it "cries out for reference to God," as Metropolitan John says.[8] Such insistence on the need for creation to transcend its "limitations" can lead to misunderstandings: but to speak of "limitations" is no insult to the material world. Nor is there the slightest suggestion that man is in any way exempt from this need. Metropolitan John is simply spelling out the consequences of the Christian doctrine of creation. The world comes *out of nothing*; so if it is to survive, it has to have a connection with something other than nothingness. And that means the One who is uncreated, "he who is."

[7]"Proprietors or Priests of Creation?" (Keynote address, Baltic Symposium, June 2003), 7–8; Cited 31 March 2009. Online: http://www.rsesymposia.org/themedia/File/1151679350-Pergamon.pdf

[8]"Preserving God's Creation" (Part 3), *Sourozh* 41 (August 1990): 35, 37.

In speaking of man's priesthood, Metropolitan John inevitably gets involved in discussion of what constitutes the divine image in man. The power of self-determination is paramount, as we have just seen; but he is particularly concerned with establishing a proper understanding of man's reason, *logos*. The Fathers are clear that "reason" is a vital distinguishing mark of man. But if "reason" is understood, as it often has been in the West, in the post-Enlightenment sense of "rationality," the implication is that man is the only thinking being in creation. And from there, it is a fatefully easy step to conclude that we are the only creature that really matters. Once the rest of creation is reduced to an inert mass of raw material, abuse of it is virtually inevitable.[9] But as Metropolitan John goes on to point out, our increasing understanding of the history of life and its evolution enables us to break out of this rationalistic captivity. It is becoming increasingly apparent to us that human intellect and consciousness differ only in degree, not in kind, from those of other animals. This means we have to look elsewhere for the specific difference that gives man a unique place in creation; and Metropolitan John locates it in our *ability to relate*. This, as he points out, actually comes very close to the fundamental sense of *logos* (which is related to the root of the word col*lect*). *Logos* is the capacity to *bring together,* to unite what is divided and so to *make sense* of the world: to make a unified and harmonious *cosmos* out of a diversified or fragmented world.[10]

[9]"Preserving God's Creation" (Part 1), *Sourozh* 39 (March 1990): 8.

[10]"Man the Priest of Creation," 182.

Priesthood and concelebration

"Priest of creation" language is embraced by others besides Orthodox, particularly Christians of the more sacramental traditions. In some quarters, however, it gives rise to misunderstandings—principally because the notion of priesthood itself means such different things to different Christians. When people take exception to the idea of man being "priest of creation," it seems to be because to them, "priesthood" implies clericalism—an exclusive class of people who control everyone else's access to God.

What idea of priesthood underlies the "priest of creation" imagery used by Orthodox Christians? It is no coincidence that this language came to prominence against the backdrop of a profound rediscovery of the Church as a *body* in which all members, and all orders, have a vital role to play. It is a body characterized by *sobornost*—unity in diversity, communion and interdependence. We should immediately recognize the similarity between this vision of how the Church community functions, and our growing understanding of how the earth community functions. In this understanding of the Church, priesthood is one ministry serving the whole body. The priest lends his hand and his voice to present an offering, which is that of the entire Church, and the presence of the laity is no less vital than his own.

The worship of the Church, then, is truly a communal action; its offering is a common offering. The depth of this consciousness was impressed upon me by a recent incident. In translating an article by a Greek theologian, I had used the term "concelebrant." The author, whose English is good, queried this: did the term I had used adequately convey his meaning of "concelebrating *clergy*"?

To his ear, "concelebrants" implied, first and foremost, *all* who join with the clergy in the offering of the Church.

So every liturgy is in some sense a *concelebration.* Even if there is only one priest, the entire body of the gathered Church joins with him in the offering, in one way or another. And the same idea can be applied to creation as a whole, when we speak of the world in eucharistic terms. As we have seen already, Archimandrite Vasileios of Iviron connects this cosmic concelebration with the "words" or inner principles of existent things, which "concelebrate with the one incarnate Word, the One who offers and is offered in the Liturgy of the whole world."[11] This cosmic liturgy is the given, the "order of service," which determines what we do with the world as "celebrants." For a priest is not one who *creates* the Eucharist or decides what form the offering is to take: he follows the established order. And by so doing, he fulfils the purpose for which Christ has assembled his Church. Similarly in the cosmos, therefore, our task is not to reorganize or redirect creation, but to *articulate* its "wordless word."

Concelebration provides the context within which we must understand the strong emphasis—characteristic especially of Metropolitan John Zizioulas—on man as *the* link between God and creation, the only being responsible for creation's fate. It would be a grave misunderstanding to see here an assertion that man as it were controls all the channels of communication or mediates God's presence in the world. The world reflects God's glory and proclaims his handiwork (cf. Ps 18.2). Its very existence testifies to the presence of God's creative energies. Yet the universe, although created "very good," is not intended to be static; it is meant to be

[11] "The Light of Christ," 23.

going somewhere, and for this "creation needs man." The existence that it enjoys by virtue of the divine energies pervading it is intended to be fulfilled in eternal life: but this is to happen not automatically, but in freedom. It therefore requires the co-working of that material creature endowed with free choice, the human being.

To speak of this task as "priestly" underlines our unique responsibility: there can be no liturgy without a priest to celebrate, however much everyone and everything else is prepared to contribute their part. But the context of concelebration reminds us of the breadth of that responsibility. In our use of the world, we are accountable not only to the Creator and to ourselves, but also to the whole body of creation that has brought its own offering and stands waiting. We find ourselves in a position to realize—or thwart—a potential in the cosmos that cries out for fulfillment.

Man can fulfill his own purpose only through matter: this too is part of the meaning of concelebration. "Man is not called to return to God as a solitary being," writes Fr Dumitru Staniloae; "he is to help his fellow man and all things to make this return."[12] So if nature cannot reach its goal without man, this is not because it is itself intrinsically valueless, but because the functioning—the *liturgy*—of creation is grounded in interdependence, not individualism.

[12]"The Foundation of Christian Responsibility in the World: The Dialogue of God and Man," in A.M. Allchin, ed., *The Tradition of Life* (London: Fellowship of St Alban and St Sergius, 1971), 68.

Exercising human priesthood: the significance of the body

The idea of cosmic Eucharist, and human responsibility for offering it, opens up various ways of thinking about our relationship with the rest of creation. These include our physical connection with the world through our body; the role of prayer, particularly the Jesus Prayer; and the *logoi* of things in relation to our use of the world.

Metropolitan John speaks for many modern Orthodox Christian theologians when he emphasizes that the fact that man is also an animal (which does not, of course, mean *only* an animal) is "the *sine qua non* for his glorious mission in creation."[13] This way of putting it might sound startling, especially if we have accepted uncritically the idea that a recognition of our animal nature somehow undermines Christian doctrine. But Metropolitan John is doing little more than restating in modern language the idea of man as microcosm, as it is used by church fathers such as Gregory of Nyssa and Maximus. Modern discoveries of just how much humans have in common with other animals—the mapping of the human genome providing the latest example—have spurred increasing interest in man's bodily nature, and the way in which he fulfils his role in creation precisely *as a bodily creature*. Here for instance is what another prominent Greek theologian, Christos Yannaras, has to say about man's "power of uniting what was divided":

> Only the reason (*logos*) and energy of man can meet and recognize in created things the polyphony of the words (*logoi*) of the divine energy. At the same time, man's body is the supreme

[13]"Preserving" (Part 3), 35.

> personal differentiation of the energies of his nature, and in that very body the principle of man's personal distinctiveness encounters the personal principle or "word" of divine creative energy. In man's body, the sacred liturgy uniting created and uncreated life has its origin and fulfillment.[14]

It would be a great mistake to think that this interest in our physical nature is a contemporary fad. One of the earliest modern Orthodox writers to explore the significance of the body in Christianity was the brilliant, if idiosyncratic, Russian priest and scientist Pavel Florensky, who perished in a prison camp in the 1930s. He starts from the point—obvious, but often ignored—that our body connects us with all the "flesh," i.e., the matter of the world: this is how the world falls and is restored along with man.[15] For it is not a disembodied human soul that is to inherit eternal life; it is a "holy body." Florensky points out that we are affirming this when we venerate relics; for a relic is nothing other than the dry and leafless seed of that holy body.[16] But how do we come to see the body and matter in this light? The key, as Florensky shows with many vivid examples, is to be found in *asceticism*. He argues passionately against the misunderstanding that sees asceticism as contempt for the material: to the contrary, Christian asceticism is a "being in love with creation." It wounds the human being with the "wound of loving pity for all things"[17]—the phrase echoes St

[14]*The Freedom of Morality* (Crestwood, NY: St Vladimir's Seminary Press, 1984), 98–9.

[15]*The Pillar and Ground of the Truth* (Princeton, NJ: Princeton University Press, 1997), 198.

[16]Ibid., 224.

[17]Ibid., 210–12.

Isaac's description of the "compassionate heart." There is of course nothing new in talking about asceticism as a remedy for a distorted view of the material world. But the significance of Florensky's approach is that asceticism becomes the antidote to a peculiarly modern (post-Enlightenment) sense of alienation from the natural world, an opposition between inert matter and human reason.

The way of thinking about our bodily existence espoused by Florensky and other Russian thinkers is not something rarified and theoretical. It is not by chance that Florensky talks about "wounding": his approach has everything to do with vulnerability, with sharing in the suffering of both the human and the natural world. We see this graphically in another victim of Soviet terror, Iulia de Beausobre. This remarkable Russian woman was imprisoned for many years under the communists, and came close to death more than once before escaping to England where she spent the latter years of her life. In her old age she became increasingly obsessed with "our task—as Christians—to use our bodies, the relics of our bodies of the resurrection, as purifiers of the earth that we increasingly pollute."[18] Spiritual and physical pollution of the earth appear seamlessly intertwined; and so the same is true of its de-pollution. Our spiritual offering of self to God makes our very body a "chemical substance" which, in God's hands, is able to effect this cleansing.[19]

The Greek theologian Panayiotis Nellas has a very similar insight.[20] He writes of death as "the means by which the human

[18]C. Babington-Smith, *Iulia de Beausobre: A Russian Christian in the West* (London: Darton, Longman and Todd, 1983), 142–3.

[19]Ibid., 182.

[20]*Deification in Christ: Orthodox Perspectives on the Nature of the Human*

body penetrates into the interior of the earth, reaching the inmost parts of creation." And then as a result, he says, creation "is dressed with a new element which, because it is a human body, is receptive of incorruption." The eschatological transformation of the universe is thus realized "from within, organically and naturally, within the human person." Few theologians talk about this so explicitly; but it is actually an insight to be found everywhere in the Orthodox Church's experience. The association between holy people and holy places is one eloquent testimony to it. We meet the same reality, less systematically expressed, particularly in accounts of holy ascetics. It is worth looking again at a source we quoted earlier, Archimandrite Vasileios of Iviron's account of the skete that was his first introduction to Athonite monasticism. Here he is talking about old Fr Pachomios, who was "a blessing for all of us and a friend to the snakes:"

> Now he sleeps in the cemetery of All Saints. He has been added to the choir of the ascetic martyrs of the Skete . . . He remains in that place as a sacred compost and a wellspring of consolation for all. From his holy relics, as from the chestnut-wood troughs they used to use for water, there will ever come a holy dew to water that place ceaselessly and give it life.[21]

So here we have some very concrete expressions of how our bodies interact with the rest of material creation; the idea that humans bear responsibility for the entire cosmos ceases to look like some arrogant metaphysical conceit. It becomes a conclusion that is

Person (Crestwood, NY: St Vladimir's Seminary Press, 1987), 65–6; translation adapted.

[21]"Reminiscences," 83.

rather hard to avoid, given what we know of the interconnection of all matter. "What is our body," Olivier Clément asks rhetorically, "if . . . not the form imprinted by our 'living soul' on the universal 'dust' which unceasingly penetrates and traverses us? There is no discontinuity between the flesh of the world and human flesh; the universe participates in human nature, as it constitutes the body of humanity."[22]

The Jesus Prayer

Our body is "dust of the universe," but it is "dust" that can enter into conscious relationship with God. One obvious way that it does this is through sacramental life, through offering and partaking of the Eucharist. But another, no less important means is through prayer, and in particular the use of the Name of Jesus ("Lord Jesus Christ, Son of God, have mercy on me" is one of its most common forms). Iulia de Beausobre records that her intuition about "de-polluting" the earth was inspired by her encounter with nuns in a Soviet prison camp, who had introduced her to "the old prayer in its new form,"[23] to the use of the Jesus Prayer to counteract humanity's accumulated pollution of creation.

Metropolitan Kallistos Ware has noted this "world-affirming" character of the Prayer. Contrary to what one might assume, prayer of the heart is anything but self-centered and inward-looking.[24] He cites, for instance, the experience of the enigmatic Russian "pilgrim" who wandered the countryside reciting the Prayer

[22]"L'homme dans le monde," *Verbum Caro* XII:45 (1958), 11–12.

[23]*Iulia de Beausobre*, 38–9.

[24]*The Power of the Name* (Oxford: SLG Press, new ed. 1986), 26–7.

and acquired the "knowledge of the speech of all creatures," the ability to hear all creatures giving glory to God.

Others have explored in greater detail the intentional use of this prayer as "an instrument of the hidden offering of everything and everyone, setting the divine seal on the world," in Nadejda Gorodetzky's words:

> We can apply this Name [of Jesus] to people, books, flowers, to all things we meet, see or think. The Name of Jesus may become a mystical key to the world . . . One might perhaps speak here of the priesthood of all believers. In union with our High Priest, we implore the Spirit: Make my prayer into a sacrament.[25]

Fr Lev Gillet, well-known for his writings on the Jesus Prayer under the name of "A Monk of the Eastern Church," quotes at length these insights of his old friend and disciple. He also takes further the underlying theology, linking the Name with the creation of the cosmos by Christ and its destiny to be transfigured into Him. "All creation mysteriously utters the Name," he writes. And so, by pronouncing it over natural things, we "speak aloud [their] secret" and "bring them to their fulfillment."[26]

It should not be thought that this contemplative approach to nature is in any way inconsistent with an active use of it, or indeed a scientific approach. This is apparent in the story that is told of a group of Orthodox physicists at the end of the Second World War who used to say the Prayer while carrying out their research. We

[25] "The Prayer of Jesus," *Blackfriars* xxiii (1942): 76.

[26] A Monk of the Eastern Church, *On the Invocation of the Name of Jesus* (London: Fellowship of St Alban and St Sergius, 1949), 15–16.

can apply to all our dealings with God's creation this "key" to its fulfillment in Christ.

Divine logoi in creation and the offering of the world

When we talk about bringing created things to their fulfillment, we are talking about the *logoi* of those things—God's will in and for his creation, which directs our proper use of it. One of the first to explore what this doctrine might imply for our relationship with the rest of creation was the distinguished Romanian theologian Fr Dumitru Staniloae. Not coincidentally, Staniloae was both a leading Maximus scholar and one the great exponents of sacramental cosmology.[27]

A central theme for Staniloae, as we have seen earlier, is the world as God's *gift* to man. It is worth saying something more about this here, especially as the whole idea is open to misunderstanding—not least because the word "gift" can be heard in very different ways. Is a gift something that the giver does not want back, and the recipient is therefore free to do what he likes with? Or is it something essentially relational, a constant reminder of the giver? Even in our everyday experience, we would probably say that the latter predominates. The value we place on a gift—be it a child's scribbly drawing, or an expensive trinket from someone trying to ingratiate themselves—has everything to do with our attitude to the giver. We treat a gift carelessly only if on some level we want to snub the giver—like the prodigal son wasting his father's legacy. This *relational* quality may explain why the world can be called a *gift to man*, despite the fact that the world manifestly serves

[27]See especially his "The World as Gift and Sacrament of God's Love," and "The Foundation of Christian Responsibility in the World," p. 210.

the needs of all its other inhabitants as well. Other creatures can benefit from God's bounty, but so far as we know they cannot consciously discern the Giver himself.

For Staniloae, and Maximus before him, the world is a "gift" in that it creates a bond of love between us and the Giver. It is the means of a constant exchange of gifts between man and the Creator. "Every one of man's possessions and he himself becomes as sacrifice, in being offered by man to God, and accepted by him. Thereupon God offers it to man by whom it is received bearing a new blessing."[28] It is through this process that the whole world comes to be seen as "the visible part of a universal and continuing sacrament."[29] And because we offer it in thankfulness, it is also a Eucharist, a means of communion with God.

Accepting the world as "gift" involves practical uses, but it is not primarily a utilitarian idea. As long as we focus on "consuming" the world, the "giving" is all in one direction. God gives, we take: there is no exchange. "Exchange of gifts" between man and God requires us to be nourished, not only by the physical resources of the world, but by their inner rationale, the wisdom and meaning within them that speaks to us of their Creator. Once again, we are brought back to the fundamental notion of the *logoi* of created things. As God's *words* in creation, the *logoi* call for a *response* to God, manifested in *responsibility*—for our neighbor, and for all creation.

What does this response consist in? Since all the "gifts" of the world are God's in the first place, how are we to offer anything as "our" gift? Staniloae answers this in two ways. On the one hand,

[28] "World as Gift", 668.

[29] Ibid., 667.

we offer God his own gifts by *sacrifice*—by being prepared to surrender them for his sake.[30] We will return to this aspect shortly. On the other hand—and this is more problematic—we are to put the seal of our "understanding and intelligent work onto creation, thereby humanizing it and giving it, humanized, back to God."[31] The "gift" of the world is equally a "task"; it is a "talent" that we are to return with interest. Economy, civilization and art would be aspects of this "interest."

Why should the idea of "the world as task" be problematic? Certainly it is positive insofar as it sees human manipulation of the world as part of the great "exchange of gifts," rather than a way of distancing ourselves from the Giver. Thus the development of a new medicine, let us say, can be seen as a way for God to extend his healing grace to more of mankind—a gift of God's love, rather than the beneficence of a pharmaceutical company. The danger of this idea lies in the implication that offering up the world—and thus fulfilling our God-given role—*necessarily* involves manipulating, altering and "developing" everything we come across. Staniloae concedes, indeed, that human efforts have not always been to the good, either in intention or in their results. But today—much more than in the 1960s when Staniloae was writing—people are coming to realize the short-sightedness of attempting to turn everything into a "human product." We discover that what Staniloae calls "the endless possibilities of the God-given understanding of [God's] servants"[32] must include the ability to recognize when to leave well enough alone.

[30]Ibid., 668.

[31]Ibid., 669.

[32]Ibid.

Let us return now to the notion of sacrifice: what does it actually mean to apply this idea to our use of the world? We might see it primarily as an *attitude,* but it also has practical implications. Since God does not stand in need of his own creations, offering him a sacrifice will also mean that we use the world's goods, or forego use of them, for the sake of our neighbor: "as you did it to one of the least of these my brethren, you did it to me." (Mt 25.40). The *logos* or fundamental principle of "the world as gift" is that we in turn should use it as a gift—offering it back to God by offering it to our neighbor. This throws some light on Staniloae's strong emphasis on "development" of the world. When he uses expressions such as "exploiting the portion of earth entrusted to us for the benefit of all,"[33] the key phrase is "*for the benefit of all.*" Whether we serve our neighbor best by "developing" a portion of the earth or by preserving it in its natural state will depend on circumstances, and may on occasion be the subject of honest disagreement. But the fundamental point is that, whatever we decide to do with it, our decision is to reflect the Giver's love for mankind—not just selfish desires of our own.

It is likely that few today would want to speak of nature "crying out to be used in the service of certain ends which man chooses."[34] Too many such choices have turned out to be disastrous, including some made with the best of intentions. Staniloae's confidence in the desirability of human intervention is likely to strike us as naive and dated; but it is important to understand what he is and is not saying. The human "choices" for which nature "cries

[33]Ibid., 671.

[34]Staniloae, *Theology and the Church* (Crestwood, NY: St Vladimir's Seminary Press, 1980), 224.

out" are not arbitrary: we are to choose the *higher* ends, out of the various possibilities available to us. And certain ends are not judged to be "higher" simply on the basis of some human moral philosophy. "Higher ends" will indeed be related to the needs of our neighbor, but not that alone. They also have to do with the fundamental nature of the matter we are dealing with. We respond to God by our use of the world; but created things are *in themselves* "replies to the creative word of God, replies analogous to the divine words, concrete and subsistent images of the *logoi* of God." They are not only "words of God towards man" but also "replies which man should make his own in a conscious manner."[35] If we are to use created things for a proper purpose, our use must bear some relation to the "reply" already embodied in the creature in its natural state.

Here, too, there is an element of sacrifice. This is how it is described by Christos Yannaras, as he tries to explore what a priestly ethos might look like in practice: there needs to be a certain sacrifice of our individual preconceptions out of respect for the nature, the *logos* of the materials we are working with. He takes Byzantine architecture as an example:

> Like the ascetic in his direct encounter with his body, the architect encounters his material with the same freedom of humility and self-abnegation; and he studies the points of resistance and also the potentialities of nature. He looks for the inner principle, the "reason" in matter which was in abeyance before the Incarnation but is now dynamic.[36]

[35]"Christian Responsibility," 65–6.

[36]*Freedom*, 245.

And as a result, Yannaras says, "Each Byzantine building is a eucharistic event. There is a certain parallel with Archimandrite Vasileios' observation, noted earlier on, about man's 'dominion' over the rest of creation: this becomes a reality, he says, only when we become 'servants and slaves of creation.' "[37] First we must submit to God, sacrificing ourselves to his purposes. No ethos that takes seriously the notion of God's *logoi,* the expressions of his will in creation, can make man the final arbiter of how creation is to be used.

Several more recent writers have taken up the theme of sacrifice, recognizing its topical importance. Patriarch Bartholomew of Constantinople has rightly identified it as the "missing dimension" in making the connection between theory and practice when confronting environmental problems.[38] But before this can make sense, it is also necessary to recover the "missing dimension" of sacrifice itself: sacrifice is not about *giving up*, but about *giving*. Staniloae's discussion of sacrifice in the context of an exchange of gifts between God and man draws us back to the original meaning of the word: to *sacri-fice* is to make sacred or holy. The Patriarch develops precisely the same idea in more detail. Sacrifice is not loss, but gain; not death, but life; not diminution, but fulfillment.[39] This is the paradox of which the Church reminds us so incessantly that we hardly notice: the instrument of *blessing* is the *Cross*. "Behold, through the Cross has joy come to all the world."[40]

[37]*Ecology and Monasticism*, 20.

[38]"Sacrifice: The Missing Dimension," in John Chryssavgis, ed., *Cosmic Grace, Humble Prayer: The Ecological Vision of the Green Patriarch Bartholomew I* (Grand Rapids, MI and Cambridge: Eerdmans, 2003), 304–8.

[39]*Cosmic Grace*, 306.

[40]Hymn following the Gospel, Sunday Matins.

Divine logoi in creation: beyond "humanizing"

The idea of sacrifice is clearly very relevant to the way we use created things. And practical use of the world and its resources is an essential part of our life, and therefore of our role in the cosmic Eucharist. But if that role really is anything like "cosmic," then use and development can hardly be the only way in which we offer creation to God. Regardless of our views on the merits or drawbacks of "development," such an idea is simply inapplicable to well over 99.9% of the universe. I recall a seminar in which we were discussing humans' offering of the world, and a physics teacher in the audience raised his hand. "That's all very well," he said gruffly, "but how do I apply this to the Horsehead Nebula?" It was a valid point: when we talk about humans in relation to "the creation," we often effectively ignore the unimaginably vast scale of the universe. In order to be taken seriously, any claims about man's cosmic purpose have to pass the Horsehead Nebula test.

The problems with "use" language apply also to that of "humanizing," employed by Staniloae and some others. If one is thinking in terms of the earth (and perhaps other parts of the solar system), "humanizing" sounds disturbing enough. The intended meaning, no doubt, is that we somehow conform other creatures to the divine image in which we ourselves were created. The way it is often heard, however, suggests that other creatures are to be absorbed in a specifically human identity: it conjures up a landscape of topiary and golf courses, of blue carnations, designer pets, and "pharm" animals genetically modified to produce the nutrients humans need. Applied to the creation as a whole, however, "humanizing" simply sounds absurd. The image of "offering up" the world means that *in some sense* we "take it in our hands": but in what sense? We need to find an interpretation that makes sense in terms both of ecology and of scientific cosmology.

More recent theologians have built on Fathers such as Maximus and modern theologians such as Staniloae to achieve such an interpretation. First of all, this involves revisiting the old idea that "the world exists for man." In its crude form—implying that nothing has value in itself—this idea is simply untenable. But there is another way of understanding it, one that is not dismissed so easily. In one of the most intriguing recent developments of Maximus' thought, it has been pointed out that the idea of the "logoi of things" combined with that of man as "cosmic unifier" is closely related to some variants of the anthropic principle.[41] The Christian view, however, is actually much less anthropocentric than the anthropic principle. According to physicist and theologian Alexei Nesteruk, "humanity is not just a purpose of creation" [cf. the "strong anthropic principle"]; "it can be understood only in the context of the promise of God for its salvation . . . as the mediating agency that is supposed to bring the whole universe through its knowledge to the new creation."[42] What this means, however, is that we cannot simply assert that the world exists for man's sake: there is equally a sense in which man exists for the sake of the world. The world can be said to serve man, to exist for

[41]cf. Andrew Louth, "The Cosmic Vision of Saint Maximus the Confessor," in Philip Clayton and Arthur Peacocke, eds., *In Whom We Live and Move and Have our Being: Panentheistic Reflections on God's Presence in a Scientific World* (Grand Rapids, MI and Cambridge: Eerdmans, 2004), 185, 194–5.

[42]*Light from the East: Theology, Science and the Eastern Orthodox Tradition* (Minneapolis, MN: Fortress Press, 2003), 230.

him—but for him to do what? The world—both this earth and the conditions in the universe on which it depends—enables man to serve the Creator's purposes for the entire creation. And that does not and cannot involve "humanizing" it in the sense that a house, a garden, a domestic animal is "humanized" nature. Rather, it involves *making it what it is*—fulfilling its own reality.

And what is that reality? Prior to man and his work in the universe, *the universe exists.* That might seem an obvious and unhelpful statement. But to exist at all is to have a connection with "him who is," the Word through whom all things were made. There is thus a continuity between the "natural" state of creation and its ultimate goal, when "Christ is all in all." It is not a matter of stamping other creatures with the mark of our own species, but of bringing them into our conscious relationship with God. Nesteruk talks about this process in language that seems initially opaque, but is ultimately less misleading. Humans have a mode of existence that is *hypostatic*: they have a concrete personal existence involving a sense of self and of otherness, and are thus able to relate to each other, to God, and to the rest of creation. This capacity to relate enables us to *relate creation to God.* In this way, we bring the rest of creation into the hypostatic mode of existence that has been bestowed on humans. In order to do this, we do not need to shape things or even to have direct contact with them: we "take them up" through our awareness and understanding of them. We are able to lead things to the existence for which they were created through our capacity to hold together the intelligible universe with the visible, to understand its meaning and to apprehend it "in its connection and unity with the primordial ground of the Logos."[43]

[43]Nesteruk, "The Universe as Hypostatic Inherence in the Logos of God," in Clayton and Peacocke, *In Whom We Live,* 174–5.

Non-human creation and its Creator

It is to the universe beyond humans that we now turn. There has been increased interest in recent years with the way in which non-human creation might relate to its Creator; and it is no coincidence that this too has gone hand in hand with the rediscovery of the doctrine of the divine "words" in creation. The *logoi* are principles of *connection*: they point us to *dia-logue* both with the Creator and with his purpose for all the creations with which we share the world. Formal theological statements tend to focus on the role of humans in this divine purpose—and this could well be seen as a matter, quite properly, of minding our own business. Yet in many important spiritual writers, there is the persistent conviction that all of matter has a connection with its Creator in ways that we can only occasionally glimpse. Metropolitan Anthony of Sourozh often spoke eloquently on this subject:

> there is not an atom in this world, from the meanest speck of dust to the greatest star, which does not hold in its core . . . the thrill . . . of its coming into being, of its possessing infinite possibilities and of entering into the divine realm, so that it knows God, rejoices in Him.[44]

We can therefore speak of a sense in which matter relates to God directly, apart from man, as the Metropolitan contends elsewhere:

> Matter [is] free to commune with God . . . because it is sinless, it is not fallen; it has become a victim of the Fall. St Theodore of Studion in one of his *Catecheses* says that the

[44]"Body and Matter," 41.

> created world, as we know it now . . . is like a good horse ridden by a drunken rider. We are the drunken rider.[45]

Many Orthodox writers would avoid such bold assertions of direct relationship between matter and its Creator. Perhaps they are wary of the heavily metaphorical language involved in speaking of "relationship" or "knowledge of God" on the part of most if not all animals, let alone the vegetable and mineral worlds. There is broad agreement, however, on an important point: the significance of miracles. Miraculous events, especially those in which the very elements obey Christ or his saints, alert us to the fact that there is more to "inanimate" creation than meets the eye. Miracles are privileged moments that allow us a glimpse through the veil of what we think of as the natural order, to what Staniloae calls "a more fundamental order that sustains the world and towards which the latter is called."[46] And what we see is what Metropolitan Anthony calls "the *normal* relationship between God and His world"; this is the order in which "things are freed from the enslavement which we have imposed on them." Miracles are not instances of nature being overpowered; rather, they can be seen as acts of "harmony" or "friendship" on the part of nature, as it hears the voice of its Lord and obeys with joy.

The same sense of a world in relationship with God's love comes across in some of the retreat addresses of Fr Lev Gillet. His emphasis is on God's side of the relationship, on the divine love which embraces every creature: it is not simply a love for us humans, manifested in the provision of good things. "Each of us and indeed

[45]Ibid., 40.

[46]*The Experience of God: Orthodox Dogmatic Theology*, vol. 2 (Brookline, MA: Holy Cross Orthodox Press, 2000), 62.

every creature, even each microscopic grain of sand, is loved by God in a divine and overwhelming manner."[47] All creatures, he says, epitomize both the evolution of the world towards the "total Christ," and "love giving Itself to us." This is why we can learn to "recognize in every creature a spring of divine love fitting to itself alone"—which is surely another way of speaking of the *logos* of that thing. This enables Fr Lev to talk about "integrating our spiritual lives with the life of the universe"—not in some pantheistic sense of dissolving into the rest of creation, but in the recognition that the Life of the universe is the One in whom we too "live and move and have our being." There is a sense, therefore, in which God's relationship with other creatures *is* our business—it is one of the foremost ways in which we come to know him and discern his will.

Animals and their Creator

How does animal creation fit into this picture? As we have seen earlier, the lives of holy people give us plenty of clues; but still, this is not a theme that many Orthodox Christians have addressed directly.

We may find some pointers in a pair of articles on the subject, by the Russian philosopher Tatiana Goricheva and the French theologian Olivier Clément.[48] Clément points out the great suffering in the animal world, and sees this as a vivid instance of the suffering of creation as a result of the fall. And he goes further; insofar as the animal sacrifices in the Old Testament are symbols

[47]*The Burning Bush* (Springfield, IL: Templegate, 1976), 35.

[48]"Les animaux dans la pensée orthodoxe," *Contacts* 145 (1989/1): 24–44.

of the sacrifice of Christ, does this not imply, he wonders, some mysterious participation in that sacrifice?

Both these writers have a sense that the relationship between animals and their Creator is a mystery to us; but both find clues in Scripture and the experience of the Church. Clément sees Adam's naming of the animals as an act of relationship, an act of bringing them into communion with God through man's mediation; Goricheva actually speaks of it as an act of raising them to some kind of personal existence. As an instance of this "personal" quality, she refers to incidents in the lives of the early martyrs, where the bodies of animals who refused to harm the saints, and were killed as a result, were themselves found to be incorrupt. Clément, too, suggests that animals may have a rudimentary "personhood." It is easier to envisage what this might mean with dogs and cats, or horses, or dolphins, than with, say, caterpillars or corals; but an important point is being made here. Most people now recognize how much we have in common with other living creatures in our biological existence; perhaps we should be open to the possibility that the commonalities carry over into the mystery of our personal existence. Animals, Clément suggests, can perhaps be seen as "an image of the image"—or, in Palamas' phraseology, an "energy" that finds its "essence" in man. Certainly, the two references in the Old Testament to covenants that include the animals would seem to imply that the latter are in some respect free agents. The passages in question are the covenant with Noah and the animals in Gen 9.8–10, and the eschatological prophesy of Hosea 2.18 ("I will make for you a covenant on that day with the beasts of the field, the birds of the air, and the creeping things of the ground"), which Clément regards as looking forward to the transfiguration of all things in Christ.

The thoughts expressed by Goricheva and Clément are undoubtedly speculative—they are not intended to be an authoritative statement of the Church's doctrine. But at the same time, they deserve to be taken seriously. Particularly since—as Goricheva is bold enough and blunt enough to point out—treatment of animals is an area where there is a disturbing gulf between the implications of our theology and tradition, and the attitudes and behavior typical of Orthodox societies.

In contrast to Goricheva and Clément's openness to the mysteries of animal nature, there are other Orthodox theologians who are very concerned to draw a sharp distinction between personhood, on the one hand, and the relationships, individuality and consciousness to be found in animals, on the other. Arguments of this sort tend to be vehement but somewhat circular, however; and they frequently show little interest in what is actually known about animal behavior. This is certainly not to deny that the differences between humans and animals are real. But perhaps the message to take away is this: humans do have a capacity for conscious relationship—above all, relationship with God—beyond that of other earthly creatures; but there is no need to underestimate the animal world in order to maintain this difference.

The sacred in creation and the challenge of paganism

There are differing ways, then, of talking about the connection between Creator and creation; and this is especially true when we are talking about the sense in which creation responds. Yet Orthodox generally agree that we live in a world which, with all its imperfections, is nonetheless shot through with divine presence. Everything reverberates with God's word.

There is a great hunger today for such a vision of the world. It is a vision that the human spirit seems to perceive intuitively; but people are at a loss for how to express it in a "reality" reduced to physical forces, genes, and economics. Hence the upsurge of interest in various forms of paganism and nature religion. To many people concerned about the state of the earth, this trend appears to be a great step forward towards a spirituality that restores the earth to its rightful place of honor. Obviously, Christians would hardly agree. But many Orthodox Christians would be struck less by the obvious errors of neo-paganism, than by the seeds of truth in it—truths deeply embedded in the Christian tradition, but long obscured, particularly in Western perceptions of Christianity. Again, Maximus' vision of creation in which "God is everything" seems to present an apt Christian response to the yearning for a sacred earth.

There is of course a crucial difference between the Christian vision and the pagan. In the Christian understanding, nature can never be sacred in and of itself, but only *because of its relation to the Creator.* And correspondingly, our reverence for nature can never stop there: it is a movement *through the creation to the Creator*, to use the title of a presentation by Metropolitan Kallistos.[49] The Metropolitan speaks unequivocally of "nature as sacred" and the world as "a sacrament of divine presence, a means of communion with God"; "the environment consists not in dead matter, but in a living relationship." Echoing Maximus, he speaks of the entire cosmos as a vast burning bush, permeated by the fire of the divine power and glory.[50] It is a world suffused with the divine,

[49]*Through the Creation to the Creator* (London: Friends of the Centre, 1996).

[50]Ibid., 9.

but not a world that *is* divine in its own nature. Bishop Kallistos goes to the heart of the difference when he contrasts a modern mystical vision of trees as somehow "alive" with Moses' vision of the Burning Bush: in the latter case, we see the created world as "the locus of an *interpersonal* encounter." As he emphasizes later on, the world acquires its true meaning only "when seen as the reflection of a reality that transcends it." And the world reveals to us, not a spiritual something, but a Someone—what Christos Yannaras characteristically calls "the personal otherness of the creative energy of its Maker."[51]

This in turn affects the way the natural world functions in our spiritual life. Our goal cannot be to become one with the universe by being dissolved into it, but to recognize its transparency. As Patriarch Ignatius of Antioch has said, the world can indeed be seen as a theophany; but this is a theophany "not with a view to some impersonal fusion . . . but with a view to personal communion."[52]

The widespread fascination with nature religions means that people often hail non-Christian indigenous religions as paragons of harmony with nature and respect for the earth, replete with a wisdom that Christianity lacks. This claim obscures the fact that pre-modern and pre-industrial societies in general showed a care and reverence for nature that the modern world has lost—this was no less true of traditional Christian societies, such as an isolated

[51]"Existential versus Regulative Approaches to the Problem of the Environment. The Environmental Issue: an Existential not a Canonical Problem," Sarah Hobson and Jane Lubchenco, eds., *Revelation and the Environment: AD 95–1995* (Singapore-New Jersey-London-Hong Kong: World Scientific, 1997), 79.

[52]"Three Sermons: A Theology of Creation; A Spirituality of the Creation; The Responsibility of Christians," *Sourozh* 38 (Nov 1989), 7.

Greek village a generation ago. But leaving that aside, a robust challenge to the idea of contrasting earth-friendly native religions with Christianity has come from Fr Michael Oleksa, who has served among the native peoples in Alaska for most of his ministry. He explores the striking congruence between the Christian understanding of divine immanence in creation and aspects of the "pre-modern world view" exemplified in Alaskan traditional beliefs; and he shows how such beliefs often could be, and were, taken up by the Russian missionaries: "They could affirm that the spiritual realities those societies worshipped were indeed *logoi*, related to the divine *Logos*, whose personal existence these societies had simply never imagined."[53] But he further points out—and this is important for us—that "there are some insights which pre-modern societies that have become Orthodox automatically understand better than we do." One such insight is the cosmic significance of our worship, offered for the whole world in recognition of "the cosmos as . . . God's icon, God's self-portrait, God's revelation to us."[54] Emphasizing the grounding of such insights in the Christian tradition, he recalls the cosmic vision of the Word in whom "all things hold together and subsist," (cf. Col 1.17) and the notion, in St Maximus, of the Word "embodied" in nature—a preparation for his incarnate coming parallel to his "embodiment" in Scripture. Oleksa also quotes words of the twentieth-century Serbian confessor St Nicolai Velimirovic testifying to the "theophanic" character of all creation:

> Theology means the word of God. Theology is all or nothing. The whole of nature is therefore theology. If the whole

[53]*Orthodox Alaska* 61

[54]"Confluence," 21.

> of nature is not theology, then theology is nothing or nature is nothing. If the whole of nature does not speak about God, who will believe Isaiah or St Paul . . . ? "Show us God," say many of our contemporaries, "and we will believe." But how? Do not these people who despise miracles demand a greater miracle? We must say to them: *Show us what is not God!*"[55]

We might well conclude that a vision of nature suffused with the sacred, far from being the preserve of nature religions, was as vividly present in the rural Serbia of St Nicolai's youth, as it is in native Alaskan cultures, including those that have embraced Orthodoxy.

God in creation and the world of science

The question of how God is active in his world is a very old one. But it becomes all the more acute today, when so much is known about the way in which physical causality operates in the universe. To express the Christian understanding of divine presence in creation, a number of contemporary theologians use the term panentheism: the belief that God is not to be identified with creation, and yet creation is in some sense *in* God, and he in it. The word "panentheism" was coined by the German idealist philosopher Friedrich Schelling, whose vision of the unity of all things struck such a chord with Russian thinkers of the nineteenth century—and led them to see their own tradition with new eyes. Confusingly, "panentheism" is used in several different senses; but it has been adopted by a number of contemporary Orthodox in two senses. It serves to indicate both that the divine energy is

[55]Ibid., 39.

in all things by virtue of their creation ("ontological panentheism"—God is fundamental to the *being* of all things), and that God is to be all in all ("eschatological panentheism"—God is the *ultimate goal* of all things).

"Panentheism" is not a traditional term. But it captures well the cosmological vision of Maximus and Palamas, as well as the sacramental cosmology explored by Schmemann and others.

Why does any of this matter? There are at least two reasons why it is more than an academic theological discussion. First, it firmly establishes a genuinely Christian sense in which creation is sacred, because it is imbued with God, and therefore is to be treated with reverence. People cannot fall back on the excuse that care for the earth and its creatures is a slippery slope towards paganism. Second—but no less important—there is a striking convergence between a "panentheist" vision of God active in the world, through his *logoi* and energies, and a scientific perspective on the capacities of matter. The Orthodox physicist and theologian Christopher Knight quotes Vladimir Lossky's statement that "the world, created in order that it might be deified, is dynamic, tending always to its final end," and observes that "this concept of an intrinsically 'dynamic' universe immediately has a strong resonance for those who acknowledge the validity of the modern scientific perception of the universe's evolutionary development. It represents, in fact, another facet of the sacramental view of matter."[56]

Such lines of thinking answer the urgent need to understand and articulate a Christian understanding of the world in a way that

[56]Christopher C. Knight, "Theistic Naturalism and the Word Made Flesh: Complementary Approaches to the Debate on Panentheism," in Clayton and Peacocke (eds.), *In Whom We Live*, 58.

takes account of scientific, empirical observation. Metropolitan John Zizioulas emphasizes that we Christians need to express our understanding of creation "in a way that will not involve logical contradictions or stumble over fundamental scientific facts, which would exclude theology from normal scientific and philosophical discourse."[57] It is all too easy for theology simply to slip into its own esoteric language, and to talk as if our knowledge of the universe had not expanded since the fifteenth century—but it is all too unhelpful in our witness to the world.

An interesting example of the parallels between a traditional theological world view and a modern scientific understanding is presented by Bishop Basil (Osborne) of Amphipolis, in an address to the symposium "The Black Sea in Crisis," which was held in 1997, under the aegis of the Patriarchate of Constantinople.[58] In this paper, he starts by talking about the nature of creation according to Dionysius the Areopagite, focusing on Dionysius' teaching about the hierarchies in creation, where each "level" mediates to the order immediately below it a part of what it has received from God. As we go down the hierarchy, each successive order only partially comprehends the order above it. Bishop Basil goes on to draw a remarkable parallel between this picture of the world, of reality as a whole, and that presented by the British physicist David Bohm,[59] in his attempt to provide an ontological interpretation of quantum theory. It is usually assumed that quantum

[57]"Preserving," Part II: 39.

[58]"Beauty in the Divine and in Nature," *Sourozh* 70 (November 1997): 28–37.

[59]See D. Bohm and B.J. Hiley, *The Undivided Universe:An Ontological Interpretation of Quantum Theory* (London and New York, NY: Routledge, 1993).

theory has to do only with *our knowledge of* reality, and not with the actual nature of things. But the result of Bohm's thinking is an image of the universe as a sort of hologram, in which each region—each level of complexity—makes possible an image of the whole. The whole universe is "enfolded" in each region—in rather the same way as when we look at a scene, and the order and details of everything there is "enfolded" in a space small enough to pass through the pupil of our eye. But behind each level, there is another level of greater subtlety. Each level or order expresses fully all that is in the order below it, and also something more. The similarity between the two visions of reality, that of Dionysius and that of Bohm, is clearly very striking.

From this, Bishop Basil draws two conclusions. Firstly, he notes that Dionysius was able to speak about the actual world around us in a language that was common to all educated people of his time and culture—however abstruse and philosophical it may seem to us today. And secondly, he points out that the understanding of the world that he has outlined gives a renewed and very concrete expression to the ancient notion of man as microcosm. Whether we call man a microcosm or a hologram, the meaning is much the same: we are saying that there is a sense in which the existence of all other creatures is "enfolded" in the deepest levels of our own being. And this means that in conforming ourselves to the will of God, which is known to us at least in part through the world, we are conforming ourselves to the deep structure of our own nature.

If we accept a connection between God's will as expressed in nature and God's will for us, this has important practical consequences. We may start to ask, for instance, what insights we might be able to draw from environmental science. As people have become aware of various aspects of environmental damage and started exploring causes and possible remedies, they discover hitherto unsuspected complexities in the web of life and the ways in which all creatures affect each other. If this conveys something of God's will for his creation, the message would seem to be one of interdependence: the activity, the well-being, or the malaise of each creature has an affect on all the rest.

If we consider what this pattern might look like reflected in our own lives, we discover that environmental science meets St Maximus. Discussing the analogy between the composition of the human being and that of the cosmos, Maximus speaks of the *particularity,* the individuality of each entity not being allowed to become a force for dissension and division. The theology of St Maximus, so fruitful for contemporary Orthodox theology of creation, points us towards a "loving affinity" that unites all things, grounded in the Creator's "invisible and unknown presence in all things," a presence that is at once single and manifested in a diversity of ways according to the variety of creatures. In a phrase that could be a road-map for our way out of successive environmental crises, he reveals that "all things belong to each other rather than to themselves."[60]

Orthodox theology and its witness

Orthodox voices have not been absent from the broader discussion about the spiritual and ethical implications of the environmental crisis. But the theologians discussed above are not the only such voices, and perhaps not even the most widely known. There

[60]See *Mystagogy* 7.

has been considerable interest in recent years, not least on the part of feminist theologians, in the theme of wisdom in creation developed most fully by Fr Sergei Bulgakov.[61] We may note, for instance, the chapters devoted to Bulgakov as representative of "ecological spirituality" in an insightful recent book on environmental ethics.[62] The attention to Bulgakov may reflect a hunger for theological and philosophical thinking that engages with the way we actually live in the world; it is significant that he combines creation mysticism with a concern for the implications of human work reflecting his original training in economics.[63]

Similar in some ways to Bulgakov's approach, the writings of Philip Sherrard have struck a chord with a wide circle of people, stretching beyond the Orthodox Church and indeed Christianity, who see the environmental crisis as symptomatic of a spiritual crisis. Sherrard affirms in the most emphatic terms the presence of God in his creation, the sacredness and sacramentality of the entire visible universe; and he no less passionately denounces the technological mentality, which he sees as a "rape of man and nature," to use the deliberately shocking title of one of his books. But as Metropolitan Kallistos remarks in a retrospective lecture, if Sherrard's work has changed people's lives, "that is above all because he himself lived what he taught."[64] His sense of the sacred

[61]See further Chryssavgis, *Beyond the Shattered Image*, 139–164.

[62]Willis Jenkins, *Ecologies of Grace: Environmental Ethics and Christian Theology* (Oxford: Oxford University Press, 2008), esp. 201–225.

[63]Most notably in his *Philosophy of Economy: The World as Household*, Catherine Evtuhov, trans., (New Haven; CT: Yale University Press, 2000).

[64]Kallistos Ware, Metropolitan of Diokleia, *Philip Sherrard: A Prophet for Our Time* [The first Annual Sherrard Lecture] (Friends of Mouth Athos, 2008), 24.

came from living in the land: whether the footpaths of Mount Athos, of which he was an articulate defender when they were first being displaced by roads, or the Greek countryside where he lived much of his life. And his life and work, especially perhaps his writing on Greek literature, testify to "a vision of the organic wholeness of life"[65] in Orthodox culture at its best—a treasure fast being lost, but greatly needed by a world groping towards a sustainable and fulfilling way of life.

The richness of Orthodox theology of creation, and its potential for giving a sense of spiritual direction at a time of environmental crisis, have become much more widely recognized in recent years. An important contributor to this process has been Patriarch Bartholomew of Constantinople, who has continued the work of his predecessor in giving high priority to environmental issues as a challenge for Christians today. Much of his writing and speaking on the subject is addressed to secular audiences, and therefore focuses more on practical exhortation than development of theological themes. But some people who might otherwise regard Orthodoxy as of merely archaeological interest are intrigued by "the Green Patriarch" and decide to explore further. Perhaps the Patriarch's most significant contribution is his unwavering insistence that the environment is a matter of *pastoral* concern. He takes seriously the role of a church leader to champion the weak and suffering, those who have no voice, whether they are victims of war and violence, poverty or environmental degradation: environmental concern is inseparable from love of neighbor. Often in a very different idiom, his witness draws us back to the core of

[65]Sherrard, *The Wound of Greece: Studies in Neo-Hellenism* (London/Athens: Rex Collings/Anglo-Hellenic, 1978), 73; quoted in Kallistos, *Prophet for Our Time,* 10.

theology that we have seen expressed so eloquently in Maximus: the "loving affinity" that defies human divisions, uniting us in love not only with all creation but also—much more demanding—with our fellow human beings.

Further reading:

Allchin, A.M., ed. *Sacrament and Image.* London: Fellowship of St Alban and St Sergius, second ed. 1987. Includes articles by Metropolitan Anthony Bloom, Bishop Kallistos Ware, Philip Sherrard.

Basil [Osborne] of Amphipolis, Bishop. *The Healing Word.* London: Darton, Longman and Todd, 2008.

Chryssavgis, John, ed. *Cosmic Grace, Humble Prayer: The Ecological Vision of the Green Patriarch Bartholomew I.* Grand Rapids, MI and Cambridge: Eerdmans, 2003.

Clayton, Philip and Arthur Peacocke, eds. *In Whom We Live and Move and Have our Being: Panentheistic Reflections on God's Presence in a Scientific World.* Grand Rapids, MI and Cambridge: Eerdmans, 2004. Includes chapters by Christopher C. Knight, Andrew Louth, Alexei Nesteruk, and Bishop Kallistos Ware.

Ignatius, Patriarch of Antioch. "Three Sermons: A Theology of Creation; A Spirituality of the Creation; The Responsibility of Christians." *Sourozh* 38 (Nov 1989) 1–14.

Knight, Christopher C., *The God of Nature,* Minneapolis, MN: Fortress Press, 2007.

A Monk of the Eastern Church (Archimandrite Lev Gillet). *The Jesus Prayer.* Crestwood, NY: St Vladimir's Seminary Press, revised ed. 1987; esp. chapters V ("The Way of a Pilgrim and The Jesus Prayer in Our Age") and VI ("On the Practical Uses of The Jesus Prayer").

Nesteruk, Alexei. *Light from the East: Theology, Science and the Eastern Orthodox Tradition.* Minneapolis, MN: Fortress Press, 2003.

Staniloae, Dumitru. *The Experience of God: Orthodox Dogmatic Theology* Vol. 2. Brookline, MA: Holy Cross Orthodox Press, 2000.

Ware, Bishop Kallistos of Diokleia. *Through the Creation to the Creator.* London: Friends of the Centre, 1996.

Zizioulas, Metropolitan John of Pergamon. "Man the Priest of Creation." A. Walker and C. Carras, eds. *Living Orthodoxy in the Modern World.* London: SPCK, 1996: 178–188.

Zizioulas, Metropolitan John of Pergamon. "Proprietors or Priests of Creation?" Keynote address, Baltic Symposium, June 2003. ‹http://www.rsesymposia.org/themedia/File/1151679350-Pergamon.pdf›

in conclusion

Living in God's Creation

We have looked at some of the riches of the Orthodox tradition, some of the many aspects of the Church's ecological vision. And this brings us to crucial questions: what does this mean for the way we live our lives? How are we to bear witness to this vision? And, finally, what difference will it make? We will suggest some answers from three angles: the Orthodox ethos, our approach to environmental issues, and the images we use for our place in creation.

But first, a note of caution. Sadly, it has to be said that the practical application of theology is an area where we Orthodox often fall down. There is a temptation to say, "Look, it's all in the Fathers" (or the liturgical texts, or sacramental life . . .) and then sit back as if the problem were solved. Yet for all the richness of our theology of creation, Orthodox countries are hardly distinguished for environmental protection, or for widespread resistance to environmentally destructive elements of the modern lifestyle. And Orthodox communities in the West largely reflect the environmental attitudes of the surrounding culture. Especially where Orthodox communities have been formed largely by upwardly mobile immigrants, there seems little appetite for rejecting the conspicuous consumption and wastefulness that society at large regards as signs of success.

Of course, there are many individual exceptions to this gloomy generalization. Particularly striking on this score are the monasteries, so many of which provide an example of environmentally sensitive living, of a love that spills out to embrace all humans and all creatures. Monks and nuns often seem to grasp swiftly and intuitively the environmental implications of Orthodox theology. But since we vigorously deny the idea of a two-tiered Christianity, with monastics set above those "in the world"—why should monasteries be the only place where the Christian life is lived out consistently?

There is no place, then, for complacency. Yet we should never underestimate the power of the Church's tradition to transform our vision in life-changing ways. I received a vivid reminder of this as I was working on the foregoing chapters, and had given a draft to a kind friend who had agreed to read it over.

> On the final morning of our vacation [as she later wrote to me], "I sat reading about how all creation praises the Lord at midnight. When the rest of my family sleepily drifted out of their beds like morning mist, my husband shepherded us all out to the beach to see the sun rise over the ocean. It was seven o'clock in the morning, but I was awed to have a perfect example of the worship of God by his creation immediately before me. I became aware of the chorus of morning bird calls, the graceful procession of the dolphins, and the changing play of light and pale stained glass colors on the sea and sky. Alone on the dock with my family, the only human representation of creation in attendance, I wished to take part in the celebration."[1]

[1]Private letter from Christine Bulko.

This contemporary response to an ancient church text illustrates well the starting point for Orthodox environmental responsibility: not a set of ethical imperatives, but an ethos of "taking part in the celebration." The vision of creation expressed in Orthodox theology should translate into a way of living that is liturgical, eucharistic and ascetic. Our actions and work are to glorify God as part of a *cosmic liturgy*, a world in which every creature glorifies its Creator in its own way. Our use of the world is to be an *offering of thanks* to its Creator, recognizing that everything we have the use of is his; it is by his mercy that it is available for our needs and the needs of others. And we are to handle the good things of the earth with *ascetic detachment*, not making them idols to which we are enslaved. An ascetic ethos is one that celebrates our freedom from the domination of "must-haves."

A eucharistic and ascetic ethos is also one of *sacrifice*—in the fullest sense of the word. It is to recall that the root meaning of "sacrifice" is not "go without" but "make sacred." "Sacrifice" and "pollution" are both originally religious notions; and, in a sense, they can be seen as opposites. We *pollute* the world in the fundamental, spiritual sense of the term when we make it an idol, the object of our own appetites—when we deny its connection with its Creator. There is an uncanny parable in the fact that this so often leads to physical pollution, as commodities are mined, energy is generated, and waste piles up in the service of those appetites. To approach natural resources with an ethos of sacrifice does not mean refraining from using them at all, but loosening our grasp. We *make them sacred* by recognizing them as God's gifts; we offer them back to him in using with gratitude what we need, but also in sharing his bounty with our neighbor and with other creatures. This too is a way of taking part in the cosmic celebration of God's creation.

How does this translate into an approach to environmental issues? First of all, we must recognize that the Church engages with contemporary issues in a very different way from any secular organization. Its concern is not with transforming structures, but with transforming human beings. The familiar motto "think globally, act locally" is for the Orthodox Christian at once too broad and too narrow. We are called to think not just globally, but *cosmically;* and to act not just locally, but *personally*. Think cosmically—be aware that our ultimate task is not to improve the world, but to transform all creation. And act personally: recognize that I am the Adam who wants to take the world as his food, to use it apart from its Creator. To see the roots of the alienation from God that is played out in abuse of his creation, I need look no further than my own heart.

We "act personally" on many levels, often simultaneously. Acting personally means working on my inner self, wrestling with the greed, selfishness, laziness, and so forth, that distort my relationship with Creator and creation alike. This is the process of *metanoia*—"change of mind," repentance—which Orthodox homilies so often invoke, and without which we cannot assume our cosmic task. And, paradoxical though this may seem, this act of turning inward to work on oneself is also the bedrock of any social and structural change. A person whose goal is freedom from passions is ready to relinquish his or her own privileges so as to serve the needs of others.

Acting personally also embraces "acting locally"—those practical works, whether on an individual level or that of the local Church, that manifest love in action. So a household, parish or diocese may feel called to work on energy efficiency, recycling, or organic gardening, just as it may feel called to reach out to the homeless and hungry. Acts of environmental responsibility are less direct than traditional acts of compassion, but no less real. In a globalized world, restricting works of mercy to the beggar at my door simply shows a myopic lack of imagination.

For the non-monastic Christian living "in the world," acting personally also involves the way we use whatever influence we may have in society. Public service, business decisions, work with charitable organizations, and indeed voting, are all ways in which we have influence and affect people's lives beyond our own immediate circle; and we have a choice how to use that influence. Will it be only to serve our own narrow interests? Or will it be to serve the well-being of other people and other creatures? Again, the answer depends in large part on how seriously we are working on ourselves.

We are "acting personally" also when we make decisions for our own lives that have much wider ramifications. This provides a way to approach one major environmental issue that Orthodox often sidestep, that of the world's rapidly growing human population. There are various possible reasons for the reluctance to face this issue. One seems to be a perception that acknowledging human numbers as a problem somehow denies the value of each human being in the eyes of God, but there seems to be a confusion here between the *intrinsic* value of the person and the *emergent* properties of the population in aggregate. If we have 500 people in a church restricted by fire regulations to a maximum of 300, this does not mean that we would wish that any given individual were not in church – but we have a problem nonetheless. Then there is also a deep-seated feeling among many pious Orthodox that the number of children one is to have should be entirely in the hands of God. Yet many other Orthodox, especially in the West, see no objection to married couples using artificial contraception to limit the size of their family. For Orthodox in America, the issue is further complicated because concern over population levels is linked in the minds of some with condoning abortion. It is quite true that many secular environmentalists support abortion as a means of birth control—because they come out of a society in which many people regard abortion as an acceptable option, regardless of whether they have any interest in the environment. But there is nothing to stop us accepting that world population growth is a problem, while insisting that certain ways of addressing it are morally unacceptable in principle. (In fact, people do this all the time, explicitly or implicitly: that is why no one suggests reducing population by banning the treatment of childhood diseases or reintroducing execution for minor offenses.)

Most Orthodox would recognize that the size of one's family does involve personal decisions, as well as an acceptance that God may have plans different from one's own. Much depends on the motives underlying our decisions. A desire to have no children, or few, may be a manifestation of selfishness, materialism or unwillingness to make a commitment to another person; and it is understandable that Christians should consider such motives unworthy. But a desire to *have* children may equally be a selfish one: and since when has the Christian tradition regarded the natural bonds of family as the ultimate form of love? Might not a couple decide to limit the size of their family out of a more all-embracing love—a concern for those other children, born and yet to be born, for whom the earth's resources are steadily being depleted? As the marriage service itself suggests, family life is intended to be not inward-looking but outward-looking;[2] and with new challenges now facing the human race, we may need to add new ways of manifesting this quality.

[2]See p. 202.

Always underlying our life in God's creation will be our image of ourselves, of how we fit into the whole. Images have power: they guide our behavior in ways that elude our consciousness. To be helpful and not a hindrance, however, an image does not only need to make theological sense; it must also be true to the physical realities of the world.

All Orthodox agree that the human role is unique, and vitally important to God's purposes for his creation. They also agree that this imposes on us an awesome responsibility to care for the world, and not to use it simply to satisfy our selfish desires. That said, however, there are striking differences of emphasis. As we have seen, there is much in church tradition and in contemporary Orthodox thought that emphasizes divine presence in creation and stresses the unity of man and the world. On the other hand, agreed statements and official pronouncements—a genre not known for being adventurous—are often given to more anthropocentric language. We are told that man is clearly distinguished from nature; humanity is superior to the rest of creation, which exists for man's sake and not *vice versa*. This is precisely the sort of language that many environmentalists point to, too hastily perhaps, as the root of human arrogance and abuse of nature. Many of the pronouncements of Ecumenical Patriarch Bartholomew contain prime examples of this language: but on the other hand, they also amply demonstrate that "anthropocentricity" of this sort has nothing in common with the idea that only humans count, that we have a right to tailor the world to our own convenience. In fact, patriarchal pronouncements repeatedly emphasize that true concern for the well-being of our fellow humans necessarily leads to concern for their environment.

The aim of such "anthropocentric" language—and it is a laudable one—is to affirm the infinite value of the human being: the person is not a means to an end, nor the accidental result of an impersonal cosmic process. He is not "just another animal," a pestilential species busy sowing the seeds of its own well-deserved extinction. But we might wonder: is it necessary or helpful to make this point by stressing a distinction between man and his environment, which, on a physical level, looks increasingly artificial? All today's environmental problems, from the build-up of toxins in our bodies, to the unintended consequences of our attempts to control nature, improve the land, or vanquish disease, seem to point in the other direction. In our physical being, we are part of an ecosystem: what we do affects every other creature, and *vice versa*. The point here is not to put human life on a par with that of an earthworm: rather, it is to underline that human "superiority" over earthworms is of limited relevance. On the small scale, it does indeed mean that the human can plough a field even though some worms will die as a result. But on the larger scale, one cannot ensure the well-being of humans without securing that of earthworms too.

There are resources within the Orthodox tradition for making sense of such an interconnected world. We may turn, for instance, to the popular image of man as priest of creation. Sometimes this image is used to express a sort of benign anthropocentrism. Man takes creation into his hands, literally or metaphorically, and offers it up to God: the implication is that creation is simply the matter of the offering, God-given, but passive. It has nothing of the dynamism of the world we see around us.

But are there not greater depths to the image of human priesthood? As we saw earlier, the logic of the metaphor requires us to recognize in nature not only the matter of the offering, but also the cosmic congregation—for a priest does not celebrate alone. This has consequences for the way we view human creativity, that characteristic quality that we increasingly recognize as a two-edged sword. The Eucharist is an offering of human work, a specifically human product. This is important in affirming that our creative work can produce a worthy offering; we are not doomed always to degrade and spoil God's handiwork. Some writers attempt to link this creativity with "priesthood," but that is to stretch the metaphor: it is not the priest who contributes the bread and the wine, but the community of which he forms part. As priest of creation, therefore, we offer also the working of nature, that great chain of transformations of which ours is only the final stage.

This way of understanding our role has two important practical consequences. Firstly: to see our working of nature in continuity with transformations within nature does not reduce human creativity and intentional action to the level of waters weathering a rock. But it does remind us that our work has its precursors: it is both new and part of a pattern. There are "precedents" that we should do well to study, so as to work with nature rather than reinventing it. The second consequence has to do with the emphasis to be placed on transforming nature through art or technology. Is this a divine imperative, or simply a part of our nature, which can be used for good or ill? If we see our primary task as being to offer up the gifts brought by the cosmos, rather than necessarily to shape them into final form, we can still affirm that our creativity can be an offering. But we shall not assume that *only* our creativity can make a worthy offering.

There are other, somewhat neglected images of man's role that can be of use to us here. I am thinking especially of St Maximus' image of man as a workshop of unity, a connecting link uniting creation and Creator. Precisely because it is *not* a personal image, it reminds us that we need not forever be turning the world into something in order to offer it to God. It is by our very nature that we carry nature with us; by being a creature of earth, an element in an ecosystem. And nature can be carried up into the divine presence precisely because there is an element in the ecosystem that yet bears the divine image.

"When we try to pick out anything by itself," writes the American conservationist and explorer John Muir, "we find that it is bound fast by a thousand invisible cords that cannot be broken, to everything in the universe."[3] This is the basic principle of ecology, which is being confirmed in ever greater detail as we become more aware of our dependence on natural systems, our intricate involvement in the web of life. Yet especially to Orthodox Christians, such an image will also seem strangely familiar. In these "invisible cords," can we not see the *logoi* or essential principles of all things, connected to each other through the Creator Word? It is this interconnection that the physical web of life reflects. To recognize that we are part of this web is only to affirm that we qualify as a link. From the "web" of nature, we are indeed a strand "picked out," a creature set apart by being endowed with the image of God. But never "by ourselves": as we draw closer to God, we draw with us the universe.

If we perceive this sort of symmetry between the world as ecosystem and the world united in the Word of God, attentiveness to the

[3]Entry for July 27, 1869; cf. *My First Summer in the Sierra* (New York, NY: The Modern Library, 2003), 211. The version quoted above is said to be Muir's original wording, later revised; Cited 31 March 2009. Online: http://www.sierraclub.org/john_muir_exhibit/writings/misquotes.html.

wisdom of nature takes on a new aspect. It is not only a matter of prudence and survival to work with nature, and not against it. It is also a way of drawing closer to its Creator, following those threads which are also the divine will expressed in every creature. And as we discover ever more deeply the sense in which we are part of our ecosystem, so we rediscover the experience of creation as gift to us. It is not a gift for our consumption; nor does it exist only for our sake. The gift, as Maximus says, is the "rationality of the world"; the patterns we discern in it, the way it functions and hangs together. We receive this as a gift when we conform our lives to it. Perhaps an awareness of interdependence, fragility and natural limits might be among the gifts awaiting our acceptance.

After all this, the question will still be asked: can anything I do really make any difference? This can be answered on two levels: we may think of them as the "global" and the "cosmic."

The figure of the dedicated environmentalist, radically committed to a sustainable way of living, reminds me of a story told by a friend. Our friend was born in India; and like most children of the British Raj, he and his brother were sent home at a tender age, in the care of their nanny, to start school. As the ship neared the end of its voyage, so many homesick expatriates crowded to the side to catch their first glimpse of the English coast that the ship began to list dangerously to starboard. Soon an announcement came over the tannoy: "Will some passengers please proceed to the port side to redress the balance of the ship." Nobody moved: except, that is, for Nanny. Seizing two reluctant small boys firmly by the hand, she marched purposefully across the deck proclaiming, "We are going to redress the balance of the ship!"[4]

[4]Reminiscence by Archimandrite Ephrem (Lash).

At first sight, the image is somewhat comical: a lonely figure waging a noble but futile struggle against insuperable odds. But the point of the story is that *Nanny was absolutely right.* Not just morally right in following the call of duty, but right about the root cause of the problem and its remedy. The imbalance of the ship, like that of our environment or even the global climate, depended on the familiar human dynamic: every individual is convinced that nothing he or she does can possibly have an effect on anything so large. And then once it becomes apparent that we have affected the whole, no one is prepared to change before everyone else does. So stalemate continues until people realize that the only remedy for the imbalance is to reverse its cause: to recognize that my own contribution counts, and act accordingly.

If it is hard to see direct results from our actions on the global level, on the cosmic level it is impossible. And yet we firmly believe that our life's work is to move toward a transfiguration in Christ in which the entire cosmos is involved. Our destiny is bound up with all the rest of creation, not just for a few million years, but for all eternity. Man's proven ability to harm nature on a global scale can be seen as a parable of this connection, albeit showing its shadow side.

It seems strange that anyone from the Christian tradition should doubt in principle that human action could affect even something so vast in scale as the global climate. The scale of human environmental impact should remind us of something basic to the story of salvation: the momentous effect of a human decision. The fall story is telling us that when humans opt for self-reliance and choose to use the world without reference to God, this is connected in some mysterious way with the suffering and disharmony of the natural world. The Annunciation reminds us of what is required to reverse this movement of disintegration: one person has to be found who with all her being says "Yes" to God's saving work.

Perhaps this puts into perspective our desire to "save the earth." When we speak of saving the earth from this or that particular threat, we are essentially talking about a movement back, not forwards. We mean returning to a state where the earth is still corruptible, still imperfect—but at least habitable. But we must ask: what is the point of this "saving" work? Our answer must be that we live on a habitable earth in order to play our part in the saving work that is God's, the work of taking all things *forward* to the Kingdom. If our task were global, then the tiny individual might well have cause to despair. But the cosmic dimension of our task relieves us of any illusion that "everything depends on me," while emphasizing to the utmost the importance of our willing assent to the task given us. We should know by now that there is no path to the Kingdom except through a thousand ordinary, humdrum decisions, whether it is sparing a kind word for somebody or recycling a sheet of paper. Every act of care and responsibility towards God's creation, human and non-human, is a practical assent to his plan of salvation. It signals our willingness to be co-workers with the Almighty in bringing his creation to the fulfillment for which it was made.

the author

Elizabeth Theokritoff was educated at Millfield School and Somerville and Wolfson colleges, Oxford, where she completed her doctorate in liturgical theology under the supervision of Bishop Kallistos (Ware). She is an independent scholar and freelance theological translator from Greek, and has served as a visiting lecturer at the Institute of Orthodox Christian Studies in Cambridge. She has had a particular interest in theology of creation since 1988, when she served as visiting Orthodox Tutor at the Ecumenical Institute, Bossey, Switzerland, for the Graduate School on "Justice, peace and the integrity of creation."